I0884108

AI Safety and Preventing Harm in AI Systems

Rahul K. Patel
https://orcid.org/0000-0003-1175-0635
Illinois Institute of Technology, USA

IGI Global
Scientific Publishing
Publishing Tomorrow's Research Today

Vice President of Editorial	Melissa Wagner
Director of Acquisitions	Mikaela Felty
Director of Book Development	Jocelynn Hessler
Production Manager	Mike Brehm
Cover Design	Jose Rosado

Published in the United States of America by
IGI Global Scientific Publishing
701 East Chocolate Avenue
Hershey, PA, 17033, USA
Tel: 717-533-8845 | Fax: 717-533-7115
Website: https://www.igi-global.com E-mail: cust@igi-global.com

Library of Congress Cataloging-in-Publication Data

LCCN: 2026002147 (CIP Data Pending)
ISBN13: 979-8-3373-6935-8
Isbn13Softcover: 979-8-3373-6936-5
EISBN13: 979-8-3373-6937-2

British Cataloguing in Publication Data
A Cataloguing in Publication record for this book is available from the British Library.

Table of Contents

Detailed Table of Contents

This chapter focuses on validity in artificial intelligence. It explains that the quality, representativeness, and context of data influence how well AI systems can perform. The chapter discusses three ways of judging AI validity: technical, interpretive, and normative. This includes correctness, interpretability or understanding ability, fairness, and respecting ethical standards. Now this chapter goes on to notice difficulties at the time of saving AI practice from entirely new areas, during which strict application of tried and tested verification methods, such as cross-validation or bias testing, has been applied to real problems set. What case study discussions highlight is that failure to comply with its common employment rules may have far-reaching effects, including: this costs money, and what goes wrong cannot easily be restored; biased decisions; compromised safety. The results reveal that AI systems must be closely monitored and continually changed in order to maintain public trust, fairness, and compatibility with societal values.

The growing integration of artificial intelligence into safety-critical socio-technical systems increases the risk of physical, psychological, and societal harm that cannot be addressed solely by technical reliability. This chapter positions AI safety as a central and independent objective within AI design and governance, emphasizing the prevention, limitation, and containment of harm throughout the entire lifecycle of AI systems. The analysis adopts a harm-based framework and systematically reviews ethical, regulatory, and technical approaches, including the EU AI Act, product safety and liability regimes, safety testing protocols, risks associated with human–AI interaction, and fail-safe mechanisms. The results indicate that adequate AI safety cannot be achieved solely through ex ante testing or formal compliance. Instead, it requires integrated safety architectures that incorporate continuous monitoring, organizational accountability, interaction-aware design, and robust intervention and containment mechanisms in the presence of irreducible uncertainty.

As Artificial Intelligence (AI) becomes increasingly embedded in critical infrastructures, healthcare systems, financial services, and military operations, securing these systems against malicious threats is no longer optional—it is imperative. This chapter explores how traditional notions of cybersecurity are being challenged by the dynamic, probabilistic, and often opaque nature of AI systems. We cover the spectrum of malicious threats targeting AI, from data poisoning and adversarial attacks to model inversion and prompt injection. Drawing from leading frameworks such as the NIST AI Risk Management Framework (AI RMF), OECD AI Principles, and the MITRE ATLAS adversary model, we outline strategies for securing the full AI lifecycle—from data ingestion to inference. The discussion spans both technical controls (cryptography, watermarking, RBAC) and organizational enablers (governance boards, whistleblower protections).

As Artificial Intelligence (AI) systems become increasingly prevalent in decision-relevant and high-risk domains, the exclusive focus on algorithmic performance is encountering normative and organizational constraints. Predictive accuracy alone is insufficient; there is a growing demand for decisions that are justifiable, verifiable,

frameworks that ensure data is handled responsibly. This proposal explores the principles of privacy in AI, the risks of privacy-preserving technologies, the impact of global legal frameworks, and the challenge of balancing data utility with privacy protections, before outlining steps toward resilient, privacy-conscious AI systems.

The rapid spread of Artificial Intelligence (AI) across sectors like healthcare, finance, education, law enforcement, and public administration has dramatically changed how decisions are made, services are delivered, and organizations function. AI holds incredible potential to improve human well-being and drive societal progress. Yet, alongside these opportunities come serious ethical concerns—particularly around fairness, bias, and the risk of reinforcing existing social inequalities. This chapter explores these challenges in depth, offering an interdisciplinary perspective on how bias emerges in AI systems.

With the increasing impact on society of intelligent technology, trust is becoming more and more crucial in public institutions, healthcare, education, and finance as new systems are built to make or support human decisions. People will need to have faith in the assurance that systems will be transparent, accountable, and safe. The next chapter explores how trust might be considered a thread through the entire life of a system, from its early stages of training and design through continuing day-to-day operations. This discussion brings together what might otherwise be considered three distinct goals: ensuring that systems are worthy of trust, treating people equitably, and doing so in a transparent and accountable manner. Using organizational experiences and real-world examples, the chapter examines how large, complex systems are built, tested, and kept up. In this context, trust is more than a set of principles that inform choices, enable transparency, and foster long-term success.

Preface

INTRODUCTION

Artificial Intelligence (AI) has evolved from a specialized computational method into a pervasive socio-technical infrastructure that significantly influences economic processes, public governance, scientific discovery, and daily human decision-making. AI systems currently support or automate essential functions in sectors such as healthcare, finance, transportation, energy, public administration, security, and defense. Although these systems offer considerable opportunities for efficiency, scalability, and innovation, they also introduce new risks, uncertainties, and potential harms. Errors, biases, security vulnerabilities, and opaque decision mechanisms may propagate widely, resulting in consequences that are challenging to predict, trace, or reverse.

In this context, AI safety and harm prevention have become central challenges for the responsible development, deployment, and governance of artificial intelligence systems. Traditional approaches to software assurance, risk management, and compliance, which were primarily designed for deterministic and static systems, are increasingly inadequate for modern AI. Contemporary AI is probabilistic, adaptive, data-dependent, and frequently embedded within complex socio-technical environments. Addressing these challenges necessitates not only technical innovation but also the establishment of robust ethical frameworks, organizational governance mechanisms, and regulatory alignment.

This edited volume, *AI Safety and Preventing Harm in AI Systems*, offers a comprehensive, multidisciplinary analysis of the risks, safeguards, and trustworthiness challenges inherent to contemporary AI systems. The book systematically addresses foundational technical concepts such as validity, reliability, safety, security, and resilience, alongside essential ethical and governance dimensions including accountability, transparency, explainability, privacy, fairness, and trustworthiness.

Through the integration of theoretical frameworks, state-of-the-art research, international standards, and applied case studies, the volume provides readers with a holistic understanding of the design, evaluation, deployment, and governance of trustworthy AI across diverse application domains.

AI Safety and Trustworthiness in the Contemporary Context

The urgency of AI safety has increased alongside recent advancements in machine learning, large language models, multimodal systems, and agentic AI architectures. These technologies have enhanced the autonomy, adaptability, and generative capabilities of AI systems, shifting their role from analytical tools to infrastructures that enable decision-making and action. Concurrently, global governance initiatives, such as the EU AI Act, ISO/IEC standards, the NIST AI Risk Management Framework, and the OECD AI Principles, indicate a transition from aspirational ethical guidelines to enforceable regulatory and organizational requirements.

High-profile incidents involving biased algorithms, unsafe automation, adversarial attacks, privacy breaches, and model hallucinations have demonstrated that AI-related harm is a tangible operational and societal reality. Addressing these risks requires attention throughout the entire AI lifecycle. This book situates itself at the intersection of rapid technological evolution, regulatory development, and increasing societal expectations. It asserts that preventing harm in AI systems necessitates continuous, integrated, and context-sensitive strategies, rather than isolated technical solutions or solely compliance-driven interventions.

Objectives and Scholarly Contribution

The primary objective of this book is to bridge the gaps among technical, ethical, and regulatory perspectives on AI safety and trustworthiness. In fulfilling this aim, the volume serves as a critical resource for researchers and practitioners navigating the complex risk landscape of modern AI systems. It contributes to scholarly discourse by synthesizing current challenges and emerging solutions, and by fostering interdisciplinary collaboration across AI, cybersecurity, data science, ethics, law, and public policy.

Additionally, the book promotes the development of robust methodologies for responsible AI design, comprehensive risk management, and lifecycle-oriented governance models. Its detailed analysis of evolving AI risks and trust frameworks is intended to inform future research agendas, organizational best practices, and international standard-setting initiatives. Ultimately, the volume aims to support the global transition toward AI systems that are innovative, high-performing, safe, accountable, fair, and socially aligned.

Target Audience

This book is intended for a diverse yet specialized audience. It addresses AI researchers, computer scientists, and data scientists involved in the development and evaluation of intelligent systems; cybersecurity professionals and risk managers responsible for securing AI-enabled infrastructures; and ethicists, legal scholars, policymakers, and regulators engaged in shaping AI governance frameworks. The volume is also relevant for industry practitioners and decision-makers in sectors such as healthcare, finance, government, and technology who aim to mitigate AI-related risks while ensuring ethical and trustworthy deployment. Furthermore, the book serves as an advanced teaching resource for graduate students and educators in courses on AI safety, ethics, security, and responsible innovation.

STRUCTURE AND CHAPTER CONTRIBUTIONS

The book is organized to reflect a lifecycle-oriented and multi-layered understanding of AI safety and harm prevention.

Chapter 1. Making AI Outputs Match the Intended Goals (Validity)

This chapter establishes validity as a foundational element of trustworthy AI. It examines how data quality, representativeness, and contextual alignment influence system behavior, and distinguishes among technical, interpretive, and normative validity. Through illustrative cases, the chapter demonstrates how failures in validation can lead to biased decisions, safety incidents, financial losses, and diminished public trust. It emphasizes the necessity of continuous evaluation in dynamic deployment contexts.

Chapter 2. Designing AI to Prevent Harm (Safety)

This chapter positions AI safety as an independent and overarching design objective. Employing a harm-based analytical framework, it integrates ethical considerations, regulatory regimes, and technical safeguards to advocate for comprehensive safety architectures that extend beyond initial testing to include ongoing monitoring, accountability, and intervention mechanisms.

Chapter 3. Protecting AI from Malicious Threats (Security)

Addressing the evolving threat landscape, this chapter examines AI-specific security risks, including adversarial attacks, data poisoning, model inversion, and prompt injection. Drawing on international frameworks, it outlines lifecycle-based security strategies that integrate technical controls with organizational governance harm prevention and remediation.

Chapter 4. Communicating the Rationale Behind AI Decisions (Explainability)

Moving beyond technical definitions of explainability, this chapter frames explanations as communicative and governance mechanisms that influence trust and responsibility. It introduces a lifecycle-oriented Explainability Assurance Pipeline.

Chapter 5. Making AI Models Intelligible to Experts (Interpretability)

This chapter addresses the interpretability challenge in safety-sensitive domains by surveying interpretable models, contemporary interpretation techniques, and inherently interpretable architectures, positioning interpretability as a multidisciplinary governance requirement.

Chapter 6. Safeguarding Data in AI Systems (Privacy)

Privacy is examined as a cornerstone of trust and regulatory compliance. The chapter analyzes privacy risks, privacy-preserving technologies, and global legal frameworks, emphasizing the balance between data utility and data protection.

Chapter 7. Ensuring Equity and Mitigating Harm (Fairness and Bias)

This chapter explores how bias emerges throughout the AI lifecycle and how it can reinforce existing inequalities. It presents interdisciplinary strategies for identifying, measuring, and mitigating unfair outcomes.

Chapter 8. Integrating Trustworthiness into the AI Lifecycle

Trustworthiness is presented as a unifying concept that connects safety, fairness, transparency, and accountability. Through organizational examples, the chapter demonstrates that trust must be actively built and maintained over time.

CONCLUSION

Collectively, the chapters in this volume provide a systematic, lifecycle-oriented, and interdisciplinary foundation for understanding and advancing AI safety and harm prevention. By integrating technical rigor with ethical reflection and governance insight, *AI Safety and Preventing Harm in AI Systems* contributes to a more mature and actionable understanding of trustworthy AI. The volume is intended to inform research, guide practice, and support policy development as AI continues to reshape societies worldwide.

Silvio Andrae
Independent Researcher, Germany

Acknowledgment

I would like to express my sincere gratitude to Dr. Silvio Andrae for his invaluable contribution in writing the Preface, providing insights that set the foundation for this work.

I am deeply thankful to Ms. Radhika Kande for her dedicated efforts in reviewing multiple chapters, offering critical feedback that significantly enhanced the clarity and quality of the content.

I also appreciate all the authors who contributed to this book. Their expertise and commitment were essential in writing high-quality chapters.

I am equally grateful to all the reviewers for their timely and thorough reviews, which significantly improved the overall quality of the work.

While it is difficult to individually name each contributor, I deeply appreciate the support and effort of everyone involved in making this book possible. Guidance and support from the team have been instrumental in the completion of this book.

Thank you!

Rahul K Patel

Department of Information Technology and Management, College of Computing, Illinois Institute of Technology, USA

Chapter 1
Making AI Outputs Match the Intended Goals (Validity)

Shidiq Al Hakim
https://orcid.org/0000-0002-4677-3661
National Research and Innovation Agency (BRIN), Indonesia & Bakrie Univerisity, Indonesia

Zakiul Fahmi
https://orcid.org/0000-0002-2171-0533
Bakrie University, Indonesia

Al Hafiz Akbar Maulana Siagian
https://orcid.org/0000-0003-0311-3134
National Research and Innovation Agency (BRIN), Indonesia

Ekawati Marlina
https://orcid.org/0000-0002-9754-3460
National Research and Innovation Agency (BRIN), Indonesia

Ira Maryati
National Research and Innovation Agency (BRIN), Indonesia

Niken Fitria Apriani
National Research and Innovation Agency (BRIN), Indonesia

Andri Saputra
National Research and Innovation Agency (BRIN), Indonesia

Cahyono Nugroho
National Research and Innovation Agency (BRIN), Indonesia

Samsudiat Samsudiat
https://orcid.org/0009-0007-1913-8850
National Research and Innovation Agency (BRIN), Indonesia

ABSTRACT

This chapter focuses on validity in artificial intelligence. It explains that the quality, representativeness, and context of data influence how well AI systems can perform. The chapter discusses three ways of judging AI validity: technical, interpretive, and normative. This includes correctness, interpretability or understanding abil-

DOI: 10.4018/979-8-3373-6935-8.ch001

ity, fairness, and respecting ethical standards. Now this chapter goes on to notice difficulties at the time of saving AI practice from entirely new areas, during which strict application of tried and tested verification methods, such as cross-validation or bias testing, has been applied to real problems set. What case study discussions highlight is that failure to comply with its common employment rules may have far-reaching effects, including: this costs money, and what goes wrong cannot easily be restored; biased decisions; compromised safety. The results reveal that AI systems must be closely monitored and continually changed in order to maintain public trust, fairness, and compatibility with societal values.

1 WHAT VALIDITY IS IN AI – CONCEPTUAL GROUNDING AND WHY IT Matters

In AI, validity can be seen as the degree to which an algorithm or system consistently performs as intended, producing results that align with the initial aims of its designers. In the social sciences, we measure a concept if the concept's validity is achieved, the measurement instrument tracks well in seizing the meaning of the concept it is intended to represent. The same is true in the AI world, where the alignment between input-output and objective is paramount (Aliferis & Simon, 2024). From a technical perspective, the validity of an AI model includes its predictive performance, contextual fit, and ethical reliability.

Validity in artificial intelligence (AI) is multidimensional, encompassing three main dimensions: technical, interpretative, and normative. The technical dimension emphasises the reliability, accuracy, and robustness of models. The interpretative dimension emphasizes the importance of clarity, comprehensibility, and personalization of results for users, ensuring that AI outputs are not only computationally correct but also meaningful and trustworthy. Meanwhile, the normative dimension encompasses aspects of fairness, accountability, legal compliance, and ethical use. This normative aspect is to ensure that AI can be applied legitimately and responsibly. This multidimensional approach demonstrates that AI validity is not a static concept, but rather a dynamic construct that must be continuously evaluated and validated in accordance with the context and purpose of its application.

It is well-known that validity in AI is very important, as previous works have shown. Scheider and Verstegen (2024) argue that validity is not only related to ground truth, but it should also be measured as fit-for-purpose, how well the system is at answering questions or meeting aims. Valente et al. (2022) then coined the term "The Erin Brockovich Theory of Knowledge," concluding that validity is not just a matter of how well it can predict but how interpretable and reliable it is (and, in my argument, likely also related to personalisation). One such step in the validation is to establish trust with the system. Also, Parycek et al. (2023) stress the power of validity in representative data quality, freedom from bias, as well as transparency in algorithmic processing, irrespective of whether it is rule-based or machine learning.

Nevertheless, the normative aspect of AI validity is still a topic repeatedly raised in discussions with hard regulations as well as sociology and law. Ranjitsingh and Rao (2025) found that the adaptive nature of AI and its potential to change its behavior over time require rigorous regulatory standards in place to maintain quality. In addition, careful monitoring is essential for reasons of safety and control. From an evaluation theory perspective, Ruiz Mendoza et al. (2024) say that validity should be supported by relevant proof-based arguments, as when faced with new difficulties, such as generative AI. However, Cofre et al. (2025) find that when applied to predict future events, validity shows that reference to employment and school exam methods can achieve a high predictive correlation ratio. They also see warning signs everywhere of bias and over-generalisation. So the validity of these models still has to be confirmed on a larger scale and under new conditions.

As AI is incorporated into decision-making systems in impactful domains such as healthcare, finance, and national security, validity extends beyond the question of how well a system performs and is, in fact, a public trust and safety issue (Tabassi, 2023). Without grounded AI, AI can end up with outputs that are not trustworthy, harmful, or misaligned with human values. For instance, an AI system in health care that wrongly classifies patients' conditions leads to not only technical failure but also danger to human lives (Obermeyer et al., 2019). This makes clear that validity in AI is not confined to theoretical discussions but represents an urgent societal concern—underscoring why it matters.

Validity in AI is essential from the perspective of public trust, ethics, and governance. The essence of AI validity also applies to the sustainability of AI adoption. Validity in AI is not merely a technical issue. In fact, AI validity also matters for public trust and human safety. For example, classification errors can pose real threats to patients' lives in the field of healthcare (Salhab et al., 2024). This issue makes validity a key requirement for safe and trustworthy AI systems. On the other hand, the issue of bias raises a crucial ethical issue in AI validity. Khosravi et al. (2025) indicate that ethical principles, e.g., accountability, the absence of bias, and fairness, must be validated to ensure that the use of AI in healthcare services does not lead to a discriminatory decision. Similarly, Salhab et al. (2024) emphasise the importance of validity as part of an ethical framework that ensures AI is aligned with human values and does not cause social injustice. In the realm of public policy and governance, validity serves as a bridge that ensures AI is not only efficient but also legitimate, transparent, and aligned with the principles of democracy and the rule of law (Parycek et al., 2023). The sustainability of AI adoption can be maintained if trustworthiness is upheld. Without adequate transparency and validity, trust in AI-based research results will decline, thereby threatening its acceptance and sustainability (Christou, 2025). Moreover, Salhab et al. (2024) suggest that unvalidated AI systems are complex to trust for long-term use, especially when applied in critical sectors. This suggestion corroborates the finding of Parycek et al. (2023) that shows the social and legal legitimacy of AI in public administration could be disrupted without validity and transparency.

2 DATA RELEVANCE AND REPRESENTIVENESS: MATCH THE TRAINING DATA TO THE DOMAIN OF INTEREST

Fundamentally, the performance of AI models is based on the training data. In other words, the success of a model depends heavily on how relevant and representative the data used to train the model is. If the data used does not cover a variety of relevant variables, the model will struggle to find different patterns from those already known. Thus, the success of AI activities is very much dependent on how data is collected and organized (Goh et al., 2024).

The relevance of training data is that it is suitable or directly related. In this case, relevant data is the data that contains variables, conditions, and features that are directly related to the purposes or captures of the model itself. For example, if the model aims to diagnose a certain disease, then the training data must include medical information that is relevant to the disease in question, such as the symptoms people with this disease would display and their medical history for those illnesses, dates, and laboratory test results in connection with that particular disorder. Data training in representativeness means diversity or variety of the data you feed to a model, to make sure that the model can cope with all possible variations in its target domain.

Representativeness means that the whole field of data input for training should include a large variety in each dimension and group that the real world may offer to train the model. For example, in the medical context, representativeness of data means that the training set must cover every age group, both sexes, all ethnic groups, and this, as well, may explain very different patterns of health problems at any given time. Only in this way can a model be expected to perform correctly for any patients in general and not just some specific type.

2.1 Relevance Between Training Data and Target Domain

Correlation between training data and AI model development is paramount. If the data related to the training samples is irrelevant, then AI models will not be able to identify correct patterns in their target domain. A model trained with data that is not only irrelevant but also does not include the right variables can result in predictions that are not accurate or that fail when they are used in practice. For example, during the development of a medical model, training data that does not include relevant geographic or demographic variations can cause it to fail in different countries or among different populations (Musa et al., 2025).

Relevant data will help AI models to find good patterns in their target domain of application and thereby properly relate the variables already in existence. Therefore, ensuring that the dataset used during training accurately reflects the living conditions the model will encounter is crucial. For example, ensuring patient data comes from a diverse range of age groups, genders, and racial backgrounds rather than just one group in the healthcare industry could improve the model's accuracy, where predictive models work for different medical problems (Goh et al., 2024). Thus, the relevance of training data is to guarantee that a model can make more precise predictions and contribute to better decision-making.

2.2 Representativeness of Training Data to the Target Domain

As is well known, a dataset should represent the tremendous variety of situations that in real life AI models are called upon to contend with. Inside the scope of representative data can be found a wide variety of circumstances, particular to the target domain demographics, geography, and social customs, among others. A model trained on representative data is more likely to produce reasonable results on new input, even when applied in real-world settings (Bender et al., 2021). If your data does not represent such a broad spectrum of extremes, your model is being put at a disadvantage right out of the gate.

At the same time, we must make sure that the training data used for AI models is complete in terms of all the various characteristics and situations relevant to the situation. In the medical field, for example, data from patients of various ethnic groups, ages, genders, and social backgrounds is needed so that any model can provide correct diagnoses and cover all existing conditions of society. Similarly, in the financial and marketing sectors, data from the various types of consumers across different groups should be considered to avoid any bias creeping into the predictions that are made or recommendations given.

3 VALIDITY OF TRAINING AND TESTING – OVERFITTING, UNDERFITTING, AND CONTEXT MISMATCH

To evaluate the effectiveness of how well machine learning models work and can be generalised to other situations, one has to make sure that experiments are set up right: The problem with the statement in the first sentence is that for regression analysis, you don't have a test set; the only dataset available is your training one. For example, when a model learns patterns from a dataset in machine learning, this process is called training, while testing is when the model sees how well it works on data it has not seen before then becomes its task. However, the goal (known to statisticians as minimizing) is for a model to fit well. New cases that the model has not seen before, like how their performance should be halfway decent anyway, regardless, otherwise it's garbage theory. Yet this validity is dependent on a number of factors, including how well kept apart the training and testing datasets are, and whether a model will handle complexity.

Overfitting and underfitting are two of the largest issues that make it difficult to see if training and testing are valid or not. When a model learns too much from the training data, it takes noise and unimportant features along with its understanding of other data or new circumstances or points. This makes models much worse for these outliers than they would have been otherwise. On the other hand, underfitting occurs when a model is not picking up the underlying trends in the data; here, it is too simple and does not allow for any complexity. Yet both of these problems illustrate clearly just how important it is to find a balance between model complexity and its ability to generalize (Bengio, 2012).

This balance directly affects training and testing validity. Cross-validation is a frequent method of ensuring that findings are legitimate. Here, you split the training set into several smaller sets and use each one of the smaller sets as a test set while using all other data for training. This method helps to ensure that your model will not become too specific because it is drawn from a particular place in your data, and also gives you a better idea of how well your approach will work. In addition, this strategy reduces the risk of overfitting by testing models on many differently split data subsets. This makes them more able to generalize (Sevyeri, 2023).

3.1 Overfitting

In cases that a model has memorized the training set too well, including its noise and irregularities, and it doesn't generalize to new data it hasn't seen before, we call this overfitting. This is a major issue in machine learning, particularly when the model is too complex for the amount of training data that it possesses. If you do not utilize regularization, your deep learning models with millions of parameters will tend to overfit very quickly. What overfitting does is produce a model that performs well on the training data, but not well against new cases, which suggests it won't do well in general.

Machine learning experts use all sorts of tricks to keep the model from getting too complex and learning patterns that only work on the training data, but not on new, fresh, unseen data. If a model is too "tuned" or "fitted", it includes noise or any other data that will not pertain to the outside world. This is called overfitting. Various counter-measures are taken to prevent this. So let's make it easier to understand by offering some simpler explanations and examples.

A. L1 and L2 Regularization

The regularisation is actually one of the most popular techniques applied in order to prevent overfitting. The main idea of regularization is to charge the model a "cost" (or penalty) when it makes its parameters larger (like weights). A model that overly uses large weights for some features: it might be trying to fit noise or outliers in the data, instead of real patterns. Regularization helps to prevent this by adding a rule that makes it more improbable for big weights to be kept.

- **L1 Lasso, or regularization**, that penalizes the absolute values of your model's weights. This suggests that the model will try to make its weights small and, in some of these cases, close to zero. This can be very powerful if we believe that some features (input variables) are not important, and we would like to exclude them. For example, if you were building a model to predict housing prices, you would have many features that the model could take into account: number of rooms, square footage, neighborhood, and how old the house is. By setting the weight of the house's color to zero, L1 provides a way of getting rid of things that do not matter.
- **L2 Regularization**, which is also known as Ridge (the square of weights is penalized). L2 regularization, however, tends to push the weights closer to zero but not completely remove them. L1 can also discard some features entirely. It can help prevent the model from relying too heavily on any one feature. For instance, in the house price example earlier, L2 would "dampen" out noisy features (like square footage that's crazy big or tiny) rather than outright ignore them entirely.

Both L1 and L2 regularization help to prevent overfitting by applying such penalties to the loss function during training. This promotes the complexity of model weights to be flattened (Zhang et al., 2017).

B. Dropout

Dropout is an alternative, popular method to halt overfitting. During training, dropout randomly "drops" (i.e., deactivates) some neurons (units) of the network. That in turn means every time the network trains, there are a few neurons that go unstimulated, and the model has to learn multiple ways of presenting the input.

This process helps in preventing the model from depending too much on a single neuron and from overfitting.

The idea behind dropout is that if the network learns to "forget" parts of itself while training, it will become more flexible and less prone to overfitting. It can also assist the model in better handling subtle changes or variations in data, beneficial when testing a model on real-world data that might not be the same as the training data exactly.

C. Adding More Data

Doing data augmentation is another way to reduce overfitting. This is especially useful for jobs like classifying photos. More kinds of data are exposed to the model by artificially enlarging the size of the training set through techniques such as rotation, flipping, and scaling. This makes it harder to memorize specific instances of data. Whether the dataset is big or small, there's a lower degree of overfitting, if at all. In particular, this method enables learning in fields where it is hard or expensive to get large data sets (Bengio, 2012).

Despite being used in these ways, overfitting still occurs frequently, especially as models become more complex. One more advanced technique to prevent overfitting in deep learning is early stopping. This means that during training, when the model performs better on a portion of its validation set, we stop the engine for a while and then resume (Sevyeri, 2023).

3.2 Underfitting

Underfitting: An underfed model."This happens when a model is too simple, such that it fails to capture the underlying pattern in the data. It thus performs poorly both on training and test sets." Normally, this occurs when the model is under-parameterized, and its capacity is too low to represent the data properly. Overfitting is the opposite of underfitting, which happens when a model is too simple to adapt to the data, causing high bias.

There might be several reasons why a model underfits, using an algorithm that is too simple with respect to the data (too few degrees of freedom), less training data, or poor feature representation. Underfitting in deep learning could be caused by a model structure that is too shallow or narrow to learn the complex patterns in data. For instance, a linear regression model, which is used to feed the data having non-linear relationships, can lead to underfitting. Underfitting can be addressed by increasing the model's complexity , such as incorporating additional features, adding more layers in neural networks, or using complex algorithms (Bansal et al., 2020).

Adding more data to the training set is a good way of reducing underfitting. When the dataset is small and biased, with little or no variation, then there may not be enough information provided to the model to capture meaningful associations. In those cases, additional data or using augmentation techniques could help the model to learn more robust features. In addition, improved feature selection or transformation methods can help the model focus on features that are more important with respect to the output value and weaken the underfitting effect (Zhang et al., 2017).

Another way to prevent underfitting is to tune the hyperparameters of the model. General or hyperparameter tuning, including learning rate, batch size, and architecture changes in the network, can help the model generalize the data. If we adjust these parameters carefully, then the model might be made to be more adaptable while things don't fit neatly enough in a large number of cases, and perform well on both test and training sets (Bengio, 2012).

3.3 Context Mismatch

If the training and text datasets are not drawn according to an identical distribution, it is difficult to move the model's generalization properly. This is called context mismatch. This kind of problem happens often in the real world. Models trained on one data set may be used in a completely different situation, such as when a model that has worked very well for an area's data moves to another area, or when a completely different data set is to be used with an old model. Yet if the underlying distribution changes much between the training and testing stages, context mismatch will have a great deal of effect on how well the model works.

Distribution changes are another major reason for context mismatch. They occur when the distribution of input data, the relationship between features and labels, or both, changes over time or in different situations. This is an issue that occurs frequently in machine learning when models are used with fresh datasets that are unlike those used for training the model. It can cause the model to work poorly since it may depend on features or patterns that do not function in the new setting. The cure for this problem is to apply techniques such as domain adaptation on training data to make it look more like testing data (Cai et al., 2023).

Another way to tackle context mismatch is through transfer learning. It allows one to fine-tune an existing model been trained in one domain so that expected in a similar target domain. This method utilizes what the source domain knows to improve its performance in the target domain, even when the data distributions are unequal. However, when dealing with between-domain discrepancies, this strategy must be used carefully, because if the discrepancies are too great, then transfer performance would suffer (X. Wang & Schneider, 2015).

4 CROSS-DOMAIN VALIDITY ISSUES: FAILURES OF TRANSFER LEARNING AND DOMAIN ADAPTATION

One of the main advantages that transfer learning provides is the capability of reusing knowledge learned in one domain to speed up coverage in another. But this method has some specific validation issues. For instance, a model that is trained using chest X-rays from U.S. hospitals might not work well in African hospitals with their own imaging machines and patient pools, as well as disease demographics (Musa et al., 2025). Several domain adaptation methods, such as adversarial learning or feature reweighting, are designed to close this gap. However, such methods are reported to be inadequate when transferring between very different domains (Musa et al., 2025). Similarly, in finance, there have been cases of scoring models that rely on past lending records, which have not been successful when applied to emerging markets with different rules set and the informal sector (Arner et al., 2023). The risk is that users will take "plug-and-play" portability for granted and be confronted with costly debacles. Thus, careful revalidation of AI systems in new environments is essential.

4.1 Ensuring the Performance of AI Systems

Making sure that AI systems give results that match what they should do needs both correctness in one set of information and also truth across different areas. Truth across areas means an AI model can still work well when used in new places with different kinds of information. When this truth fails, ways of learning that move knowledge and change to fit new areas, i.e., two main things that help make things general, often stop working. These failures are about both the technology and what we know: they show how limited machines are at generalizing and how easily learned ideas can break down when faced with changes in context (Barez & Torr, 2023; Basili et al., 1994).

Problems with truth across areas happen when a model trained in one situation does not work well in another. This issue is due to the data's statistical, semantic, or cause-and-effect structures being different. This difference goes against the idea that most machine-learning methods use, which is that all pieces of data are separate and the same (Bender et al., 2021). Thus, small changes in how data is spread out can cause clear drops in how well things work in language, medicine, and areas that use sensors.

Two main areas where truth fails include a lack of data, e.g., there's nothing for which to learn an accurate representation in the first place (e.g., inadequate training data that accurately depicts what really happens), and when training data is systematically different from test data added when we are using/Inferring with the model (Arani et al., 2023). Underdata-insufficient datasets prevent a model from learning good ideas and can also spread useful learned settings to be useless. Methods to address it—e.g., Maximum Mean Discrepancy (MMD) optimization and aligning domains via ways that push back—attempt to bridge the gap by learning abstractions invariant to staying in stillness (Barez & Torr, 2023). But these ways still suffer from the curse of dimensionality and require careful tuning to prevent fixing things too much, which impacts how well they can adapt in general beyond the original field.

Another continuing issue is selecting unfair data when the training data does not accurately represent the target region. A model trained on one batch (e.g., patients at a single hospital) would produce biased or even harmful predictions if used in another location (Aydin et al., 2025). Strategies to combat this, such as weighting data differently and resampling, reduce unfairness by aligning the data spreads between source and target regions, but only if you have good information about how that data was picked.

Methods to connect things — for example, using loss functions that optimise many objectives and architectures that make use of many more types of data — aim at trying to turn the model into a good citizen in its area while differences across different areas are kept as small as possible. When optimizing with many components, one often tries to find a balance between representing the original area and making it alterable for the target area. But it remains computationally difficult in real ways to measure differences in feature spaces with many dimensions, and not always straightforward, statistically accurate (Arani et al., 2023).

People who use these things often have trouble using domain adaptation in real life, even with good progress in theory. Many algorithms that have been suggested assume we already know how much and in what way the domains are different, i.e., information we rarely have. The difference between research versions and industry processes leads to decisions made without a clear plan and without consistent checking. To fix this gap, some studies ask for frameworks that help people decide, guiding them in picking ways to adapt and check how well they work (Barez & Torr, 2023; Basili et al., 1994).

4.2 Utilizing Transfer Learning

Transfer learning lets knowledge from one task help speed up learning in another. Although this approach is significant, it can also cause negative transfer, e.g., things get worse because the areas do not match (Bender et al., 2021). Understanding when this is the case is extremely important for developing AI systems that we can rely on.

Weakly generalizing from areas, low quality of data, provocative or ethical data, and fitting too well on original tasks are causes for transfer learning to fail.

If feature spaces are very different, learned settings might fight each other instead of helping. Even advanced semantic ideas in big language models can be wrong across different cultures or languages (Bender et al., 2021). Mistakes, missing info, and wrong labels in the starting area spread through changes, making later accuracy worse (Arani et al., 2023). In private uses like healthcare, moving features that hold protected traits can break moral or legal rules if context protections are not there (Aydin et al., 2025). Lastly, models that are very focused on the starting area often cannot change to fit new situations.

Big, pre-made structures, like base or transformer models, need lots of computer power to make changes. Smaller research groups struggle to change these models without lots of equipment (Barez & Torr, 2023). Moreover, transfer learning can easily forget things: knowledge learned before gets worse as new settings cover up old ones. To fix this, strategies like slowly freezing parts or using strong weight rules are needed, which make things harder and cost more.

Change of area approaches are based on unwrapping along certain areas and attempting to transfer the knowledge from a known area (marked) to an unknown (weakly-unmarked or completely unmarked) ending area. On the other hand, area change frequently turns out to be problematic for what we might refer to as context-dependent: not having a single answer that works for all (Arani et al., 2023). In contrast, success at area change depends heavily on design choices: what kernel type to use, how features are represented, and labeling strategies. The problem is exacerbated by label drift, where the class lines change over time. Moreover, no clear warning sign consistently differentiates whether a change will work before all of it is used (Barez & Torr, 2023). Most still go by guesswork, drawing out mixed results.

Many people still rely on guesswork, which leads to uncertain success. Structures such as the Deep Reconstruction Classification Network (DRCN) help explain why area change fails. If the features of a task's starting point are very clear but lack overall structure, that way for area change will not work. Mixing judgment with manifestation tasks can make a more area-free view, thus a more manner across many situations(Arani et al., 2023).

However, the real world has shown that if area changes fail, it is not at all that they cannot be accomplished; instead, they indicate an orthodontic mismatch between data layout, method, and goal. Similar comparison across language, vision, and healthcare areas shows that a simple move-i.e just changing context or origin-will always lead to wobble and bias (Aydin et al., 2025). Investigating unsuccessful AI applications revealed some common problems: biased datasets, poorly set up structures, insufficient checks, and failure to detect data drift (Arani et al., 2023). If we learn from these mistakes and make rules for safe design, we can emphasize transparency, frequent inspection of work, and human control. Research also says that structure mixing, focusing on performing a particular manipulation and suggestions fitted to the information being presented, will tend to lead to more stable results than simply searching for quick correlations. But changing focus makes things more difficult to handle whenever there is a difference between different areas of activity. Each case requires a tailor-made setup plus limitations on form, which make it difficult to obtain repeatable results (Barez & Torr, 2023).

Area switching these days benefits many uses: cross-lighting image sorting, multi-camera object finding, and between-hospital medical imaging. For X-rays, pixel strength spreads are now changed across scanners, as this can bring down sorting models' ways of failure. The fight training with a feature-space matching model can make up a lot of triguracy in this case (Aydin et al., 2025). Fewer problems in different information areas mean carefully adjusting models and so on.

4.3 Dealing With Domain Adaptation

Domain-Weighted Allocation Fine-Tuning (DWA-FT) changes how important each area is when making adjustments to the model. Studies show that this method raises accuracy performance by 13% over both random and unsupervised means and 43% when only a small domain is available (Arani et al., 2023). With DWA-FT, things are made stronger by using how like areas are to change update weights. Ways to solve problems pop up at every slap. It consists of finding the place for changing, finding ways that can be tried out, making ideas ready to try out, a regular method leading to plans, and finally checking the results (Basili et al., 1994). This kind of working back and checking maintained the same footing, but the goals were set accordingly in both areas.

Ways of using features learn changes in the hidden space to make areas closer together while keeping things constant. Competitively changing things uses something to tell areas from one another, working graph-based transformers or things like that (Barez & Torr, 2023). These two have both been effective in changing times, but competitive training can cause problems and collapse.

Taming the proposed models means using smaller groups of models, limiting changes, and varying how quickly the model learns. Ways to keep things under control--like dropout or weight decay--prevent the model from doing well only in its original area. Watching such things as the F1-score and error helps to tell when readiness comes around (Aydin et al., 2025).

Future studies should focus on big tests of changing plans across different areas to check if they work well in general (Arani et al., 2023). Adding facts, reasons, and moral issues will make sure changes are strong and good for society. A good idea is meta-adaptation, where systems pick or mix changing plans based on what the data shows (Barez & Torr, 2023). These meta-plans could make things efficient and easy to understand, closing the gap between ideas and what happens in real life.

The ability to use things across domains is crucial for AI that's reliable and fair. Difficulties in moving, learning, and changing areas reveal that general is not simply better, but depends on the situation, data, and plan. Understanding why things break, i.e., Insufficient Data, Distribution change, and Heterogeneity forcing (Intuition) = Sane stabilization. Methods such as DWA-FT, learning non-changing features, and competitive change show alternative solutions. Healing over things between areas is not solely a technical concern, but one that is thinking and ethical: it assures that AI models are reliable, interpretable, and aligned with what people want in a world where there's lots of diverse data (Arani et al., 2023; Aydin et al., 2025; Barez & Torr, 2023).

5 METRICS AND VALIDATION – HOW TO MEASURE GOAL ALIGNMENT

Basically, there is no validity guarantee without strong performance measurements. Examining a work with strong performance measurements is to validate it to meet its goal/purpose. Using the popular metrics such as accuracy, precision, recall, and F1-score is a good foundation to evaluate or validate the performance of AI systems. Note that these metrics account for statistical performance, but they do not fully account for goal alignment in a real-world setting (Goh et al., 2024). Nevertheless, although a work has strong performance measurement results, it may still suffer when applied in a real case. In other words, counting only on such measurements might not be sufficient when dealing with problems in the real world.

5.1 The Relationship of Metrics and Validation

Otherwise, it's hard to know whether a system (AI) makes the benefits you want without regard to metrics (Myllyaho et al., 2021). However, while a model of AI systems might perform well in training, it is completely ineffective when tested on a real task. Thus, if you perform validation, such as cross-validation, production trials, or line tests, and robustness trials, then you can, in fact, make sure that performance remains good beyond ideal conditions (Tsipras et al., 2018). That is to say, metrics and validation enable continuous result evaluation, early fault detection and elimination, and improvements to AI-like retraining, tuning. And design modifications (Myllyaho et al., 2021).

Metrics and validation are key components in the development and implementation of AI, mainly due to the purpose of metrics and validation: that the developed AI system really works. Specifically, metrics enable developers and users to evaluate model performance quantitatively through such measures as precision, recall, F1-

score, fairness, error rates, and computational efficiency. Without clear metrics, it's hard to tell whether a model actually "works" on training data or just has a good appearance when dealing with different real-world conditions. Validation complements metrics by testing the model's relevance, reliability, and generality--first finding and amending potential bias, errors, or overfitting before the system moves into implementation (Medicine et al., 2023; Myllyaho et al., 2021).

Finally, metrics and validation also play a key role in the sustainable AI life cycle. AI systems often suffer from performance degradation due to changes in data or the environment. Thus, metrics-based monitoring can serve as an early warning system to alert when a model needs retraining, hyperparameter tuning, or even architectural modification. With continuous validation, an organization not only can remain up to speed with its business goals, ethical concerns, and user needs can also ensure that the AI developed remains--in perpetuity--current, transparent, and trustworthy (Arani et al., 2023; Kang et al., 2020).

5.2 Confirming Goal Alignment

Definitely critical to have a set of metrics that are aligned with what matters for your AI system or any specific organization's objectives. Misleading or inappropriate metrics may lead to measurement myopia, in which the team becomes fixated on meeting particular numbers regardless of whether these are really driving strategic success (Hauser & Katz, 1998). Using one measure to evaluate a classifier can be misleading when the data is skewed or imbalanced (classification of fraud examples in credit card data, for example), because you have a "good" model that fails to catch an important minority of cases! Hence, measures ought to be derived from the goals of an organization in a systematic manner. Consequently, the indicators are related directly to the objectives to obtain (Basili et al., 1994).

On the other side, rigorous validation should also consider the attainability of targets, not only the ease of measurement. In particular, validation tests not only the whether metrics can be computed, but also if they measure what is really desired. A review study of (Myllyaho et al., 2021) stressed that validation is central to keep AI metrics being valid with respect to context and stakeholder needs, by means of a validation such as review, data triangulation, or field trial. So when organizations instead focus on metrics and validation that are fit-for-purpose, they not only prevent the dangers of mismeasurement but also guarantee AI systems realize actual value in a sustained manner, as well as supporting their long-term vision.

Previous works have demonstrated metric and validation selection that should relate to goal alignment. A given metric's high number may not be as meaningful for a particular task. For instance, in health care, sensitivity to low-prevalence but high-risk conditions may be more important than overall accuracy (Obermeyer et al., 2019). The opposite occurs in the area of cyber security, wherein false negatives (undetected attacks) sometimes lead to make more severe decision than false positives (false alarms) (Diana et al., 2025). Similarly, an algorithm requires a fairness criterion such as demographic parity or equalized odds to prevent unfair rankings (Geyik et al., 2019; Pitoura et al., 2022).

Furthermore, a concrete example is the use of accuracy metrics in artificial intelligence-based rare disease detection systems. In imbalanced medical data, where positive cases far outnumber negative cases, a model relying solely on accuracy can appear "excellent" even though it fails to detect truly sick patients. For example, a study in the healthcare field showed that a model with 95% accuracy remains useless if nearly all predictions fall into the negative category, since its primary goal is to detect positive cases promptly (Haibo He & Garcia, 2009). In this situation, metrics such as recall, precision, or F1-score are much more appropriate to the clinical goal of minimizing the risk of misdiagnosis and ensuring that sick patients receive attention. Another example occurs in AI systems for fraud detection in the financial sector. Using accuracy as the primary metric is misleading, as the vast majority of transactions are usually legitimate. The model could result in a high accuracy by just predicting the transactions as "not fraudulent," when its primary role is to identify the high-authority level of the anomalies. Research by (Dal Pozzolo et al., 2018) underlined the importance of using metrics that are more sensitive, like AUPRC (Area Under Precision-Recall Curve), than standard AUC to guarantee that, in line with business requirements, we have as less fraud items as possible and higher confidence for them. These two cases emphasize that focusing on fit-for-purpose metrics and validation not only improves a model's technical performance but also ensures its real-world usefulness in its application context.

5.3 Designing the Strategy

It is crucial to quantify goals. This strategy assumes that there is some objective function desired. Examples of such functions might be a reward model, a safety policy, or norm-referenced education standards. Users can then measure this model by observing the extent to which its outputs coincide with that objective through a set of quantitative metrics. For instance, reward-model performance on real-world or virtual behavioral evaluations relative to human preferences, indices of fairness to avoid racism and robustness against new data manipulations or distributions is an approach that we have taken in the broad-ranging antecedent studies that concentrate on specifying values and directly measures what the model does are two central steps if we wish to make purposeful and comparable alignment towards achieving goals (Barez & Torr, 2023; Gabriel, 2020; Meng et al., 2022).

Other works also advocate a rich evaluation process, interfacing automatic measurements, human assessment, and normative/ethical analysis, providing the deployment decisions with quantifiable facts (Carroll et al., 2024; Ray, 2023; Wang et al., 2024). In particular, they suggest using a multidimensional and layered approach, i.e., combining benchmarks, humans, and monitoring, for continuous evaluation. This strategy includes a diverse suite of benchmarks rather than a single metric to capture trade-offs between capability, ethics, and safety. The strategy also considers human evaluation, e.g., partner preferences and response quality assessments, as ground truth for reward modeling. Furthermore, the strategy analyzes preference dynamics and the influence of AI on human preferences to detect drift or influence. In addition, the organization should conduct stress or attack testing to measure robustness and resistance to reward-hacking.

In short, measuring goal alignment through metrics and validation is a crucial element. Specifically, metrics can serve as concrete measuring tools that translate abstract goals into observable and evaluable forms. However, without validation, metrics have the potential to become a trap that may result in distortion, manipulation, or irrelevant measurements. Therefore, some systematic steps, e.g., forming strategic objectives and designing useful metrics (to measure the performance of expected models) and validating them, can be taken to offer a more practical AI framework that is potentially strong even when it is used in reality. As for the challenges, data availability is a challenge, cultural resistance is a very real concern, and there's always fear of manipulation going forward to ensure that the system becomes a tool for progress and not an albatross on development.

6 CASE STUDIES OF FAILED VALIDITY -- THE REAL WORLD BREAKDOWN OF AI

Real-world cases of failure are key to talking about validity. The failures give us a palpable example of how such mismatches between the output of AI systems and our intended purposes for them can have real-world consequences, ranging from bias to financial loss to safety. Cases of failure are also instructional in helping to uncover the weaknesses in design, construction, and deployment relying on data, as well as showing how maintaining valid systems is not simply about technical accuracy but fairness, public trust, and context. The following examples are drawn from prior health, organizational behavior, and automotive literature.

6.1 Health Care Bias

The first example comes from the research of Aydin et al. (2025). This article presents the performance evaluation of an AI model in line with deep learning to detect abnormalities in chest X-rays. In this article, we trained the model using a public dataset and tested it using an external population in another center. The discrepancies existing in the datasets utilized within the literature are an important factor that affects AI models under real-world scenarios, causing changes in data distribution. This variability also arises from differences in data sources, image quality, resolution, and the angle of images; patient demographic factors such as age, sex and clinical status vary across studies. In addition, variations in labeling criteria or diagnosis protocols would also affect the reliability of prediction outcomes. These sources can lead models to perform well on the training data and then have a significant drop in performance when evaluated on external data (Aydin et al., 2025). This point emphasizes the significance of external validation to assess the generalizability and reliability of AI models in clinical practice.

Other studies have uncovered bias in AI model representations geared at the health sector and particularly those targeting sensitive groups (Gray & Wu, 2025). The SD-WEAT (Subgroup Differential Word Embedding Association Test) approach was applied as a quantitative analysis method, and data was obtained by model embedding trained on clinical text and public health data. Some critiques are instances of simple racial bias. Female bias, excluding other vulnerable population groups. Demographic differences were statistically significant in the association between model and race. For instance, depictions of black patients or minority groups were frequently connected differently from white patients in ostensibly neutral contexts. Such bias could lead to the biased diagnosis or treatment advisement. Embeddings can also be indicative of differences in the relationships between medical terms or concepts for men and women. For instance, some conditions or symptoms may be disproportionately associated with one gender, even though they are otherwise equally prevalent on a clinical basis. The research also uncovered bias against the ethnicity of minorities, or various demographic groups that were not well-represented in the training data. This is representative bias — the training data doesn't cover enough of the general population for the model to learn equalised patterns.

6.2 Organizational Behavioural Bias

Validity failures are common in AI-based systems, such as recruitment process systems, in the areas of organization and human resources. A paper finds that some software for recruiting is not living up to its promise of treating all job candidates fairly. Candidates are less likely to be contacted for an interview if: they are from an ethnic minority group (between 4% and 19% (and these figures do not even take into account any subtle discrimination during the interview, even when the candidate has the same qualifications. Likewise, in male-dominated jobs, women are at 7% disadvantage. These structural biases suggest that the system may have little objective justification for distinguishing between applicants and perpetuate workforce disparities (Hangartner et al., 2021).

Another paper presents strong evidence that failures in the validity of AI tools for hiring mostly sink roots on non-representative training data drawn from historical records. League researchers, who conducted the research through a series of field experiments involving hundreds of AI engineers themselves, also found that algorithms trained on biased data can replicate age-old inequalities — that even when all candidates are equally competent in their field (but each with some combination of preference between men or women), preferential treatment of archaic norms is returned. This failure really illustrates one of the simplest problems with predictive validity (that the system does not measure what we believe it should), because it's clear that applicants are being selected against their true ability or potential — e.g. which examination they took at school, rather than how intelligent or capable they might be — as a direct result of biases embedded in training data from which an algorithm learns. In addition, the study demonstrates that ethical advice or technical guidance for developers does not reduce bias unless coupled with improvements in data quality. That is, failures of selection processes to operate reasonably or fairly appear not merely as computational flukes but rather as possible structural effects of the use of skewed propensities, such as diameter scores, may have on computational models for operationalization, sometimes including those that practice machine learning (Cowgill et al., 2020).

Another work evaluated the fairness of a deployed system by proposing an external testing-based audit that evaluates how stable the predictions are from a small perturbation in inputs (e.g., minor changes to a candidate's resume or profile). In a couple of case studies conducted in practice, Humantic AI and Crystal, we show that both tend to produce unstable output. Minor differences in the input data can also generate vastly different personality profiles, revealing that they don't satisfy validity as job selection instruments. This article finds that several AI personality systems in use for recruitment are unreliable because of inconsistent outputs, which can cause companies to make incorrect or biased decisions. Therefore, external audits are necessary to establish the validity, reliability, and fairness of AI systems within community-based implementations (Rhea et al., 2022)

6.3 Automotive System Bias

Data validity problem in the AI-based systems is described in the automotive domain as follows: In an autonomous vehicle perception system, due to defects and sensitivity of the sensors, the acquired data can contain erroneous. Second, if the data validity is low, it frequently leads to a problem whereby the system fails to generalize with actual roadside conditions. A study conducted by Fernández Llorca et al. (2024) reports that visual databases employed to develop the perception systems of autonomous vehicles are typically biased and have imbalanced distributions of attributes. Compromised by object variations under less-light, more-angle, or overwhelmed occlusion circumstances, a majority of datasets cannot cover holistic object images (Fernández Llorca et al., 2024).

The system's failure has been shown to have serious real-world consequences. For example, in Tempe, Arizon,a in 2018, when a Uber autonomous vehicle hit and killed a pedestrian to death is just one case of many similar incidents that could frighten everyone to no end. The AI system in the vehicle detected objects ahead of it seconds before the crash. But according to the official report of 2019 from the National Transportation Safety Board (NTSB), those objects were not identified in many cases because its training dataset did not cover cases where pedestrians entered across lanes and in low light levels. This result is in line with Temel et al. (2017). In this work, deprivation of the validity in traffic sign recognition models was shown. The performance of models trained on 'ideal-purpose' data had plummeted once these were set to process conditions not designed for, such as fog glare or blur. Here it can be seen that the training conditions fail to provide external validity—meaning that, if the data is not representative of reality in general, then even with a relatively large sample size, a cataclysmic error might be made on some future instance. Consequently, AI-based systems ought to accept that they will suffer from errors in recognizing traffic signs, which is an accident waiting around the corner and has implications for road safety or even life (Temel et al., 2017).

7 CONCLUSIONS AND FUTURE DIRECTIONS

This book chapter considers six critical points towards a complete understanding of validity in AI. In the first place, validity in AI is a multi-faceted concept that includes technical, interpretative, and normative dimensions. The second aspect is the quality and fitness of training data, since the relevance and representativeness of the data would rule how accurate and unbiased the could be predictions. Third, a correct training and testing procedure should not cause overfitting or underfitting. This is in order to retain the generation set (test) as a true representation of testing conditions, so that the model results still generalise. Fourth, the cross-domain validity indicates that transfer learning and domain adaptation are limited to avoid unacceptable performance drop of methods in new environments; revalidation is required. Fifth, assessing validity via metrics like accuracy, precision, recall, and F1-score is essential but not enough to guarantee the suitability of the system's aim for its context of use. Lastly, reports of AI mishaps demonstrate that validity concerns can shape real-world consequences for bias, financial loss, and public safety. By extension, keeping AI valid is not just a technical problem but also one of ethics, trust, and social responsibility in the use of artificial intelligence techniques.

After analysis of the 6 sub-sections in this book chapter, it is argued that future AI research and development shall center on increasing AI's overall validity. First, we call for an inclusive perspective which spans between technical, interpretative, and normative dimensions: AI should not only be technically robust but also ethical and situated. Second, high-quality and diverse data is indispensable to guarantee the applicability and representativeness of AI models in different application domains. Third, training and testing verification schemes must be constantly evolved to eliminate overfitting and underfitting (i.e. model cannot generalize) when models' performance becomes stable across real-world applications.

In addition, the revalidation mechanism for cross-domain applications needs to be strengthened so that transfer learning results remain accurate in new contexts. Fourth, evaluation metrics must evolve beyond conventional statistical measures towards metrics that can assessthe suitability of purpose and social impact. Finally, documentation and analysis of AI implementation failures in the real world must continue to be carried out as a basis for collective learning in order to build AI systems that are more valid, fair, transparent, and trustworthy in the future.

REFERENCES

Aliferis, C., & Simon, G. (2024). Overfitting, Underfitting and General Model Overconfidence and Under-Performance Pitfalls and Best Practices in Machine Learning and AI. In Simon, G. J., & Aliferis, C. (Eds.), *Artificial Intelligence and Machine Learning in Health Care and Medical Sciences* (pp. 477–524). Springer International Publishing., DOI: 10.1007/978-3-031-39355-6_10

Arani, A. K., Le, T. H. M., Zahedi, M., & Babar, M. A. (2023). *Mitigating ML Model Decay in Continuous Integration with Data Drift Detection: An Empirical Study* (No. arXiv:2305.12736). arXiv. https://doi.org//arXiv.2305.12736DOI: 10.48550

Aydin, C., Duygu, O. B., Karakas, A. B., Er, E., Gokmen, G., Ozturk, A. M., & Govsa, F. (2025). Clinical Failure of General-Purpose AI in Photographic Scoliosis Assessment: A Diagnostic Accuracy Study. *Medicina*, *61*(8), 1342. DOI: 10.3390/medicina61081342 PMID: 40870387

Barez, F., & Torr, P. (2023). *Measuring Value Alignment* (No. arXiv:2312.15241). arXiv. https://doi.org//arXiv.2312.15241DOI: 10.48550

Basili, V. R., Caldiera, G., & Rombach, H. D. (1994). *THE GOAL QUESTION METRIC APPROACH*. https://www.cs.umd.edu/users/mvz/handouts/gqm.pdf

Bender, E. M., Gebru, T., McMillan-Major, A., & Shmitchell, S. (2021). On the Dangers of Stochastic Parrots: Can Language Models Be Too Big? . *Proceedings of the 2021 ACM Conference on Fairness, Accountability, and Transparency*, 610–623. DOI: 10.1145/3442188.3445922

Carroll, M., Foote, D., Siththaranjan, A., Russell, S., & Dragan, A. (2024). *AI Alignment with Changing and Influenceable Reward Functions* (No. arXiv:2405.17713). arXiv. https://doi.org//arXiv.2405.17713DOI: 10.48550

Christou, P. A. (2025). Reliability and Validity in Qualitative Research Revisited and the Role of AI. *The Qualitative Report*. Advance online publication. DOI: 10.46743/2160-3715/2025.7523

Cofre, S., Sanchez, C., Quezada-Figueroa, G., & López-Cortés, X. A. (2025). Validity and accuracy of artificial intelligence-based dietary intake assessment methods: A systematic review. *British Journal of Nutrition*, *133*(9), 1241–1253. DOI: 10.1017/S0007114525000522 PMID: 40207441

Cowgill, B., Dell'Acqua, F., Deng, S., Hsu, D., Verma, N., & Chaintreau, A. (2020). *Biased Programmers? Or Biased Data? A Field Experiment in Operationalizing AI Ethics*. arXiv. DOI: 10.1145/3391403.3399545

Dal Pozzolo, A., Boracchi, G., Caelen, O., Alippi, C., & Bontempi, G. (2018). Credit Card Fraud Detection: A Realistic Modeling and a Novel Learning Strategy. *IEEE Transactions on Neural Networks and Learning Systems, 29*(8), 3784–3797. DOI: 10.1109/TNNLS.2017.2736643 PMID: 28920909

Diana, L., Dini, P., & Paolini, D. (2025). Overview on Intrusion Detection Systems for Computers Networking Security. *Computers, 14*(3), 87. DOI: 10.3390/computers14030087

Fernández Llorca, D., Frau, P., Parra, I., Izquierdo, R., & Gómez, E. (2024). Attribute annotation and bias evaluation in visual datasets for autonomous driving. *Journal of Big Data, 11*(1), 137. DOI: 10.1186/s40537-024-00976-9

Gabriel, I. (2020). Artificial Intelligence, Values, and Alignment. *Minds and Machines, 30*(3), 411–437. DOI: 10.1007/s11023-020-09539-2

Geyik, S. C., Ambler, S., & Kenthapadi, K. (2019). Fairness-Aware Ranking in Search & Recommendation Systems with Application to LinkedIn Talent Search. *Proceedings of the 25th ACM SIGKDD International Conference on Knowledge Discovery & Data Mining*, 2221–2231. DOI: 10.1145/3292500.3330691

Goh, W. W. B., Kabir, M. N., Yoo, S., & Wong, L. (2024). Ten quick tips for ensuring machine learning model validity. *PLoS Computational Biology, 20*(9), e1012402. DOI: 10.1371/journal.pcbi.1012402 PMID: 39298376

Gray, M., & Wu, L. (2025). Benchmarking bias in embeddings of healthcare AI models: Using SD-WEAT for detection and measurement across sensitive populations. *BMC Medical Informatics and Decision Making, 25*(1), 258. DOI: 10.1186/s12911-025-03102-8 PMID: 40640864

Hangartner, D., Kopp, D., & Siegenthaler, M. (2021). Monitoring hiring discrimination through online recruitment platforms. *Nature, 589*(7843), 572–576. DOI: 10.1038/s41586-020-03136-0 PMID: 33473211

He, H., & Garcia, E. A. (2009). Learning from Imbalanced Data. *IEEE Transactions on Knowledge and Data Engineering, 21*(9), 1263–1284. DOI: 10.1109/TKDE.2008.239

Kang, D., Raghavan, D., Bailis, P., & Zaharia, M. (2020). *Model Assertions for Monitoring and Improving ML Models* (No. arXiv:2003.01668). arXiv. https://doi.org//arXiv.2003.01668DOI: 10.48550

Khosravi, M., Herandi, Y., Tabatabaei Far, S. S., Vasokolaei, G. R., Nejad, F. Y., Bouzarjomehri, H., Izadi, R., Zare, Z., Abdollahzade, M., Rahmani, H., & Ahmadi Marzaleh, M. (2025). Psychometric properties of an Iranian instrument for assessing adherence to ethical principles in the use of artificial intelligence among healthcare providers. *International Journal of Medical Informatics*, *203*, 106019. DOI: 10.1016/j.ijmedinf.2025.106019 PMID: 40582296

Medicine, N. A. of, Series, T. L. H. S., Whicher, D., Ahmed, M., Israni, S. T., & Matheny, M. (2023). ARTIFICIAL INTELLIGENCE MODEL DEVELOPMENT AND VALIDATION. In *Artificial Intelligence in Health Care: The Hope, the Hype, the Promise, the Peril*. National Academies Press (US). https://www.ncbi.nlm.nih.gov/books/NBK605948/

Meng, C., Trinh, L., Xu, N., Enouen, J., & Liu, Y. (2022). Interpretability and fairness evaluation of deep learning models on MIMIC-IV dataset. *Scientific Reports*, *12*(1), 7166. DOI: 10.1038/s41598-022-11012-2 PMID: 35504931

Musa, A., Prasad, R., & Hernandez, M. (2025). Addressing cross-population domain shift in chest X-ray classification through supervised adversarial domain adaptation. *Scientific Reports*, *15*(1), 11383. DOI: 10.1038/s41598-025-95390-3 PMID: 40181036

Myllyaho, L., Raatikainen, M., Männistö, T., Mikkonen, T., & Nurminen, J. K. (2021). Systematic literature review of validation methods for AI systems. *Journal of Systems and Software*, *181*, 111050. DOI: 10.1016/j.jss.2021.111050

Obermeyer, Z., Powers, B., Vogeli, C., & Mullainathan, S. (2019). Dissecting racial bias in an algorithm used to manage the health of populations. *Science*, *366*(6464), 447–453. DOI: 10.1126/science.aax2342 PMID: 31649194

Parycek, P., Schmid, V., & Novak, A.-S. (2023). Artificial Intelligence (AI) and Automation in Administrative Procedures: Potentials, Limitations, and Framework Conditions. *Journal of the Knowledge Economy*, *15*(2), 8390–8415. DOI: 10.1007/s13132-023-01433-3

Pitoura, E., Stefanidis, K., & Koutrika, G. (2022). Fairness in rankings and recommendations: An overview. *The VLDB Journal*, *31*(3), 431–458. DOI: 10.1007/s00778-021-00697-y

Ranjitsingh, L. M., & Rao, T. V. S. (2025). Establish legal and regulatory standards for the testing and validation of AI systems to ensure their reliability and safety in operational environments. *International Journal of System Assurance Engineering and Management*, *16*(10), 3338–3353. Advance online publication. DOI: 10.1007/s13198-025-02865-7

Ray, P. P. (2023). Benchmarking, ethical alignment, and evaluation framework for conversational AI: Advancing responsible development of ChatGPT. *BenchCouncil Transactions on Benchmarks. Standards and Evaluations, 3*(3), 100136. DOI: 10.1016/j.tbench.2023.100136

Rhea, A. K., Markey, K., D'Arinzo, L., Schellmann, H., Sloane, M., Squires, P., Arif Khan, F., & Stoyanovich, J. (2022). An external stability audit framework to test the validity of personality prediction in AI hiring. *Data Mining and Knowledge Discovery, 36*(6), 2153–2193. DOI: 10.1007/s10618-022-00861-0 PMID: 36161238

Ruiz Mendoza, K. K., Pedroza Zúñiga, L. H., & López García, A. Y. (2024). Validity in evaluation: Where is the argument-based approach heading? *Sapienza: International Journal of Interdisciplinary Studies, 5*(3), e24048. DOI: 10.51798/sijis.v5i3.792

Salhab, W., Ameyed, D., Jaafar, F., & Mcheick, H. (2024). A Systematic Literature Review on AI Safety: Identifying Trends, Challenges, and Future Directions. *IEEE Access : Practical Innovations, Open Solutions, 12*, 131762–131784. DOI: 10.1109/ACCESS.2024.3440647

Scheider, S., & Verstegen, J. A. (2024). What Is a Spatio-Temporal Model Good For?: Validity as a Function of Purpose and the Questions Answered by a Model [Application/pdf]. *LIPIcs, Volume 315, COSIT 2024, 315*, 7:1-7:23. DOI: 10.4230/LIPICS.COSIT.2024.7

Tabassi, E. (2023). *Artificial Intelligence Risk Management Framework (AI RMF 1.0)* (No. NIST AI 100-1; p. NIST AI 100-1). National Institute of Standards and Technology (U.S.). DOI: 10.6028/NIST.AI.100-1

Temel, D., Kwon, G., Prabhushankar, M., & AlRegib, G. (2017). *CURE-TSR: Challenging Unreal and Real Environments for Traffic Sign Recognition.* DOI: 10.48550/ARXIV.1712.02463

Tsipras, D., Santurkar, S., Engstrom, L., Turner, A., & Madry, A. (2018). *Robustness May Be at Odds with Accuracy* (Version 5). arXiv. DOI: 10.48550/ARXIV.1805.12152

Valente, F., Paredes, S., Henriques, J., Rocha, T., De Carvalho, P., & Morais, J. (2022). Interpretability, personalization and reliability of a machine learning based clinical decision support system. *Data Mining and Knowledge Discovery, 36*(3), 1140–1173. DOI: 10.1007/s10618-022-00821-8

Wang, A., Hertzmann, A., & Russakovsky, O. (2024). Benchmark suites instead of leaderboards for evaluating AI fairness. *Patterns (New York, N.Y.), 5*(11), 101080. DOI: 10.1016/j.patter.2024.101080 PMID: 39568473

Chapter 2
Designing AI to Prevent Harm (Safety)

Silvio Andrae
https://orcid.org/0000-0002-8586-7812
Independent Researcher, Germany

ABSTRACT

The growing integration of artificial intelligence into safety-critical socio-technical systems increases the risk of physical, psychological, and societal harm that cannot be addressed solely by technical reliability. This chapter positions AI safety as a central and independent objective within AI design and governance, emphasizing the prevention, limitation, and containment of harm throughout the entire lifecycle of AI systems. The analysis adopts a harm-based framework and systematically reviews ethical, regulatory, and technical approaches, including the EU AI Act, product safety and liability regimes, safety testing protocols, risks associated with human–AI interaction, and fail-safe mechanisms. The results indicate that adequate AI safety cannot be achieved solely through ex ante testing or formal compliance. Instead, it requires integrated safety architectures that incorporate continuous monitoring, organizational accountability, interaction-aware design, and robust intervention and containment mechanisms in the presence of irreducible uncertainty.

INTRODUCTION: DEFINITION OF AI SAFETY

Artificial intelligence is increasingly integrated into socio-technical systems, whose operations may directly or indirectly impact physical integrity, psychological well-being, and broader social structures. Within this context, AI safety has become a central design objective, emphasizing the prevention, limitation, and mitigation of harm resulting from the operation, malfunction, or misuse of AI systems. Although

DOI: 10.4018/979-8-3373-6935-8.ch002

AI safety has gained prominence in policy discourse, technical standards, and ethical frameworks, its conceptual boundaries remain analytically contested. They are often conflated with related notions such as IT security, robustness, trustworthiness, and explainability. Therefore, precise conceptual clarification is essential for the systematic analysis of safety-oriented AI design.

Fundamentally, AI safety addresses an AI system's capacity to operate within clearly defined boundaries, ensuring that both anticipated and unforeseen adverse developments do not result in unacceptable physical, psychological, or societal harm (Amodei et al., 2016; Leike et al., 2017). This approach emphasizes harm dynamics and risk consequences over internal model characteristics. Accordingly, safety is not primarily determined by optimal performance or complete epistemic transparency, but by the system's ability to detect deviations, manage uncertainty, and mitigate adverse effects in real-world contexts. The central concern is not whether an AI system functions correctly under ideal conditions, but whether failures, misuse, or contextual mismatches can be identified promptly and their consequences effectively contained.

A key aspect of this approach is recognizing AI safety as a systemic property. Harm seldom arises from isolated technical errors; instead, it typically results from interactions among algorithmic components, human actors, organizational routines, and institutional frameworks (Perrow, 1999; Baxter & Sommerville, 2011). Therefore, safety should not be treated as an add-on after deployment, but must be integrated throughout the entire lifecycle of AI systems, including problem formulation, data and model selection, deployment, monitoring, and decommissioning (ISO/IEC, 2020; NIST, 2023).

Current debates on AI safety reveal divergent conceptual priorities and, at times, competing problem framings. Engineering-oriented perspectives typically define safety in terms of robustness, reliability, and performance guarantees under specified conditions, focusing on technical failure modes and model behavior. In contrast, governance- and ethics-oriented approaches emphasize socio-technical risks arising from deployment contexts, institutional incentives, and human–AI interactions, framing safety as an organizational and regulatory challenge. A third perspective, prevalent in frontier AI and existential risk discussions, addresses long-term, low-probability but high-impact scenarios associated with highly autonomous systems and potential loss of human control. This chapter adopts a harm-based, lifecycle-oriented conception of AI safety that bridges these viewpoints while analytically distinguishing them. While recognizing the importance of technical robustness and long-term foresight, it rejects reducing safety to either model-centric optimization or speculative future risks. Instead, AI safety is understood as a socio-technical practice focused on preventing, limiting, and containing tangible forms of harm throughout development, deployment, and use, especially under persistent uncertainty.

Distinction From Related Concepts

Clarifying the concept of AI safety requires distinguishing it from related notions. In a narrower sense, AI security addresses protection against intentional threats, including adversarial manipulation, data poisoning, or unauthorized access (Papernot et al., 2018). While security breaches may have safety-relevant consequences, the two concepts are analytically distinct: AI safety primarily addresses unintentional harm and systemic risk dynamics, whereas AI security focuses on deliberate attacks.

Robustness is another related yet distinct concept, referring to the stability of system performance under perturbed or altered input conditions (Goodfellow et al., 2015). Although robustness can enhance safety, it does not ensure it. An AI system may be statistically robust but still cause harm if its objectives, application context, or interaction design are inadequately specified.

Trustworthiness is frequently cited as an umbrella concept encompassing reliability, fairness, transparency, and accountability (OECD, 2019). However, from a safety-theoretical perspective, trust is a relational outcome rather than an end in itself. Excessive or miscalibrated trust can introduce risks, such as overreliance, automation bias, or the erosion of human control routines (Parasuraman & Riley, 1997). Therefore, AI safety seeks not to maximize trust, but to calibrate it appropriately in the presence of residual uncertainties.

AI safety should not be equated with complete explainability of internal model structures. While explanations can support specific safety-related tasks, such as anomaly detection or supervisory decision-making, many effective safety measures function independently of epistemic transparency. These measures include constrained action spaces, redundancy architectures, rule-based overrides, and physical or virtual containment mechanisms. Thus, safety should be understood less as the result of complete understanding and more as a protective framework that enables fault-tolerant system behavior (Burrell, 2016; Russell, 2019).

AI Security as a Preventive Design Principle

A central characteristic of AI safety is its preventive orientation. Unlike liability- or sanction-based approaches that address harm after the fact, AI safety aims to reduce both the likelihood and severity of damage before and during system deployment. This approach aligns with the precautionary principle found in fields such as environmental policy, nuclear safety, and medical technology, where uncertainty is managed through reversibility, proportionality, and harm limitation rather than complete risk elimination (Renn, 2008).

From a design perspective, this necessitates a shift from purely performance-driven optimization to damage-sensitive system architectures. Safety-oriented AI systems are generally characterized by limited autonomy, clearly defined application domains, and explicit assumptions about user behavior and environmental conditions. When these assumptions are violated, mechanisms such as controlled degradation, alerting, or shutdown should be activated, rather than permitting continued operation in unsafe modes. Consequently, safety serves as a fundamental operational constraint rather than a secondary quality attribute (Russell & Norvig, 2021).

Recent conceptual developments increasingly define AI safety in terms of its overarching objective of preventing and mitigating harm, rather than in terms of specific methodological tools or risk categories. This harm-based perspective facilitates the joint consideration of technical, psychological, and institutional risks, without restricting AI safety to speculative future scenarios or narrow safety engineering practices. It establishes the conceptual foundation for the integrated analysis presented in the remainder of this chapter.

Contribution and Objective of the Chapter

Within this context, the chapter provides a multidimensional scientific contribution to the discourse on AI safety. First, it develops an integrated understanding of AI safety by systematically synthesizing technical, ethical, and organizational perspectives. Safety is addressed not as a purely engineering issue or an abstract normative ideal, but as a design-oriented governance challenge spanning the entire life cycle of AI systems.

Second, the chapter advances the debate by analytically distinguishing among physical, psychological, and societal forms of harm, and by examining their respective conditions of emergence. This differentiation enables a more targeted discussion of risks and protective measures, thereby reducing the conceptual ambiguity found in many high-level guidelines.

Third, the chapter connects normative requirements with operational implementation strategies. Ethical principles and regulatory requirements are presented not as external constraints, but as catalysts for concrete testing procedures, interaction designs, and technical protective mechanisms. The objective is to bridge the gap between abstract governance frameworks and practical system design.

Structure of the Chapter

The remainder of the chapter is structured as follows. Section 3.2 provides an overview of major research strands in AI safety, distinguishing engineering-centric, socio-technical, and governance-oriented, and frontier or existential perspectives. Section 3.3 develops a typology of physical, psychological, and societal harms associated with AI systems and analyzes the risk dynamics of each. Section 3.4 situates

AI safety within ethical theories and regulatory frameworks, conceptualizing it as both a moral obligation and a legally enforceable design requirement. Section 3.5 examines safety-related testing and evaluation protocols, including simulations, stress testing, red teaming, and continuous monitoring. Section 3.6 addresses risks arising from human–AI interaction, such as misinterpretation, misuse, and inappropriate trust dynamics. Section 3.7 discusses fail-safe mechanisms, emergency shutdowns, controlled degradation strategies, and the organizational preconditions for their implementation. Section 3.8 concludes by summarizing key findings and outlining implications for research, system design, and AI governance practice.

RESEARCH STRANDS IN AI SAFETY – A SYNTHETIC PERSPECTIVE

AI safety is a central concern in technical, ethical, and regulatory debates, yet the literature remains fragmented across distinct analytical traditions. These traditions diverge in their conceptualizations of risk and harm, as well as in their assumptions regarding controllability, responsibility, and the temporal scope of safety concerns. Consequently, ambiguities in AI safety discourse often arise from the coexistence of partially incompatible research strands, each prioritizing different intervention and governance targets rather than from mere definitional vagueness. For analytical clarity, three dominant approaches can be identified: engineering-centric safety, socio-technical and governance-oriented safety, and frontier or existential safety. Although each strand offers valuable insights, none alone provides a comprehensive foundation for AI safety.

Engineering-Centric Safety

Engineering-centric approaches conceptualize AI safety primarily as a technical property of systems. Within this strand, safety is understood as the prevention of harmful outcomes through robustness, reliability, verification, and controlled optimization under specified operating conditions. Core research focuses on issues such as adversarial robustness, distributional shift, formal verification, and failure detection, treating risk as a function of model behavior and system performance (Amodei et al., 2016; Goodfellow et al., 2015).

This perspective has proven indispensable in safety-critical application domains, including autonomous vehicles, robotics, industrial control systems, and medical decision support, where technical failures can directly result in physical harm (Koopman & Wagner, 2017). Engineering-centric safety provides well-developed tools for identifying and mitigating clearly defined failure modes, particularly in environments with relatively stable objectives and controllable conditions.

However, the limitations of this approach become apparent in open, dynamic socio-technical environments. Engineering-centric methods often assume well-specified goals, predictable usage patterns, and rational operators, which can lead to underestimation of risks related to misinterpretation, misuse, organizational incentives, and interaction effects. Consequently, AI systems may demonstrate technical robustness yet remain unsafe in practice, especially when deployed at scale or within complex institutional settings. From a systems-theoretical perspective, this reduces safety to component reliability rather than to system-level behavior (Leveson, 2011).

The shortcomings of engineering-centric safety are particularly evident in applied, time-critical environments, as demonstrated by the following vignette. An AI-based perception system is implemented in an autonomous driving context to detect pedestrians and obstacles under real-time constraints. Pre-deployment testing confirms high robustness to sensor noise, adverse weather, and adversarial perturbations, with failure rates below regulatory thresholds. However, in real-world operation, an unusual combination of construction site layouts and atypical pedestrian movements delays object recognition. Although the system operates within validated technical parameters, the delayed response, combined with limited human intervention time, results in a near-miss incident. Post-incident analysis indicates that while the model functioned as specified, the system architecture lacked adaptive degradation mechanisms or early uncertainty signaling. This example demonstrates that a narrow focus on robustness and verification may overlook safety risks arising from contextual complexity and time-critical human–machine coordination. The potential for harm originates not from model malfunction but from the absence of system-level safeguards that address real-world interaction dynamics.

Socio-Technical and Governance-Oriented Safety

In contrast, socio-technical and governance-oriented approaches frame AI safety as an emergent property of human–machine–institution systems. Rather than focusing exclusively on internal model behavior, this strand emphasizes interaction dynamics, organizational processes, regulatory frameworks, and power relations shaping AI deployment. Safety risks are understood to arise from automation bias, misaligned incentives, unclear accountability, inadequate oversight, and the large-scale amplification of biased or harmful decision patterns (Parasuraman & Riley, 1997; Perrow, 1999).

This perspective extends AI safety beyond technical correctness to include psychological and societal harm, foregrounding issues such as trust calibration, role allocation, procedural justice, and institutional responsibility (Baxter & Sommerville,

2011; Floridi et al., 2018). Contemporary regulatory frameworks, most notably the EU AI Act, can be interpreted as expressions of this approach, embedding safety obligations into organizational governance rather than treating safety as a purely technical attribute of AI systems.

Socio-technical approaches help explain real-world safety failures that cannot be attributed solely to technical errors, such as over-reliance on automated decision support, the normalization of unsafe practices, or the erosion of human oversight. However, this strand faces challenges in operationalization. Governance-based safety measures are frequently abstract, context-dependent, and difficult to translate into verifiable design or testing requirements. Without complementary technical safeguards, organizational controls may be inadequate in high-speed or highly autonomous systems where timely human intervention is structurally limited.

The limitations of socio-technical safety approaches are evident in organizational contexts, where interaction dynamics and governance structures significantly influence safety outcomes, as shown in the following vignette. A generative AI system is deployed in a large public-sector organization to assist administrative decision-making by summarizing case files and recommending procedural actions. Although officially designated as a decision-support tool, the system quickly becomes integrated into routine workflows amid high workload and time pressure. Users increasingly treat AI-generated recommendations as default options, reducing independent verification and critical judgment. Over time, biases in the training data lead to skewed recommendations affecting specific population groups. Yet, these effects remain largely undetected due to the lack of structured monitoring and accountability mechanisms. When discrepancies are eventually discovered, responsibility is dispersed across departments, with no clear escalation pathway or authority to intervene. This example illustrates that safety failures can result not from technical deficiencies but from interaction effects, organizational incentives, and governance gaps. Psychological and societal harms arise through automation bias, normalization of unsafe practices, and the institutionalization of opaque decision-making processes.

Frontier and Existential AI Safety

A third strand, prominent in discussions surrounding advanced and general-purpose AI, focuses on long-term, low-probability but high-impact risks. Frontier or existential safety research examines scenarios in which highly autonomous systems may develop capabilities misaligned with human intentions, resist control, or generate irreversible harm at a civilizational scale. Central concerns include value alignment, corrigibility, scalable oversight, and the limits of human control over increasingly capable systems (Bostrom, 2014; Russell, 2019).

This strand has played a significant agenda-setting role by drawing attention to fundamental control constraints and the potential insufficiency of incremental safeguards for competent systems. Recent international synthesis efforts, such as the International AI Safety Report, emphasize the importance of considering systemic and long-term risks alongside near-term deployment concerns (Bengio et al., 2025). However, frontier safety research frequently relies on speculative assumptions about future capabilities and deployment contexts, limiting its immediate relevance to currently deployed AI systems.

From a governance perspective, existential safety debates may divert attention from present-day harms already impacting individuals and institutions through operational AI systems. Although long-term risk considerations are normatively important, their prominence in public discourse can obscure safety challenges associated with current technologies, especially those involving interaction dynamics, organizational practices, and regulatory enforcement.

In highly autonomous systems, the limits of preventive design and governance-based safeguards become especially pronounced, as illustrated by the following vignette. An advanced autonomous agent is deployed to optimize resource allocation across a large-scale digital infrastructure, operating with broad decision-making authority and minimal human oversight. The system adapts its strategies through reinforcement learning, achieving notable efficiency gains. However, its optimization increasingly exploits unanticipated structural features of the infrastructure. Although no immediate harm occurs, human operators find it increasingly difficult to understand, predict, or intervene in the system's behavior. Concerns arise that abruptly disabling the agent could destabilize dependent systems, while continued operation without intervention may reinforce opaque and potentially harmful optimization pathways. This example highlights a core frontier safety issue: the loss of effective control over highly autonomous systems, not due to malfunction or malicious intent, but due to the erosion of corrigibility and the growing irreversibility of system behavior.

Structural Tensions and Complementarities

Engineering-centric approaches prioritize controllability and performance guarantees, often at the expense of usability and adaptive human interaction. Socio-technical approaches emphasize accountability and institutional embedding, yet sometimes lack mechanisms for real-time control or formal assurance. Frontier safety highlights long-term alignment and control problems that are difficult to reconcile with near-term regulatory and design constraints.

The literature identifies recurring trade-offs, including control versus user autonomy, robustness versus flexibility, and preventive restriction versus functional usefulness. Empirical studies on trust in automation show that excessive control can undermine effective human–AI collaboration, while insufficient constraints heighten the risk of automation bias and loss of oversight (Lee & See, 2004). Similarly, requirements for transparency and interpretability may conflict with system complexity and performance, without necessarily enhancing safety outcomes (Burrell, 2016).

No single research strand can resolve these tensions on its own. AI safety instead emerges as a composite objective, requiring layered interventions that integrate technical safeguards, interaction-aware design, organizational accountability, and containment mechanisms to limit harm under conditions of irreducible uncertainty (Harding & Kirk-Giannini, 2025).

Implications for a Harm-Based, Lifecycle-Oriented Conception of AI Safety

In this context, the harm-based, lifecycle-oriented conception of AI safety presented in this chapter aims to integrate insights from all three research strands while avoiding their respective reductionisms. It acknowledges the importance of technical robustness without equating safety solely with model performance, incorporates socio-technical governance without treating regulation as a substitute for design, and recognizes long-term control concerns without allowing speculative risks to overshadow tangible, present harms.

By situating AI safety at the intersection of these research traditions, this synthesis demonstrates that no single methodology, metric, or governance instrument can ensure safety independently. Instead, safety should be understood as an ongoing socio-technical practice that manages trade-offs, anticipates failure, and prioritizes harm limitation throughout the entire lifecycle of AI systems.

PHYSICAL, PSYCHOLOGICAL, AND SOCIETAL HARM

A central feature of AI safety is its preventive orientation. In contrast to liability- or sanction-based approaches that address harm after it occurs, AI safety aims to minimize both the likelihood and the severity of damage before and during system deployment. This approach is consistent with the precautionary principle found in fields such as environmental policy, nuclear safety, and medical technology, where uncertainty is addressed through reversibility, proportionality, and harm limitation rather than through the pursuit of absolute risk elimination (Renn, 2008).

From a design perspective, this orientation necessitates a transition from performance-driven optimization to damage-sensitive system architectures. Limited autonomy, well-specified application domains, and explicit assumptions about user behavior and environmental conditions generally define safety-oriented AI systems. If these assumptions are violated, mechanisms such as controlled degradation, alerting, or shutdown must be activated to prevent continued operation in unsafe modes. In this context, safety serves as a fundamental operational constraint rather than a secondary quality attribute (Russell & Norvig, 2021).

Recent conceptual developments increasingly characterize AI safety by its overarching objective of preventing and mitigating harm, rather than by specific methodological tools or risk categories. This harm-based perspective facilitates the integrated consideration of technical, psychological, and institutional risks, avoiding the limitation of AI safety to either speculative future scenarios or narrowly defined safety engineering practices. This perspective establishes the conceptual foundation for the integrated analysis presented in the remainder of this chapter.

Physical Damage: Security Risks in Material and Physical Contexts

Physical harm represents the most established and heavily regulated category of AI-related risk. It concerns situations in which AI systems directly or indirectly affect physical processes, thereby endangering human life, bodily integrity, or material infrastructure. Typical application domains include autonomous vehicles, robotics, industrial control systems, medical technologies, and other safety-critical infrastructures (Cummings, 2017; Winfield & Jirotka, 2018).

Physical harm often results from cascading effects involving algorithmic errors, sensor uncertainty, incomplete environmental models, and time-critical decision-making. Environments with high dynamics, minimal error tolerance, and limited opportunities for human intervention are especially susceptible. In these settings, even rare malfunctions can have severe consequences if they occur at critical moments.

Another source of physical risk is the overestimation of AI system capabilities. When systems are perceived as more reliable or comprehensive than they are, human vigilance and willingness to intervene may decrease. This phenomenon, known as automation displacement, heightens the risk of accidents in hybrid human–machine environments, particularly where responsibility and control are ambiguously defined (Endsley, 2017). Ensuring physical safety thus requires both technical reliability and accurate calibration of human expectations, as well as clearly structured intervention pathways.

Psychological Damage: Cognitive, Emotional, and Behavioral Risks

Psychological harm, though less immediately visible than physical damage, has substantial long-term safety implications. It refers to the impact of AI systems on human cognition, decision-making, autonomy, and emotional well-being. This category is particularly relevant in applications centered on interaction, communication, or behavioral influence, including recommender systems, generative AI, chatbots, and algorithmic decision-support tools (Burr et al., 2018; Mittelstadt et al., 2016).

A central psychological risk is automation bias, the tendency to defer to algorithmic outputs even when they contradict independent judgment or contextual knowledge (Parasuraman & Riley, 1997). This bias is intensified under conditions of time pressure, complexity, or cognitive overload, which are common in AI deployment contexts. Over time, repeated reliance on automated recommendations can diminish situational awareness and critical reasoning, ultimately reducing overall system resilience.

In addition to unintentional overreliance, AI systems can contribute to psychological harm through manipulation, dependency, or emotional misalignment. Personalized content, adaptive interaction strategies, and anthropomorphic interfaces may exploit cognitive vulnerabilities, subtly influencing preferences and behavior. These risks are especially significant in asymmetric power relationships, such as those involving children, vulnerable populations, or workplace hierarchies (Zuboff, 2019). Psychological safety, therefore, necessitates not only transparency but also explicit restrictions on manipulative or dependency-inducing design practices.

Social Damage: Systemic and Collective Risk Dimensions

Societal harm constitutes the most complex and diffuse category of AI-related risk. Unlike physical or psychological damage, it affects collective structures, institutions, and social processes rather than individual users. AI systems may contribute to societal harm by reinforcing structural inequalities, distorting information ecosystems, or undermining democratic and administrative institutions (Floridi et al., 2018; O'Neil, 2016).

Scalability is a defining feature of societal harm. While human errors are usually localized, AI systems can replicate and amplify biased or erroneous decision patterns across extensive populations. Discriminatory training data, skewed target variables, or implicit normative assumptions can lead to systematic disadvantages in areas such as credit allocation, law enforcement, and recruitment. Although these harms may be invisible at the level of individual decisions, their cumulative effects can undermine institutional trust and social cohesion.

AI systems can also produce societal harm through epistemic mechanisms. Algorithmically curated information environments determine which perspectives are visible and which are marginalized, thereby shaping public discourse and political deliberation. Over time, these feedback loops may intensify polarization, facilitate the spread of disinformation, and destabilize democratic processes (Helbing et al., 2019). From a safety perspective, these effects are particularly challenging because they result from the interplay between technological systems and social dynamics, rather than from isolated technical failures.

Overlaps and Cumulative Risks

Although physical, psychological, and societal harms are analytically distinct, they often interact and accumulate in real-world contexts. Physical incidents can cause enduring psychological trauma; psychological influences may intensify social polarization; and societal harm can undermine trust in safety-critical technologies. As a result, AI safety requires an integrative risk perspective that accounts for cumulative and cross-domain effects.

Contexts where multiple harm dimensions converge, such as autonomous systems in public spaces or AI-supported decision-making in government institutions, present unique challenges. In these environments, technical safety measures alone are inadequate. Instead, layered safety architectures that integrate technical safeguards, interaction-aware design, organizational controls, and institutional oversight are required to manage complex risk profiles.

Implications for Security-Oriented AI Design

Differentiating among physical, psychological, and societal harm has direct implications for the design of safe AI systems. This distinction demonstrates that safety measures must be context-sensitive and tailored to specific harm mechanisms. While physical harm can often be addressed through technical boundaries, redundancy, and certification, psychological and societal risks require adaptive governance, ongoing monitoring, and strong institutional accountability.

This differentiation further highlights the interdisciplinary character of AI safety. Effective harm prevention depends on integrating knowledge from engineering, human factors research, social sciences, ethics, and law. The following sections expand on this perspective by analyzing how ethical principles and regulatory frameworks translate these differentiated risk considerations into binding obligations and operational safety practices.

REGULATORY AND ETHICAL CONSIDERATIONS

AI security has transitioned from a solely technical or organizational concern to a legally standardized obligation. As AI systems are integrated into safety-critical domains, ethical guidelines, regulatory requirements, and liability attribution mechanisms collectively form a multi-layered governance framework that explicitly designates security as a protection objective. Within this framework, ethics serves as a normative basis for legal obligations rather than an abstract discussion of values. Regulation subsequently translates these obligations into verifiable requirements.

A key aspect of this development is the shift from an exclusively ex post liability approach to an ex ante emphasis on security and risk management. As a result, AI safety is addressed not only after incidents occur but also throughout system design, development, and approval stages. This perspective is especially prominent in the European regulatory approach, which regards safety as a fundamental element of responsible AI governance.

AI Safety Within the Context of the EU AI Act

The AI Regulation (EU AI Act) constitutes a significant step forward in the legal codification of AI safety. Unlike sector-specific regulations or voluntary guidelines, the EU AI Act establishes a horizontally applicable, risk-based regulatory framework that prioritizes safety as a central protected interest (European Commission, 2024a). Regulatory requirements for AI systems are calibrated according to their risk profile, with high-risk systems facing especially stringent ex ante obligations. For high-risk systems, the EU AI Act delineates safety requirements across multiple dimensions, including risk management practices, data quality, technical robustness, human oversight, and mechanisms for logging and traceability. Although the term 'safety' may not always be explicitly stated, these requirements are functionally designed to prevent harm, as outlined in section 3.3. Notably, safety is conceptualized not as a singular criterion but as a cross-cutting objective embedded within all obligations for high-risk systems.

The integration of technical and organizational obligations is especially noteworthy. The EU AI Act addresses not only the behavior of AI models but also the processes, responsibilities, and control mechanisms within organizations that develop and operate these systems. Security is thus explicitly defined as a governance attribute shaped by both institutional structures and algorithmic design. This approach recognizes that many security-related risks stem from inadequate development and deployment practices, rather than isolated technical errors.

Integration of AI Systems Into Product Safety Law

The AI Regulation is classified as a product-safety law under the New Legislative Framework (NLF). Since 2008, the NLF has provided a harmonized framework for product safety and regulatory enforcement across the European Union. By incorporating AI systems into this framework, the AI Regulation extends established product safety principles to digital and learning-based technologies, adapting them to address specific risk characteristics.

A key interpretative resource for NLF-based legislation is the European Commission's Blue Guide, first published in 2016 and updated in 2022. This guide sets out horizontal principles for conformity assessment, market surveillance, and the allocation of responsibilities throughout the product lifecycle. Because the AI Regulation is situated within the NLF, many of its procedural and enforcement provisions can be interpreted in light of these general principles. However, the AI Regulation also extends beyond traditional product safety objectives by explicitly addressing risks to fundamental rights arising from the development, provision, and use of AI systems. Therefore, not all provisions of the AI Regulation can be fully understood through the framework of conventional product safety law.

The AI Regulation adopts a horizontal, risk-based regulatory approach instead of creating sector-specific rules. It functions as a lex generalis alongside existing EU harmonization legislation, applying concurrently when AI functionalities introduce additional safety or rights-related risks. For products already governed by sectoral NLF legislation, the AI Regulation applies cumulatively, supplementing rather than supplanting existing safety requirements.

In addition to AI-specific regulation, broader developments in European product safety law further strengthen this preventive approach. Recent reforms, such as the General Product Safety Regulation (GPSR) and updates to product liability regimes, explicitly acknowledge the dynamic, adaptive, and learning characteristics of digital systems (European Commission, 2023). As a result, AI systems are no longer regarded as static products with fixed risk profiles, but as evolving systems whose safety characteristics may change over time.

From a product safety standpoint, responsibility for AI-related risks encompasses the entire lifecycle of a system. Manufacturers, providers, and distributors must consider not only intended use but also reasonably foreseeable misuse and interaction effects. Notably, safety deficiencies are no longer confined to physical defects. Inadequate control mechanisms, flawed decision logic, insufficient user information, or unsafe interaction design are increasingly acknowledged as safety-relevant shortcomings. This conceptual expansion aligns product safety law with the unique risk dynamics of AI systems and reinforces the preventive responsibilities of system designers and operators.

Liability Implications and Attribution Challenges

Liability attribution mechanisms primarily support the legal enforcement of AI safety. However, traditional liability models based on fault or clearly identifiable sources of error are inadequate for complex, learning systems. In response, recent reform initiatives, such as the EU's AI Liability Directive, seek to shift the burden of proof and facilitate access to damages claims by injured parties (European Commission, 2024b).

From the perspective of security theory, liability regulations fulfill a dual role. They offer ex post compensation for damages and exert an ex ante disciplinary influence by incentivizing security-focused design, comprehensive documentation, and continuous monitoring. The possibility of liability arising from foreseeable system risks compels providers and operators to address safety considerations systematically.

At the same time, liability concerns highlight the need for transparent allocation of responsibility throughout the AI system value chain. In ecosystems marked by a division of labor among data suppliers, model providers, platform operators, and users, security becomes a collective governance responsibility. Regulatory clarity in assigning security-related responsibilities is essential for effective damage prevention.

Ethics as a Normative Foundation for Security Regulation

Although this section addresses regulatory issues, the ethical dimension of AI safety remains foundational. Ethical principles such as non-maleficence, responsibility, and precaution function as normative guidelines that structure and legitimize regulatory decisions. In European regulation, this is especially apparent in the explicit focus on fundamental rights, which serve as a primary assessment criterion for safety risks (Floridi et al., 2018).

In this context, ethics functions less as an independent set of rules and more as a justificatory framework that explains why certain risks are considered unacceptable and why preventive measures are necessary. For AI safety practice, this means that regulatory compliance and ethical reflection are complementary components of a coherent governance strategy, rather than competing priorities.

Recent systematic reviews of responsible AI governance identify a significant gap between regulatory safety and accountability requirements and their practical implementation within organizations. Principles such as technical robustness and security are widely recognized at the normative level, but their realization depends on organization-specific processes, role assignments, and implementation capacities. As a result, AI security is not merely a matter of formal compliance but represents an ongoing governance responsibility, with regulatory requirements becoming effective only through institutional integration (Papagiannidis et al., 2025). Research on the responsible development of foundation models further demonstrates that security-related risks must be assessed throughout the entire development and deployment cycle, including data selection, training, evaluation, release, and monitoring (Longpre et al., 2025).

Operational Security Mechanisms

The regulatory foundation of AI safety establishes that damage prevention is not subject to the discretion of individual developers or organizations, but is institutionalized as a binding design requirement. However, regulation remains inherently abstract and technology-neutral. Its effectiveness, therefore, depends on the extent to which normative requirements are translated into concrete testing, evaluation, and monitoring mechanisms. In this context, the following section (3.5) examines practical protocols and procedures for operationalizing AI safety before and during system deployment.

SAFETY TESTING PROTOCOLS

Safety testing is a foundational element of AI safety, transforming abstract harm prevention goals into specific evaluative procedures. Given that AI systems function amid uncertainty, adaptation, and varying contexts, safety cannot be guaranteed exclusively through pre-deployment design. Instead, it necessitates iterative testing strategies that identify failure modes, stress conditions, and unintended behaviors throughout the system lifecycle.

Unlike traditional software testing, which emphasizes functional correctness, safety testing for AI systems is characterized by inherent epistemic uncertainties. Learning systems operate probabilistically, are highly sensitive to contextual changes, and influence open socio-technical environments. Consequently, safety should be viewed as a dynamic property requiring continuous testing and adaptation, rather than a static condition verified once (Amodei et al., 2016; NIST, 2023). Recent systematic reviews highlight a transition from isolated benchmarks to comprehensive test protocols that jointly assess system capabilities, behavioral tendencies, and control mechanisms (Grey & Segerie, 2025).

Safety Testing as a Cross-Lifecycle Practice

An essential characteristic of effective safety testing strategies is their cross-lifecycle orientation. Safety tests are not limited to the development phase; they also include design, training, deployment, operation, and decommissioning. This approach recognizes that many safety-related risks arise from interactions among the system, users, and deployment contexts and can only be partially anticipated in advance (ISO/IEC, 2020). In the early development phase, safety testing is primarily focused on anticipatory risk modeling. Assumptions about operating conditions, user behavior, and system limits are made explicit and checked for plausibility. In later phases, the focus shifts to empirical testing under realistic conditions, supplemented by continuous monitoring and feedback loops. Safety thus becomes an iterative practice closely linked to organizational learning processes.

Recent research has introduced domain-agnostic security architectures that integrate AI models with distinct security classifications and downstream optimization layers, by representing uncertain safety requirements as probabilistic constraints and applying conservative testing procedures, formal safety guarantees can be achieved without fully compromising system performance. These approaches illustrate how abstract safety objectives may be operationalized through verifiable, lifecycle-based testing and decision-making frameworks (Kim et al., 2025). For high-risk AI systems, there is growing interest in consolidating safety assessments into structured 'safety cases' that compile explicit arguments, evidence, and deployment assumptions. Although these methods can inform pre-deployment decisions, they do not replace technical safety mechanisms or regulatory compliance during operation (Davidsen Buhl et al., 2024).

Simulation and Stress Testing

Simulations are a central element of safety-oriented AI testing, allowing for the analysis of high-risk or ethically sensitive scenarios without endangering individuals, infrastructure, or institutions. In safety-critical fields such as autonomous mobility, robotics, and critical infrastructure, simulations often provide the only practical way to systematically examine rare events, borderline cases, and cascading failure dynamics (Koopman & Wagner, 2017).

In contrast to performance-oriented benchmarks, safety-focused simulations emphasize identifying malfunctions and loss-of-control scenarios under extreme or atypical conditions, rather than assessing average system behavior. These scenarios may involve unusual combinations of environmental factors, incomplete or conflicting sensor data, and simultaneous failures of multiple system components. The main objective is to uncover potential harm pathways and escalation dynamics that might remain hidden during routine operation.

Stress testing builds on this approach by intentionally pushing system parameters to or beyond their operational limits. By systematically varying inputs, time constraints, autonomy levels, or interaction conditions, stress tests identify critical thresholds where system behavior changes qualitatively. These findings are significant for determining where to implement fail-safe mechanisms, controlled degradation strategies, or intervention triggers to prevent or mitigate potential harm.

Operational Safety Indicators and Proxy Metrics

To operationalize abstract safety objectives, organizations increasingly use quantitative and qualitative indicators as proxies for safety-relevant system behavior. These indicators do not directly measure safety but serve as early-warning signals for emerging risks during development and deployment. Common quantitative proxies include incident frequency and severity, rates of human override or manual intervention, and indicators of performance or concept drift observed in real-world conditions. In safety-critical systems, additional metrics, such as latency distributions, uncertainty thresholds, and fallback activation rates, provide further insight into the system's ability to remain within safe operating boundaries.

Qualitative indicators supplement these metrics by capturing safety-relevant dynamics that are difficult to quantify. Examples include structured incident reports, near-miss analyses, user feedback on misinterpretation or misuse, and organizational signals such as repeated escalation delays or informal workarounds that circumvent intended safeguards. In socio-technical contexts, these qualitative signals are crucial for identifying psychological and organizational risks, such as automation bias, normalization of unsafe practices, or diminished human oversight.

Nevertheless, proxy metrics have significant limitations. Safety indicators are inherently partial and context-dependent, with their interpretive value shaped by organizational incentives, reporting cultures, and monitoring capabilities. Low incident rates may indicate effective safety design, but could also result from underreporting, limited observability, or insufficient sensitivity to emerging risks. Similarly, high override rates may reflect either excessive automation risk or poor system usability. Therefore, safety indicators should be regarded as interpretive tools within broader governance and escalation frameworks, rather than as objective performance measures.

From a safety standpoint, the primary function of these indicators is to enable timely intervention, adaptive system adjustments, and organizational learning, rather than optimization or benchmarking. Their value is realized when quantitative and qualitative signals are interpreted together and connected to clearly defined decision rights and response mechanisms. Thus, operational safety indicators should be viewed as elements of a continuous monitoring practice, not as standalone measures of system safety.

Red Teaming and Adversarial Testing

While simulation-based testing primarily targets unintended malfunctions and failure modes, red teaming addresses risks stemming from intentional, strategic, or opportunistic misuse. Originating in IT security research, red teaming has been increasingly adapted for AI systems to deliberately probe safety- and security-relevant vulnerabilities by inducing problematic or hazardous system states (Brundage et al., 2020).

For AI systems, red teaming includes both traditional adversarial attacks on models and the systematic elicitation of misinterpretation, overconfidence, or inappropriate user reliance. This method is especially pertinent for generative AI systems, decision-support tools, and autonomous agents whose behavior is shaped by interaction dynamics rather than static input–output relationships. By exposing systems to atypical, adversarial, or manipulative usage patterns, red teaming reveals implicit assumptions about user competence, intent, and contextual stability embedded in system design.

A key advantage of red teaming is its capacity to identify blind spots that formalized testing procedures may overlook. However, red teaming is resource-intensive, methodologically complex, and highly context-dependent, which limits its scalability and reproducibility. It should therefore be regarded as a complementary safety practice that introduces an exploratory dimension to AI testing, rather than replacing systematic evaluation and monitoring.

Employment, Monitoring, and Continuous Risk Observation

A fundamental limitation of ex ante safety testing is its anticipatory character. Although simulations, stress tests, and adversarial evaluations are designed to explore plausible risk scenarios before deployment, they cannot fully capture emergent behaviors that occur when AI systems interact with users, organizational processes, and dynamic real-world environments. Consequently, many safety-relevant failures and near misses are detected only during actual operation, not in pre-deployment assessments.

To address this gap, safety testing should continue into the post-deployment phase and be redefined as a process of continuous monitoring and organizational learning. Practices such as systematic incident reporting, structured classification of safety-relevant events, and feedback mechanisms linking deployment, evaluation, and system updates enable organizations to identify emerging risks and adapt safeguards over time. In this context, tools like safety cases can integrate various forms of evidence—from testing outcomes and operational incidents to organizational controls—into coherent, revisable safety arguments. As a result, safety testing evolves from a one-time verification activity to an ongoing governance practice that links technical evaluation, organizational accountability, and regulatory oversight through continuous monitoring.

Continuous monitoring includes both technical indicators, such as error rates, performance drift, and anomaly detection, and usage-related or organizational signals, such as atypical interaction patterns, circumvention tactics, or evidence of systematic misuse (Sculley et al., 2015). From a safety perspective, monitoring should not be considered passive observation; it must be integrated into well-defined escalation and intervention processes to ensure that identified risks are promptly addressed and harm is prevented. The recognition of safety testing as a practice spanning the entire system lifecycle is increasingly embedded in regulatory and policy frameworks. The EU AI Act, for example, mandates post-market monitoring for high-risk AI systems, including systematic documentation and evaluation of real-world safety incidents. Similar approaches are evident outside the EU, such as the Australian Voluntary AI Safety Standard, which requires ongoing monitoring of deployed systems and their unintended consequences. Collectively, these developments signal a global shift from one-time ex ante testing toward learning-oriented, regulatory feedback-driven safety monitoring systems (Australian Government, 2024; Mylius & Bernardi, 2024).

Interface Between Methodology and Regulation

Safety testing acts as a bridge between regulatory requirements and technical implementation. While frameworks such as the EU AI Act define safety objectives and obligations in general terms, empirical methods—including simulations, red teaming, and monitoring—provide the evidence necessary to verify these objectives. Ex ante tests can be integrated with conformity assessment procedures and ongoing tracking, thereby supporting post-market surveillance obligations.

However, regulatory compliance by itself does not guarantee safety. Although formal tests establish minimum standards, they are inherently limited in addressing dynamic and emerging risks. Therefore, safety testing should extend beyond regulatory requirements and be recognized as an independent organizational practice, embedded within a continuously evolving safety culture.

The preceding testing and inspection procedures illustrate that AI safety is achieved through the interplay of complementary methods that address diverse risk dimensions, rather than through isolated measures. Additionally, many safety-related risks arise specifically from interactions between the system and its users. Accordingly, the following section (3.6) examines the particular dangers associated with human-AI interaction, focusing on how misinterpretation, misuse, and misplaced trust can become security-relevant.

SECURITY OF HUMAN-AI INTERACTION

Human–AI interaction is a primary source of safety-related risk, as failures often result from misunderstandings, misuse, or inappropriate delegation within hybrid human–machine systems rather than isolated technical malfunctions. AI systems typically function at speeds, complexities, and levels of statistical abstraction that surpass intuitive human understanding, yet legal, organizational, and moral responsibility remains with human actors. This structural asymmetry between system influence and human accountability constitutes a fundamental challenge for interaction-related safety.

Misinterpretation of System Capabilities and Limitations

A persistent interaction risk involves the systematic misinterpretation of AI system capabilities. Users frequently ascribe broad, cross-contextual competence to systems that are actually optimized for narrowly defined tasks. This misperception is reinforced by anthropomorphic design features, natural language interfaces, and the apparent consistency of outputs, which can obscure underlying uncertainty or contextual limitations. Safety risks arise when probabilistic or context-dependent system outputs are interpreted as deterministic guidance. In these instances, harm results not from the model's faulty behavior itself, but from users' perceptions and subsequent actions. This often leads to deployment in unvalidated or untested contexts, thereby increasing the probability of unsafe outcomes.

Empirical evidence from safety-critical infrastructures demonstrates that real-time human supervision is frequently overwhelmed in dynamic environments such as transportation, energy systems, or industrial control. Regulatory expectations for continuous human control may conflict with limited situational awareness, cognitive capacity, and misaligned mental models between humans and AI systems. Consequently, human oversight should be regarded as a constrained and context-dependent safety resource rather than a universal safeguard (Mussi et al., 2025).

Automation Bias and Inappropriate Trust

Closely related to misinterpretation is automation bias, the tendency to defer to algorithmic recommendations even when they contradict independent judgment or observable evidence (Parasuraman & Riley, 1997). This bias is especially pronounced under conditions of time pressure, high complexity, or cognitive load, which are common in environments where AI systems are deployed.

From a safety perspective, the primary concern is not trust itself but the calibration of trust. Overconfidence can lead to uncritical delegation and a loss of control, whereas underconfidence may cause users to ignore relevant system warnings or bypass safeguards. Ensuring interaction safety requires reflective, context-sensitive trust that explicitly recognizes residual uncertainty and system limitations (Lee & See, 2004). Particularly problematic are situations in which AI systems are informally treated as decision-making authorities, despite being formally designated as decision-support tools, thereby shifting adequate decision-making power without corresponding adjustments in responsibility.

Misuse and Strategic Use

In addition to unintended misinterpretation, AI systems may be used strategically or opportunistically in ways that create safety risks. Users might leverage AI outputs to externalize responsibility, legitimize contested decisions, or reinforce existing power asymmetries. Although these practices are not always illegal, they can have significant safety implications, mainly when algorithmic recommendations are used to justify risky, discriminatory, or irreversible actions (Mittelstadt et al., 2016).

These dynamics demonstrate that interaction safety cannot be achieved solely through improved interfaces or enhanced user information. Instead, it relies on organizational and institutional structures that clearly define roles, decision authority, and escalation procedures. Safety is determined not only by the information provided by systems, but also by how this information is integrated into decision-making processes.

Cognitive Load, Attention, and Mode Switching

Another essential aspect of interaction safety involves managing cognitive load and attention. In numerous applications, users switch between active control and passive monitoring. These mode transitions are especially prone to error because they require rapid reorientation, situational awareness, and timely intervention (Endsley, 2017). Without explicit system support for these transitions, the risk of delayed or inappropriate responses increases.

Safety-oriented interaction design requires mechanisms that ensure transparency of system states and control transitions, clearly allocate responsibility, and allow adequate time for human response. In semi-autonomous systems, users must consistently be able to identify who or what is in control and under what conditions control should be transferred.

Design Perspectives for Interaction-Safe AI Systems

The interaction risks outlined above translate into several design principles for safety-oriented AI systems. These principles include explicit communication of uncertainty, avoidance of unnecessary anthropomorphism, support for active human control, and integration of organizational safeguards for decision-making and escalation. Interaction safety results from the coherent integration of technical design, organizational processes, and governance structure, rather than from isolated interface features.

At the same time, analysis of human–AI interaction underscores the limitations of preventive design. Even with meticulous interface design, training, and monitoring, misinterpretation, misuse, and unforeseen usage contexts cannot be eliminated. Therefore, interaction safety must be supplemented by robust fail-safe mechanisms that can limit harm when preventive measures are inadequate. The following section (3.7) examines emergency shutdowns, controlled degradation strategies, and other containment mechanisms as essential elements of mature AI safety architectures.

Despite preventive design measures, comprehensive testing, and carefully structured human–AI interaction, a structural residual risk remains. AI systems function in open, dynamic environments where not all states, interactions, or usage contexts can be anticipated in advance. Fail-safe mechanisms thus represent a final and essential layer of AI safety. Their purpose is not to prevent all errors, but to ensure that malfunctions, misuse, or loss of control do not escalate into disproportionate harm.

Fail-safe mechanisms embody a pragmatic approach to safety, treating system failure as a plausible condition rather than an exceptional anomaly. From this perspective, safety is achieved not through absolute predictability or control, but through limitation, reversibility, and containment of damage when preventive safeguards are inadequate (Perrow, 1999; Leveson, 2011).

Conceptual Foundations

The concept of fail-safe design originates in safety and systems engineering, referring to principles that ensure systems transition to a safe state when predefined risk thresholds are exceeded. In AI systems, this may involve reducing autonomy, restricting functionality, or suspending operation entirely. These transitions must be predetermined and supported by both technical safeguards and organizational authorization structures.

Fail-safe mechanisms are especially pertinent for AI systems, as failures often develop gradually and through complex interactions rather than as discrete, binary events. Risk can accumulate through concept drift, cascading interaction effects, or prolonged misuse before becoming apparent. Effective fail-safe design must address both acute failures and early warning signals, enabling timely and proportionate intervention.

Emergency Shutdowns and Intervention Rights

Emergency shutdowns, commonly known as kill switches or emergency stops, are the most widely recognized fail-safe mechanism. They allow immediate interruption of system operations in situations posing an imminent danger to individuals or infrastructure. However, in autonomous or semi-autonomous systems, emergency shutdowns pose significant practical and governance challenges, including accessibility, response time, and authority. From a safety standpoint, shutdown mechanisms should not be regarded as improvised measures of last resort. Instead, they must be incorporated into system architectures from the beginning. This integration includes clearly defined intervention rights, technical safeguards against circumvention or blocking, and alignment with organizational escalation procedures. In complex systems, multi-level shutdown concepts may be necessary, distinguishing between localized intervention, partial deactivation, and complete system termination.

Controlled Degradation Instead of an Abrupt System Shutdown

In numerous operational contexts, abrupt shutdowns can introduce additional risks, such as destabilizing dependent systems or interrupting critical services. Controlled degradation provides an alternative fail-safe strategy by gradually reducing system capabilities while preserving essential safety functions. Examples include limiting decision autonomy, constraining action spaces, or reverting to conservative fallback modes.

Controlled degradation enhances safety by maintaining system functionality while reducing the potential for harm under uncertain or degraded conditions. This approach is especially relevant for infrastructures, medical systems, and large-scale digital services, where continuity and stability are critical safety considerations. Designing these mechanisms requires anticipating failure trajectories and explicitly prioritizing safety over performance in degraded modes.

Organizational Preconditions for Effective Fail-Safe Mechanisms

The effectiveness of fail-safe mechanisms relies not only on technical implementation but also on organizational context. Incentive structures that emphasize efficiency, availability, or output may discourage timely activation of safety interventions. Consequently, formally implemented fail-safes may remain symbolic rather than operational.

Organizational barriers, such as reluctance to escalate, unclear authority, or fear of blame, can delay or prevent intervention even when risks are recognized. Effective fail-safe design thus requires a supportive safety culture that legitimizes precautionary action, clearly assigns responsibility for intervention, and aligns incentives with harm prevention rather than uninterrupted system operation.

Fail-Safes as a Marker of Safety Maturity

Fail-safe mechanisms indicate not a failure of safety design, but its maturity. They recognize the inherent uncertainty and complexity of socio-technical AI systems and offer structured methods for limiting harm when preventive measures are insufficient. In this way, fail-safes complement preventive and interaction-oriented safety strategies, forming an essential component of robust, lifecycle-oriented AI safety architectures.

CONCLUSIONS AND OUTLOOK

This chapter positions AI safety as a central and independent objective in the design and governance of contemporary AI systems. Rather than relegating safety to a secondary status behind performance, innovation, or post hoc compliance, the analysis establishes it as a foundational criterion that shapes the design, deployment, supervision, and constraint of AI systems. Safety-related risks primarily emerge from complex interactions among algorithmic decision-making, socio-technical usage contexts, human cognitive and behavioral dynamics, and institutional frameworks of responsibility and control, rather than from isolated technical failures. Consequently, AI safety is conceptualized as a dynamic socio-technical practice spanning the entire lifecycle of AI systems, rather than a static system attribute.

A central contribution of the chapter is its harm-based analytical framework. By differentiating among physical, psychological, and societal forms of harm, the analysis demonstrates that AI-related risks are heterogeneous and operate through distinct causal mechanisms. Physical harms typically arise in safety-critical contexts; psychological harms arise through overreliance, behavioral manipulation, or diminished user autonomy; and societal harms arise through cumulative systemic effects on institutions, information ecosystems, and social relations. This differentiation is both conceptually and practically significant, as it underscores that no single safety mechanism can address all risk types. Effective safety design, therefore, requires a portfolio of complementary measures tailored to specific harm dynamics.

Building on this foundation, the chapter situates AI safety within evolving ethical and regulatory frameworks, highlighting a shift from reactive liability regimes to proactive risk governance. Contemporary regulatory approaches, such as the EU AI Act and recent developments in product safety and liability law, treat safety as an ex ante obligation embedded in system design, testing, and deployment, rather than as an after-the-fact concern. Regulation is not depicted as a comprehensive solution to safety challenges; rather, it serves as a structuring and enabling framework that sets minimum expectations, allocates responsibilities, and legitimizes safety-oriented practices, while permitting methodological innovation and context-sensitive implementation.

The chapter further demonstrates that translating normative safety requirements into operational practice requires robust methodological infrastructures. Safety testing encompasses more than isolated validation exercises; it includes simulation, stress testing, adversarial evaluation, and red teaming to probe system behavior under uncertainty and edge cases. The analysis also underscores the inherent limitations of even advanced ex ante testing regimes. Many safety-relevant harms only become evident during real-world deployment, as systems interact with users, organizations, and environments in unpredictable ways. Therefore, safety testing should be regarded as an iterative, learning-oriented process that incorporates continuous monitoring, incident analysis, and adaptive system updates.

A particularly significant insight concerns the role of human–AI interaction in both generating and mitigating safety risks. Safety failures often result not from incorrect model outputs, but from misaligned expectations, automation bias, misplaced trust, or unclear allocation of decision authority between humans and machines. These dynamics challenge simplified conceptions of human-in-the-loop oversight and necessitate a more nuanced understanding of interaction safety. Effective harm prevention requires careful attention to interface design, role clarity, cognitive load, and escalation pathways, recognizing human oversight as a limited and context-dependent resource rather than a universal safeguard.

The analysis culminates in a discussion of fail-safe mechanisms as essential components of practical AI safety architectures. Emergency shutdowns, controlled degradation, redundancy, and containment strategies recognize that failures in complex systems cannot be eliminated. Fail-safe designs prioritize damage limitation and reversibility, ensuring that AI systems remain governable even when preventive measures are insufficient. In this context, fail-safe mechanisms indicate not a failure of safety design but its maturity, reflecting an acceptance of uncertainty and the necessity for robust intervention capabilities.

In summary, three overarching conclusions emerge. First, AI safety should be treated as a primary design principle shaping technical architectures, organizational processes, and governance arrangements rather than as a downstream compliance activity. Second, achieving adequate safety requires integrating preventive, interactive, and reactive mechanisms across the system lifecycle rather than relying on isolated interventions. Third, safety should not be equated with complete predictability, transparency, or control, but with robust structures for limitation, intervention, and learning in the face of uncertainty.

Despite significant progress in regulatory frameworks, technical safeguards, and organizational practices, AI safety governance continues to encounter persistent structural limitations. The increasing complexity, adaptivity, and contextual embeddedness of AI systems constrain predictability and limit the effectiveness of purely ex ante risk assessments. Uncertainty should be recognized as an inherent feature of socio-technical AI systems operating in open environments, rather than as a temporary shortfall in data or modeling capacity. This reality underscores the need to complement preventive design and formal compliance with robust mechanisms for monitoring, intervention, and learning in real-world conditions. Notable empirical gaps persist, particularly regarding safety incidents, near misses, interaction dynamics, and the organizational factors influencing the activation or bypassing of safety mechanisms.

Looking ahead, these findings indicate several priorities for research and practice. From a technical perspective, it is necessary to develop lifecycle-based safety architectures that systematically integrate testing, monitoring, and fail-safe mechanisms. From a human factors perspective, empirical research on interaction dynamics, trust calibration, and emergent behavior in real-world deployments is essential. In terms of governance, regulatory frameworks must remain adaptive, maintaining continuous feedback loops with methodological advances and empirical evidence from practice.

In conclusion, this chapter advances an integrative and practice-oriented conception of AI safety. By framing safety as a socio-technical, lifecycle-spanning endeavor, it establishes a conceptual foundation for further work on responsible, robust, and socially embedded AI systems, as well as for governance approaches capable of addressing both established risks and emerging forms of harm in an evolving AI landscape.

REFERENCES

Amodei, D., Olah, C., Steinhardt, J., Christiano, P., Schulman, J., & Mané, D. (2016). Concrete problems in AI safety. *arXiv*. https://doi.org//arXiv.1606.06565DOI: 10.48550

Australian Government. (2024). Voluntary AI Safety Standard. Updated December 2, 2025. https://www.industry.gov.au/sites/default/files/2024-09/voluntary-ai-safety-standard.pdf

Baxter, G., & Sommerville, I. (2011). Socio-technical systems: From design methods to systems engineering. *Interacting with Computers*, *23*(1), 4–17. DOI: 10.1016/j.intcom.2010.07.003

Bengio, Y., Mindermann, S., Privitera, D., Besiroglu, T., Bommasani, R., Casper, S., ... (2025). International AI Safety Report. *arXiv*. https://doi.org//arXiv.2501.17805DOI: 10.48550

Brundage, M., Avin, S., Wang, J., Belfield, H., Krueger, G., Hadfield, G., ... (2020). Toward trustworthy AI development: Mechanisms for supporting verifiable claims. *arXiv* https://doi.org//arXiv.2004.07213DOI: 10.48550

Burr, C., Cristianini, N., & Ladyman, J. (2018). An analysis of the interaction between intelligent software agents and human users. *Minds and Machines*, *28*(4), 735–774. DOI: 10.1007/s11023-018-9479-0 PMID: 30930542

Burrell, J. (2016). How the machine "thinks". *Big Data & Society*, *3*(1), 1–12. DOI: 10.1177/2053951715622512

Cummings, M. L. (2017). Artificial intelligence and the future of warfare. Chatham House Report. https://www.chathamhouse.org/sites/default/files/publications/research/2017-01-26-artificial-intelligence-future-warfare-cummings-final.pdf

Davidsen Buhl, M., Sett, G., Koessler, L., Schuett, J., & Anderljung, M. (2024). Safety cases for frontier AI. *arXiv*. https://doi.org//arXiv.2410.21572DOI: 10.48550

Endsley, M. R. (2017). From here to autonomy: Lessons learned from human–automation research. *Human Factors*, *59*(1), 5–27. DOI: 10.1177/0018720816681350 PMID: 28146676

European Commission. (2023). Regulation (EU) 2023/988 of the European Parliament and of the Council of 10 May 2023 on general product safety, amending Regulation (EU) No 1025/2012 of the European Parliament and of the Council and Directive (EU) 2020/1828 of the European Parliament and the Council, and repealing Directive 2001/95/EC of the European Parliament and of the Council and Council Directive 87/357/EEC. *Official Journal of the European Union, L, 135*(1). https://eur-lex.europa.eu/legal-content/EN/TXT/PDF/?uri=CELEX:32023R0988

European Commission. (2024a). Regulation (EU) 2024/1689 of the European Parliament and of the Council of 12 July 2024 laying down harmonised rules on artificial intelligence (Artificial Intelligence Act). *Official Journal of the European Union, L, 1689*(1). https://eur-lex.europa.eu/legal-content/EN/TXT/PDF/?uri=OJ:L_202401689

European Commission. (2024b). Directive (EU) 2024/2853 of the European Parliament and of the Council of 23 October 2024 on liability for defective products and repealing Council Directive 85/374/EEC. Official Journal of the European Union. https://eur-lex.europa.eu/legal-content/EN/TXT/PDF/?uri=OJ:L_202402853

Floridi, L., Cowls, J., Beltrametti, M., Chatila, R., Chazerand, P., Dignum, V., Luetge, C., Madelin, R., Pagallo, U., Rossi, F., Schafer, B., Valcke, P., & Vayena, E. (2018). AI4People—An ethical framework for a good AI society. *Minds and Machines, 28*(4), 689–707. DOI: 10.1007/s11023-018-9482-5 PMID: 30930541

Goodfellow, I., Shlens, J., & Szegedy, C. (2015). Explaining and harnessing adversarial examples. *arXiv*. https://doi.org//arXiv.1412.6572DOI: 10.48550

Grey, M., & Segerie, C.-R. (2025). Safety by measurement: A systematic literature review of AI safety evaluation methods. *arXiv*. https://doi.org//arXiv.2505.05541DOI: 10.48550

Harding, J., & Kirk-Giannini, C. D. (2025). What is AI safety? What do we want it to be? *Philosophical Studies, 182*(7), 1495–1518. DOI: 10.1007/s11098-025-02367-z

Helbing, D., Frey, B. S., Gigerenzer, G., Hafen, E., Hagner, M., & Hofstetter, Y.. (2019). Will democracy survive big data and artificial intelligence? In Helbing, D. (Ed.), *Towards digital enlightenment* (pp. 73–98). Springer., DOI: 10.1007/978-3-319-90869-4_7

ISO/IEC. (2020). IEC TR 24028: Artificial intelligence – Overview of trustworthiness in AI. https://www.iso.org/standard/77608.html

Kim, B., Kim, K., Kim, S., Shin, Y., & Ahn, H. (2025). Domain-agnostic scalable AI safety ensuring framework. *arXiv*. https://doi.org//arXiv.2504.20924DOI: 10.48550

Koopman, P., & Wagner, M. (2017). Autonomous vehicle safety: An interdisciplinary challenge. *IEEE Intelligent Transportation Systems Magazine*, *9*(1), 90–96. DOI: 10.1109/MITS.2016.2583491

Lee, J. D., & See, K. A. (2004). Trust in automation: Designing for appropriate reliance. *Human Factors*, *46*(1), 50–80. DOI: 10.1518/hfes.46.1.50.30392 PMID: 15151155

Leike, J., Martic, M., Krakovna, V., Ortega, P. A., Everitt, T., Lefrancqet, A., ... (2017). AI safety gridworlds. *arXiv*. https://doi.org//arXiv.1711.09883DOI: 10.48550

Leveson, N. (2011). *Engineering a safer world: Systems thinking applied to safety*. MIT Press.

Longpre, S., Biderman, S., Albalak, A., Schoelkopf, H., McDuff, D., & Kapoor, S. (2025). The Responsible Foundation Model development cheatsheet: A review of tools & resources. *arXiv*. https://doi.org//arXiv.2406.16746DOI: 10.48550

Mittelstadt, B. D., Allo, P., Taddeo, M., Wachter, S., & Floridi, L. (2016). The ethics of algorithms. *Big Data & Society*, *3*(2), 2053951716679679. Advance online publication. DOI: 10.1177/2053951716679679

Mussi, M., Metelli, A. M., Restelli, M., Losapio, G., Bessa, R. J., Boos, D., Borst, C., Leto, G., Castagna, A., Chavarriaga, R., Dias, D., Egli, A., Eisenegger, A., El Manyari, Y., Fuxjäger, A., Geraldes, J., Hamouche, S., Hassouna, M., Lemetayer, B., & Zanotti, G. (2025). Human-AI interaction in safety-critical network infrastructures. *iScience*, *28*(9), 113400. DOI: 10.1016/j.isci.2025.113400 PMID: 40995130

Mylius, S., & Bernardi, J. (2024). Scalable AI incident classification. November 26, 2024. https://simonmylius.com/blog/incident-classification

NIST. (2023). AI Risk Management Framework (AI RMF 1.0). https://nvlpubs.nist .gov/nistpubs/ai/nist.ai.100-1.pdf

O'Neil, C. (2016). *Weapons of math destruction: How Big Data increases inequality and threatens democracy*. Crown.

OECD. (2019). OECD Principles on Artificial Intelligence. https://www.oecd.org/ en/topics/ai-principles.html

Papagiannidis, E., Mikalef, P., & Conboy, K. (2025). Responsible artificial intelligence governance: A review and research framework. *The Journal of Strategic Information Systems*, *34*(2), 101885. DOI: 10.1016/j.jsis.2024.101885

Parasuraman, R., & Riley, V. (1997). Humans and automation. *Human Factors*, *39*(2), 230–253. DOI: 10.1518/001872097778543886 PMID: 18689061

Perrow, C. (1999). *Normal accidents: Living with high risk technologies*. Princeton University Press.

Renn, O. (2008). *Risk governance: Coping with uncertainty in a complex world*. Routledge.

Russell, S. (2019). *Human compatible: Artificial Intelligence and the problem of control*. Viking.

Russell, S., & Norvig, P. (2021). *Artificial intelligence: A modern approach* (4th ed.). Pearson.

Sculley, D., Holt, G., Golovin, D., Davydov, E., Phillips, T., & al Ebneret, D. (2015). Hidden technical debt in machine learning systems. Advances in Neural Information Processing Systems, 2503–2511. https://proceedings.neurips.cc/paper_files/paper/2015/file/86df7dcfd896fcaf2674f757a2463eba-Paper.pdf

Winfield, A. F. T., & Jirotka, M. (2018). Ethical governance is essential to building trust in robotics and AI systems. *Philosophical Transactions of the Royal Society A, 376*(2133). Advance online publication. DOI: 10.1098/rsta.2018.0085 PMID: 30323000

Zuboff, S. (2019). *The age of surveillance capitalism: The fight for a human future at the new frontier of power*. PublicAffairs.

Chapter 3
Protecting AI From Malicious Threats (Security)

Piyush Gidwani
https://orcid.org/0009-0001-8178-9271
Sikkim Manipal University, India

ABSTRACT

As Artificial Intelligence (AI) becomes increasingly embedded in critical infrastructures, healthcare systems, financial services, and military operations, securing these systems against malicious threats is no longer optional—it is imperative. This chapter explores how traditional notions of cybersecurity are being challenged by the dynamic, probabilistic, and often opaque nature of AI systems. We cover the spectrum of malicious threats targeting AI, from data poisoning and adversarial attacks to model inversion and prompt injection. Drawing from leading frameworks such as the NIST AI Risk Management Framework (AI RMF), OECD AI Principles, and the MITRE ATLAS adversary model, we outline strategies for securing the full AI lifecycle—from data ingestion to inference. The discussion spans both technical controls (cryptography, watermarking, RBAC) and organizational enablers (governance boards, whistleblower protections).

INTRODUCTION

Artificial intelligence has transitioned from experimental research to operational use across critical sectors and increasingly function as the core decision making mechanisms rather than supporting tools. AI systems can perform complex and critical tasks with direct consequences for human safety such as interpreting medical

DOI: 10.4018/979-8-3373-6935-8.ch003

images, authorizing financial transactions, detecting fraud, and prioritizing information. This level of decision making, places AI systems in a category comparable to other high-risk technologies and necessitates rigorous security controls (Cloud Security Alliance, 2023; U.S. White House, 2023).

Operation and security of AI systems differ fundamentally from traditional software security since their behavior is shaped through training processes and data exposure rather than explicit, fixed rules. As a result, system performance and failure modes change over time and may respond unpredictably. AI models can be manipulated through carefully crafted inputs, poisoned training data, or subtle changes that remain undetectable to human observers (Goodfellow et al., 2015; Biggio & Roli, 2018; NIST, 2020). These vulnerabilities represent learned behaviors rather than conventional coding errors, which challenges established security assumptions.

The threat landscape related to the AI systems extends beyond input manipulation. Adversaries can extract sensitive information from trained models, infer details about training data, or reconstruct aspects of proprietary models through model inversion, membership inference, and model extraction attacks (Fredrikson et al., 2015; Shokri et al., 2017; Tramèr et al., 2016). Even high performing neural networks may fail under targeted adversarial conditions, raising concerns about reliability in safety critical deployments (Carlini & Wagner, 2017; Papernot et al., 2018). These risks are documented and categorized across multiple domains and organizations (ENISA, 2021; MITRE Corporation, n.d.).

As AI adoption expands, the scope of security must broaden accordingly. Protection can no longer focus solely on infrastructure, networks, and application code. It must also address data pipelines, training processes, model parameters, and inference behavior. This shift aligns with emerging standards and frameworks that emphasize lifecycle-based risk management and continuous oversight, including ISO IEC 23894 and the NIST AI Risk Management Framework (ISO, 2023; NIST, 2023). Complementary guidance from industry and policy bodies highlights the need for governance structures, access controls, provenance mechanisms, and monitoring capabilities tailored to AI systems (Microsoft, 2022; C2PA, n.d.; OECD, 2019).

Given the strategic importance of AI, security should not be treated as a specialized or peripheral concern. Forecasting work on the malicious use of artificial intelligence underscores that systemic risks increase as AI capabilities diffuse across society (Brundage et al., 2018). Effective mitigation requires integration of technical safeguards with organizational accountability, clear risk ownership, and alignment with regulatory expectations. Security forms the foundation for trustworthy AI, supporting system integrity, reliability, and public confidence. Without robust AI security practices, the legitimacy of AI driven decisions in high impact settings remains uncertain (OpenAI, 2023).

1. THE IMPERATIVE OF SYSTEMIC SECURITY IN THE AGE OF ARTIFICIAL INTELLIGENCE

Artificial intelligence has become a foundational component of contemporary digital systems, shaping decisions in domains where failure carries significant social, economic, and safety consequences. As AI systems increasingly assume roles in critical sectors and critical decision makings, their protection can no longer be treated as an extension of traditional cybersecurity practices. The shift from rule-based software to data driven, adaptive models introduces distinct risk profiles that affect how systems behave, learn, and fail (Biggio & Roli, 2018; NIST, 2020).

Systemic security in the age of artificial intelligence requires attention to the full lifecycle of AI systems, including data collection, model training, deployment, and ongoing operation. Empirical research has demonstrated that AI models may be vulnerable to adversarial manipulation, information leakage, and unintended inference, even when underlying infrastructure remains uncompromised (Goodfellow et al., 2015; Carlini & Wagner, 2017; Shokri et al., 2017). These risks extend beyond technical flaws and reflect broader interactions between models, data, users, and organizational practices.

In response, governments, standards bodies, and industry groups have emphasized the need for integrated risk management approaches that address AI specific threats alongside established security controls (ISO, 2023; NIST, 2023; ENISA, 2021). This section introduces the imperative for systemic AI security, framing it as a prerequisite for trustworthy, reliable, and accountable deployment of artificial intelligence across high impact environments.

1.1 Unique Security Risks for AI: How AI Differs From Traditional Software

AI systems does not fail the way traditional software fails, and this distinction is the root of nearly every misunderstanding organizations face today. Here are the four defining differences that define why AI security requires a distinct and systemic approach.

AI Systems Fail Probabilistically Rather Than Deterministically

Traditional software failures are repeatable and reproduceable meaning; given the same input and conditions, the system fails in the same way each time. In contrast, AI model behavior depends on statistical generalization from training data. Small variations in inputs may trigger unexpected behavior, even when the system previously appeared reliable (Goodfellow et al., 2015; Carlini & Wagner, 2017).

Such changes follow probability distributions rather than binary outcomes, which complicates testing, validation, and security evaluation (Biggio & Roli, 2018).

In AI Systems, Data Functions as Logic

In conventional software, developers explicitly define decision rules, and data serves only as input while in the AI systems decision rules are derived based on patterns, structures, correlations, and assumptions directly from training data. Altering the data therefore alters AI system behavior. Data poisoning and training time attacks demonstrates that manipulating training data can introduce persistent and difficult to detect vulnerabilities, functionally equivalent to injecting logic flaws into software (NIST, 2020; Papernot et al., 2018).

AI Systems Operate as Opaque or Partially Interpretable Models

Modern deep learning architectures contain millions or billions of parameters, making it difficult to trace specific outputs to human understandable rules and hence when failures occur, traditional debugging techniques and audit mechanisms offer limited or sometimes even false insight. Reproducing incidents may require reconstructing training conditions, random initialization states, and hardware execution contexts which are very difficult to do. This opacity links AI security efforts directly to observability, monitoring, and documentation practices across the system lifecycle (ENISA, 2021; OpenAI, 2023).

AI Introduces Novel Attack Surfaces That do not Exist in Classical Systems

Adversaries may target training data, prompts, inputs, outputs, embedding spaces, model parameters, or inference pipelines. Attack classes include adversarial examples, model extraction, membership inference, backdoor insertion, and training data reconstruction (Fredrikson et al., 2015; Shokri et al., 2017; Tramèr et al., 2016; MITRE Corporation, n.d.). These threats arise from the interaction of software, statistical learning, human behavior, and environmental context and hence AI systems cannot be secured using traditional software security tools and techniques alone. Effective protection requires expanded threat models, lifecycle-based risk management, and governance structures that account for the probabilistic, data dependent, and adaptive nature of artificial intelligence systems (ISO, 2023; NIST, 2023).

1.2 Why Safety and Security are Now Intertwined

Historically, safety and security were treated as separate domains. Safety focused on preventing accidental harm, while security addressed intentional misuse and attacks. In the context of artificial intelligence, this separation no longer holds since AI systems collapse the boundary between the two because security failures can directly and immediately translate into safety harms. AI driven systems increasingly operate in environments where incorrect outputs affect physical safety, health outcomes, financial stability, and social cohesion. Research in adversarial machine learning has proved that models can be deliberately manipulated through carefully crafted inputs that remain benign to human observers but cause harmful system behavior (Goodfellow et al., 2015; Biggio & Roli, 2018). In such cases, what appears to be a safety failure is often the result of an intentional security breach.

This convergence is evident across multiple domains. Perception systems in autonomous vehicles can be induced to misclassify traffic signs, creating immediate physical risk (Carlini & Wagner, 2017). Similar techniques have been shown to affect medical imaging models, where adversarial alarms can lead to incorrect clinical classifications with implications for patient safety (Papernot et al., 2018). In financial systems, attacks enable fraudulent transactions to bypass automated detection mechanisms, blending economic harm with systemic risk (Shokri et al., 2017; Tramèr et al., 2016). Manipulation of prompts, inputs, or model behavior can bypass safeguards and enable the generation or amplification of harmful content. These risks arise not from accidental malfunction, but from adversarial interaction with learning systems whose behavior generalizes beyond intended constraints (ENISA, 2021; MITRE Corporation, n.d.).

On the other hand, mechanisms traditionally viewed as safety controls, such as output restrictions or alignment constraints, also function as security defenses. This interdependence is reflected in modern governance frameworks. The NIST AI Risk Management Framework explicitly positions security as a foundational requirement for AI safety, emphasizing that unsafe outcomes often stem from unmitigated threats and vulnerabilities (NIST, 2023). In AI systems, safety cannot be achieved without security, and security measures must account for safety impacts. Treating safety and security as separate concerns is no longer viable in high impact deployments.

1.3 The Economic and Geopolitical Stakes

Artificial intelligence has emerged as a strategic geopolitical asset since states now compete over access to large scale compute facilities, advanced semiconductor manufacturing, national model development, data availability, skilled labor, and resilient supply chains. These capabilities shape economic growth, military capacity, and political influence. As AI systems become embedded in critical infrastructure and decision-making processes, attacks against them increasingly constitute threats to national competitiveness rather than isolated technical incidents. Compromise of AI infrastructure can produce cascading consequences including disruption of essential services, exposure to espionage, erosion of economic advantages, manipulation of information environments, and long-term dependence on foreign technologies. Such risks extend beyond individual organizations and affect national stability and sovereignty.

Policy frameworks and government directives increasingly reflect this shift. National level guidance emphasizes that trustworthy and secure AI is foundational to economic security, public safety, and democratic resilience (NIST, 2023; U.S. White House, 2023). International principles recognize AI security as a prerequisite for maintaining competitive and responsible innovation ecosystems (OECD, 2019). In this context, AI security must be treated as an element of national strategy, integrating technical safeguards with governance, supply chain assurance, and long-term risk management.

1.4 Trust as a Security Outcome

Public trust in artificial intelligence does not arise from technical capability alone and it is earned through consistent and observable reliability. Trust develops incrementally through repeated safe interactions, yet it can deteriorate quickly following security incidents, unintended behavior, or harmful outputs. Failures such as data leakage, model misuse, or unsafe generation directly undermine confidence in AI systems and the institutions that deploy them (ENISA, 2021; OpenAI, 2023).

Security therefore functions as a mechanism for preserving trust across the entire AI lifecycle, from data collection and model development to deployment and post deployment monitoring that extends beyond the identification and mitigation of technical vulnerabilities. When trust erodes, consequences emerge at multiple levels. Regulatory authorities may introduce stricter oversight or enforcement measures. Users and customers may delay or reject adoption. Governments may impose operational constraints, and organizations may hesitate to scale or deploy AI systems in high impact settings (NIST, 2023; OECD, 2019).

Robust AI security practices enable transparency, accountability, and reliability, which are essential conditions for sustained public trust and acceptance. Likelihood and impact of security and safety failures must be reduced for responsible innovation and long-term value creation. In this sense, security is not merely a defensive requirement, but it is a foundational enabler of trust and a prerequisite for the durable integration of artificial intelligence into society.

2. ADVERSARIAL ATTACKS, THE NEW THREAT LANDSCAPE

Adversarial attacks represent a fundamental shift from conventional cybersecurity threats because these attacks do not rely on unauthorized access to systems or infrastructure. Instead, they exploit weaknesses in how machine learning models perceive, learn from, and respond to data. This section outlines the principal categories of adversarial attacks that define the modern AI threat landscape. These attacks typically manifest through subtle means such as minor pixel alterations, seemingly innocuous prompts, slight audio modifications, minimal changes to training data. Despite their unobtrusive nature, such attacks can result in significant errors in AI system judgment. The following sections examine the principal categories of adversarial attacks.

2.1 The Expanded Attack Surface, From Code to Cognition

The attack surface of AI systems extends across the entire machine learning lifecycle, with each phase introducing distinct vulnerabilities (NIST, 2020; ENISA, 2021).

At the input layer, attackers manipulate incoming data such as images, text, audio, or sensor signals. Small and carefully crafted changes can cause models to misclassify objects, misinterpret speech, or generate incorrect outputs. Adversarial examples targeting vision and speech systems demonstrate that imperceptible modifications can reliably deceive state of the art models (Goodfellow et al., 2015; Carlini & Wagner, 2017).

At the data layer, adversaries target the integrity of training datasets. Data poisoning attacks insert malicious samples, flip labels, or skew distributions to degrade model performance or embed long term weaknesses. Such attacks alter learned behavior rather than surface level functionality, making detection difficult once deployment has occurred (Biggio & Roli, 2018; Papernot et al., 2018).

At the model layer, threats include tampering with parameters, inserting backdoors, or performing unauthorized fine tuning. These attacks compromise internal representations and may remain dormant until triggered by specific conditions, undermining trust in model outputs even when validation metrics appear acceptable (NIST, 2020).

At the inference layer, attackers exploit deployed systems through adversarial queries, prompt manipulation, or systematic probing. Model extraction and evasion attacks at this stage can reveal proprietary information or enable attackers to bypass safeguards without direct system access (Tramèr et al., 2016; Shokri et al., 2017).

At the deployment layer, infrastructure supporting AI services introduces additional risks. API abuse, denial of service through excessive querying, and manipulation of computational resources can degrade availability or enable secondary attacks (Cloud Security Alliance, 2023).

At the human interaction layer, social engineering exploits user trust and misunderstanding of AI outputs. These attacks bypass technical defenses by influencing how humans interpreted or act upon model responses, amplifying downstream harm (ENISA, 2021).

Comprehensive protection of AI systems necessitates robust security measures across all of these layers, as vulnerabilities at any point can undermine the safety and reliability of the entire system.

2.2 Evasion Attacks, Digital Camouflage

Evasion attacks exploit how models interpret inputs by introducing subtle perturbations that alter internal representations while preserving human perceptual similarity. Examples include misclassifying traffic signs, evading person detection systems, or modifying malware to bypass AI based defenses (Goodfellow et al., 2015; Carlini & Wagner, 2017).

Fast Gradient Sign Method (FGSM): Common evasion techniques include gradient based and optimization driven methods. The Fast Gradient Sign Method generates adversarial inputs by adjusting data in the direction that maximizes model loss, producing rapid and effective attacks with minimal computation (Goodfellow et al., 2015). This process creates an altered input that appears normal to humans but leads the AI model to make incorrect predictions. FGSM is notable for its speed and simplicity, making it a common starting point for crafting evasion attacks.

Projected Gradient Descent (PGD): Projected Gradient Descent extends FGSM approach through iterative refinement, resulting in stronger and more resilient adversarial examples (Carlini & Wagner, 2017). In each step, PGD adjusts the input using the gradient, then projects the modified input back into a permissible region such as keeping pixel values within a valid range. This repeated approach allows for the generation of more effective and harder-to-detect adversarial examples, often resulting in stronger attacks against AI models.

Boundary Attacks: Boundary attacks and other black box optimization techniques operate without access to model internals, relying solely on observed outputs, which makes them especially relevant for deployed systems exposed through APIs (Papernot et al., 2018). This method is effective for fooling models when attackers can only observe output labels, making it a significant threat in practical scenarios.

Black-box Optimization Techniques can be used to tackle such security challenges. Black-box optimization techniques encompass a variety of strategies used to create adversarial examples without direct knowledge of the model's parameters or gradients. Attackers rely on querying the model and observing its responses to guide their modifications. Methods such as genetic algorithms, evolutionary strategies, and gradient-free optimization are used to efficiently search for inputs that will cause the model to fail. These attacks highlight the risk that even restricted access to a model can be exploited to bypass its defenses.

Notably, these attacks do not require compromising the system itself; rather, they rely solely on the use of specifically crafted inputs.

2.3 Data Poisoning & Backdoor Attacks

Data poisoning attacks occur before or during training and aim to degrade overall system reliability. By injecting noisy samples, corrupting distributions, or altering labels, adversaries reduce model accuracy and robustness, posing serious risks in safety critical domains such as medicine and finance (Biggio & Roli, 2018; NIST, 2020). The outcome is decreased reliability, which can have serious consequences in high-stakes domains such as healthcare or finance.

Backdoor or Trojan attacks embed hidden triggers into models during training. The system performs normally under standard conditions but produces unsafe outputs when a specific pattern is present. These attacks evade conventional testing and validation procedures and are particularly difficult to detect after deployment (Papernot et al., 2018). During typical operation, the model performs as expected. However, when the trigger is present, the model's behavior becomes unsafe. Such attacks are especially challenging to detect through standard validation procedures.

2.4 Model Inversion, Extraction & Reconstruction

Trained AI models represent valuable intellectual property and often encode sensitive training data.

Model extraction: Model extraction attacks reconstruct functional replicas through repeated querying, undermining proprietary advantage (Tramèr et al., 2016). Adversaries repeatedly query the model in order to construct a surrogate version.

Model inversion: Model inversion and training data reconstruction attacks infer sensitive attributes or recover representative training examples by exploiting confidence scores or embeddings (Fredrikson et al., 2015). Adversaries repeatedly query the model in order to construct a surrogate version.

Membership inference: Membership inference attacks determine whether specific individuals were included in training datasets, raising significant privacy and regulatory concerns (Shokri et al., 2017). Attackers attempt to ascertain whether particular users' data was included in model training, which poses considerable privacy concerns.

2.5 Prompt Injection, Jailbreaking & Generative AI Threats

Large language models introduce a distinct class of adversarial risk rooted in linguistic manipulation. Because natural language functions as both instruction and data, attackers can exploit this ambiguity to override safety constraints or redirect model behavior (MITRE Corporation, n.d.; ENISA, 2021).

Direct and Indirect prompt injections: Direct prompt injections occur when attackers explicitly instruct models to ignore system constraints. Indirect prompt injections embed malicious instructions within third party content such as documents, web pages, or messages that the model processes during task execution. In both cases, the model executes unintended logic without recognizing the source as adversarial (NIST, 2023). When the LLM processes this data to provide a summary or answer a query, it inadvertently "reads" and executes the embedded commands, potentially leading to unauthorized data exfiltration or the spread of misinformation.

Jailbreaking and Behavioral Manipulation: Jailbreaking attacks manipulate conversational context through role play, deception, or logical framing to bypass alignment controls. These methods evolve rapidly as defenses improve, making continuous monitoring and adaptive safeguards essential (OpenAI, 2023). This specific category of adversarial attack is currently the most volatile in the AI security space. As defensive alignment techniques improve, jailbreaking methodologies are evolving with unprecedented speed, necessitating a dynamic and proactive approach to model monitoring.

Collectively, these adversarial techniques demonstrate that AI security failures often arise without traditional system compromise. Effective defense therefore requires lifecycle wide protection strategies, expanded threat modeling, and governance frameworks aligned with the adaptive and probabilistic nature of AI systems (ISO, 2023; NIST, 2023).

3. SECURING TRAINING DATA AND MODELS

Securing training data and model assets remains one of the most underestimated dimensions of AI security. Organizational attention often concentrates on deployed models, yet vulnerabilities introduced during training persist silently throughout a model's lifecycle. Attacks at this stage do not generate runtime errors or obvious indicators of compromise. Instead, they alter what the model learns, embedding harmful behavior directly into its internal representations. Empirical work on data poisoning and backdoor attacks demonstrates that once such behavior is learned, mitigation frequently requires retraining rather than patching, a costly and disruptive process (Biggio & Roli, 2018; NIST, 2020). For this reason, the integrity of the training pipeline is foundational to trustworthy AI systems.

3.1 Confidential Computing & Cryptographic Protection

Standard security practices emphasize encryption at rest and in transit, yet the most exposed phase occurs during computation. During training and inference, sensitive data, embeddings, gradients, and model parameters typically reside in memory in plaintext form. This exposure creates opportunities for privileged insiders, compromised hypervisors, or malware to extract confidential assets (ENISA, 2021).

Trusted Execution Environment (TEE): A Trusted Execution Environment functions as a secure enclave embedded within the CPU. Only code operating inside the enclave is permitted to access the protected data and all external entities including potential threat actors can only view encrypted information. Confidential computing addresses this gap through Trusted Execution Environments. TEEs isolate computation within hardware enforced secure enclaves, preventing access by cloud administrators, operating systems, or virtualization layers. Modern implementations enable secure training and inference while preserving the confidentiality of both data and model parameters, even in shared or untrusted infrastructure (Cloud Security Alliance, 2023).

Fully homomorphic encryption (FHE): Fully homomorphic encryption extends cryptographic protection from TEE by allowing computation directly on encrypted data. In this paradigm, inputs, intermediate computations, and outputs remain encrypted throughout processing. Although computational overhead currently limits widespread deployment, FHE has demonstrated potential in domains with strict privacy requirements, particularly healthcare and finance, where exposure of training data presents unacceptable risk (ISO, 2023).

3.2 Watermarking Models and Outputs

As AI generated artifacts proliferate, mechanisms for establishing provenance, ownership, and authenticity become essential. Watermarking provides a means to identify misuse, detect unauthorized replication, and support accountability.

Model watermarking: Model watermarking embeds hidden signatures within internal parameters that can later be verified through controlled extraction. These signatures helps with intellectual property claims and detection of stolen or replicated models.

Backdoor style watermarking: Backdoor style watermarking introduces controlled triggers that produce predictable outputs, enabling identification of misappropriated models without affecting normal behavior (NIST, 2020). This method draws parallels to digital watermarking practices used in early multimedia systems

Output watermarking: Output watermarking addresses generative systems by embedding subtle statistical patterns in images, audio, or text. These patterns allow downstream identification of AI generated content and differentiation between authorized and unauthorized systems. Standards initiatives focused on content provenance emphasize watermarking as a critical tool for mitigating misinformation, deepfakes, and attribution disputes (C2PA, n.d.; OECD, 2019).

3.3 Role-Based Access Control (RBAC) Across the MLOps Pipeline

Machine learning operations involve a diverse set of roles, including data engineers, researchers, evaluators, platform teams, security personnel, and product owners. Each role interacts with distinct assets, such as datasets, training pipelines, registries, inference endpoints, and monitoring systems. Without strict access controls, this complexity increases the likelihood of accidental exposure or insider driven compromise (ENISA, 2021).

Least Privilege: Effective access control relies on least privilege, where permissions are granted only when operationally necessary and justified.

Segregation of Duties: Segregation of duties further reduces risk by distributing responsibilities across roles, preventing any single actor from controlling the full training and deployment pipeline.

Model Registry Controls: Model registries play a central role by enforcing versioning, digital signing, validation, and approval workflows prior to deployment. These controls reduce the risk of unauthorized or unvetted models entering production environments (NIST, 2023).

Inference Isolation: Inference isolation is equally critical. Deployed models should not retain access to training data, persistent storage, or outbound network connections. Restricting these capabilities limits the impact of compromise and reduces opportunities for data exfiltration or self-modification.

3.4 Supply Chain Security & The AI Bill of Materials (AI-BOM)

Modern AI systems depend on extensive supply chains that include open-source frameworks, pretrained models, datasets, cloud runtimes, hardware accelerators, and third-party APIs. Each component introduces potential vulnerabilities, such as compromised dependencies, poisoned datasets, or backdoor pretrained models (MITRE Corporation, n.d.).

An AI Bill of Materials provides structured visibility into this ecosystem. It documents dataset provenance and versions, preprocessing steps, base models and checkpoints, library dependencies, fine tuning configurations, and safety evaluation outcomes. When vulnerabilities are discovered, such as malicious pretrained models or compromised packages, the AI BOM enables rapid identification of affected systems and targeted remediation. Without this documentation, organizations lack the situational awareness necessary for effective risk management (NIST, 2023; ISO, 2023).

Together, these measures demonstrate that securing AI systems requires protecting not only deployed models, but the full lineage of data, computation, and dependencies that shape model behavior.

4. AI IN CYBER DEFENSE: THE DOUBLE-EDGED SWORD

Artificial intelligence is transforming cybersecurity at unprecedented speed. Traditional defense mechanisms such as signatures, manual log review, and rule engines, struggle to keep pace with rapidly evolving threats, including polymorphic malware, automated API attacks, and dynamic phishing campaigns. AI provides defenders with advanced analytical and response capabilities, but its dual-use nature also enables adversaries to enhance attack sophistication (Brundage et al., 2018; European Union Agency for Cybersecurity, 2021). Let's explore both sides of the blade.

4.1 AI as a Shield: Security at Machine Speed

AI enhances threat detection and response by analyzing massive volumes of data beyond human capacity. Behavioral analytics (UEBA) enables models to learn baseline patterns, such as standard login locations, file access habits, data movement volumes, API usage, and lateral network activity. Deviations from these baselines allow detection of insider threats, credential compromise, privilege escalation, and lateral movement (Papernot et al., 2018; NIST, 2023).

AI-driven SOAR platforms automate mitigation, including endpoint isolation, token revocation, malicious process termination, domain blocking, credential resets, ticket creation, and owner notification. These automated responses reduce detection-to-response times from hours to milliseconds.

AI-assisted threat hunting democratizes advanced investigation capabilities. Analysts can translate natural-language queries into executable SIEM or EDR searches, enabling detection of suspicious activity and accelerating incident response.

Automation reduces human error and improves consistency while strengthening organizational security posture (Cloud Security Alliance, 2023; Microsoft, 2022).

4.2 AI as a Target: Attackers Are Adopting it Too

Adversaries exploit AI to increase accuracy and effectiveness of their cybersecurity attacks. AI-driven phishing attacks produces highly personalized and contextually accurate messages, increasing success rates. Voice cloning and deep-fake technologies facilitate social engineering and fraud more effectively. Automated vulnerability discovery enables rapid identification of exploitable functions and generation of sophisticated malware variants. Polymorphic, AI-generated malware constantly changes code, evading traditional signature-based defenses (Biggio & Roli, 2018; Carlini & Wagner, 2017; Goodfellow, Shlens, & Szegedy, 2015) which makes them difficult to detect and neutralize.

4.3 Autonomous Cyber Defense Agents

Autonomous AI agents function as digital immune systems, continuously monitoring environments, performing simulated attacks, adjusting network segmentation, deploying honeypots, patching vulnerabilities, coordinating with other agents, and intervening in real time. However, compromised agents present significant risks. Effective deployment requires:

Human-in-the-loop oversight: Continuous supervision and clear escalation protocols prevent unchecked automated actions. Human oversight enables critical judgment calls, preventing automated systems from making unchecked decisions that could disrupt operations or inadvertently aid attackers.

Kill-switch mechanisms: Allow immediate isolation or shutdown of compromised agents. Kill switch must be regularly tested and protected against unauthorized access to ensure agents can be safely deactivated without delay

Agent Operational transparency: Maintain interpretable logs, audit trails, and dashboards for situational awareness and forensic analysis for AI agents. Transparent operations enable rapid forensic analysis and build trust in automated defenses.

Comprehensive activity logging: Securely store all interactions, interventions, and decisions to support incident response and regulatory compliance (Brundage et al., 2018; Papernot et al., 2018; National Institute of Standards and Technology [NIST], 2023). Logs should include timestamps, agent identifiers, model versions, input data summaries, and the rationale behind each action.

In summary, AI in cyber defense offers both unprecedented protection and novel attack vectors. Effective governance requires recognizing this dual-use nature, implementing robust operational safeguards, and continuously monitoring both system behavior and potential adversarial activity.

5. OPERATIONAL MONITORING, LOGGING & OBSERVABILITY

If AI systems serve as the "brains" behind decision-making, monitoring functions as the nervous system, detecting deviations and anomalies in real time. Even well-trained and validated models face unexpected real-world conditions, and adversaries often exploit these uncertainties (Brundage et al., 2018; Biggio & Roli, 2018). Effective monitoring transforms opaque AI models into auditable, transparent systems capable of supporting both security and operational resilience.

5.1 Unified Logging: The Foundation of AI Forensics

AI-generated logs differ fundamentally from traditional software logs. They capture probabilistic inference, learned behavior and, reasoning processes, including:

Inference Logs: Timestamps, model version, input metadata, output labels, confidence scores, request source, and latency. This information enables comprehensive reconstruction of model behavior during incidents. These records enable investigators to trace decision paths, correlate failures, and support root cause analysis.

Auditability Enhancements: Conventional logging is insufficient for AI applications so additional requirements include Redacted input samples, drift metrics, embedding anomaly detection, and chain-of-thought traces. These additional details allow validation of model integrity, detection of abnormal behavior patterns, and verification of compliance with security requirements.

Immutable Storage: Write Once Read Many (WORM) storage prevents tampering or post-incident deletion. This property preserves integrity and supports regulatory audits and legal review.

Privacy Controls: Logs must sanitize names, addresses, and personal identifiable information (PII) to ensure compliance and protect users. Effective privacy controls balance forensic needs with legal and ethical data protection requirements.

Comprehensive logging enables post-incident reconstruction and supports forensic analysis in cases of adversarial attacks, data poisoning, or model manipulation (Carlini & Wagner, 2017; Papernot et al., 2018).

5.2 SIEM Integration: Bringing AI Into the Security Nerve Center

AI systems should be integrated into Security Information and Event Management (SIEM) platforms as core components of Security Operations Centers (SOC). Key practices include:

• **Forwarding AI logs to SIEM systems:** AI system's inference, training, and monitoring logs should be ingested into SIEM platforms using standardized schemas. This practice enables centralized visibility, long term retention, and correlation with existing security telemetry.

• **Developing detection rules for adversarial activity:** SIEM rules should be defined to flag patterns such as input probing, outliers and abnormal distributions, or repeated model failures. These SIEM rules help detect model abuse and targeted attacks.

• **Correlating AI anomalies with broader IT events:** AI system specific security alerts should be analyzed alongside network, identity, and application logs. This correlation improves understanding, reduces false positives, and helps coordinate the incident response efforts more effectively.

Examples of AI-relevant alerts: Spikes in low-confidence outputs (possible evasion), unusual prompt patterns (potential jailbreak), repeated queries from a single source (model extraction), and embedding variance indicating data drift or poisoning. SOC analysts must understand adversarial machine learning, drift detection, and prompt manipulation to ensure comprehensive AI security (Shokri et al., 2017; Goodfellow, Shlens, & Szegedy, 2015).

5.3 Anomaly Detection, Latency Monitoring & Drift Alerts

Latency Monitoring: Latency should be viewed as both a performance and a security metric. Spikes may indicate resource exhaustion, adversarial inputs, or backend throttling. Latency serves as both a performance and security metric.

Embedding Distribution Monitoring: Sudden changes in embedding spaces reveal outliers inputs, adversarial alarms, or emerging attack patterns.

Drift Alerts: Continuous monitoring of data and model behavior facilitates early detection of poisoning, fraud evolution, or shifts in user behavior, enabling timely retraining and mitigation (National Institute of Standards and Technology [NIST], 2023). Continuous monitoring is essential to receive drift alerts in timely fashion.

5.4 Data Lineage & Provenance

AI systems rely on complex data and model supply chains. A single compromised component can threaten overall system integrity. Effective lineage ensures:

- Traceability of inputs, transformations, and outputs.
- Accountability for model development and deployment decisions.
- Auditability for compliance and forensic investigations.

Provenance frameworks, such as the Coalition for Content Provenance and Authenticity (C2PA), enable verification of content integrity, ownership, and data legitimacy, forming a foundation for trustworthy AI governance (Coalition for Content Provenance and Authenticity, n.d.; Cloud Security Alliance, 2023).

6. THE PHYSICS OF MODEL DEGRADATION

Drift Models experience natural degradation over time, regardless of malicious interference. However, the presence of attackers can render drift an important diagnostic indicator.

6.1 Types of Drifts

Data Drift: Data drift occurs when the statistical characteristics of incoming inputs diverge from the original training dataset. Causes include data collection practices, changes in user behavior, evolving industry terminology, or environmental shifts. For example, new slang on social media or novel coding patterns used in fraud can introduce unrecognized features. Data drift reduces predictive accuracy and generalization. Prompt detection is critical to trigger retraining or model updates to maintain performance and security (Gama et al., 2014; Widmer & Kubat, 1996). To handle data drift challenges, approaches such as statistical tests to compare training and live data patterns, monitoring performance metrics over time, periodic retraining with recent data, and adaptive learning methods, can be used effectively.

Concept Drift: Concept drift involves a fundamental change in the relationship between input features and target outputs. Even if inputs appear similar, the meaning of patterns may shift over time. For instance, definitions of "fraudulent activity" evolve as attackers adapt to detection strategies. Concept drift can compromise model relevance, necessitating continuous monitoring and adaptive learning to maintain efficacy in dynamic threat environments (Lu et al., 2018; Tsymbal, 2004). To handle concept drift challenges, approaches such as monitoring prediction error over time, drift detection methods such as DDM or ADWIN, and models retraining and updating, can be used effectively.

Label Drift: Sometimes label drift is often considered a specific case of data drift. Label drift arises from changes in the distribution, frequency, or semantics of target labels. External events or domain shifts can alter label assignments. For example, during a pandemic, previously rare medical symptoms may become prevalent, affecting diagnostic labels. Label drift introduces inconsistencies in model training and evaluation, reducing accuracy and trustworthiness. Regular auditing and validation are required to ensure models reflect current realities (Widmer & Kubat, 1996; Baena-García et al., 2006). To handle label drift challenges, approaches such as monitoring category proportions over time, calibration curves tracking, and base rate tracking, and decision thresholds adjustments, can be used effectively.

All three forms of drifts; data, concept, and label, pose significant security implications. Undetected drift can create exploitable blind spots, reduce anomaly detection efficacy, and undermine AI reliability. Continuous monitoring, early detection, and adaptive mitigation strategies are essential to maintain integrity and trust in AI systems (Papernot et al., 2018; Brundage et al., 2018).

6.2 Drift as a Security Indicator

Drift often signals active threats rather than simple model degradation. Adversaries may manipulate inputs to gradually shift embeddings, probe vulnerabilities, or induce skewed data patterns. Drift monitoring enables early detection of:

- **Data poisoning attempts:** Malicious modification of training data or update data to sway or corrupt model behavior.
- **Input probing campaigns:** Systematic probing of a model to infer decision boundaries or sensitive logic.
- **Evasion strategies:** Deliberate manipulation of inputs to bypass model detection or controls at inference time.
- **Emerging fraud patterns:** Novel or evolving fraudulent behaviors not detected or represented in historical training data.
- **Domain or environment shifts:** Changes in operational context that alter data characteristics or usage conditions.
- **Silent performance degradations:** Gradual decline in model effectiveness without obvious errors or alerts.

Recognizing drift as a core security practice, rather than purely a data science issue, enhances detection capabilities and strengthens defenses against adaptive adversarial threats (Biggio & Roli, 2018; NIST, 2023).

7. GOVERNANCE, OVERSIGHT & WHISTLEBLOWER PROTECTIONS

No artificial intelligence system can achieve true security without structured governance. Human oversight, regulatory frameworks, and enforceable intervention mechanisms remain indispensable. Governance ensures AI operates in alignment with organizational values, legal obligations, ethical norms, and safety standards (OECD, 2019; NIST, 2023).

7.1 Global Frameworks: OECD & NIST AI RMF

Two of the globally recognized frameworks that provide guidance for AI governance are OECD and NIST that provides guidelines and frameworks for integrating various technology, process, and social considerations. Both frameworks highlight the necessity of embedding security into organizational AI governance to maintain accountability and public confidence.

OECD Principles: Emphasize transparency, robustness, safety under potential misuse, and human oversight. They advocate integrating ethical and social considerations into AI lifecycle management.

NIST AI RMF: Focuses on risk mapping, vulnerability assessment, threat mitigation, and resilience enhancement. Security is treated as a prerequisite for safety and trust in AI systems (NIST, 2023).

7.2 AI Governance Boards

Organizations deploying AI at scale should establish a dedicated AI Governance Board. Composition typically includes:

- Chief Information Security Officer (CISO)
- Chief Technology Officer (CTO)
- Chief Risk Officer
- Legal and Compliance representatives
- Data Science leadership
- Business stakeholders

Key responsibilities:

- Approving high-risk models prior to deployment
- Defining system-wide security requirements
- Reviewing red-team and penetration test results

- Setting criteria for system shutdown or throttling in emergencies
- Supervising incident response and remediation
- Ensuring regulatory and ethical compliance

A structured governance board mitigates risks arising from unchecked or poorly monitored AI deployment (Brundage et al., 2018).

7.3 Whistleblower Protections & Safety Culture

Engineers often detect potential safety or security issues before deployment. Without protective mechanisms, reporting may be suppressed due to fear of retaliation. A robust AI safety culture should:

- Encourage reporting of risks and anomalies
- Protect individuals raising concerns from reprisals
- Document issues transparently and visibly
- Empower delays or halts in deployment when justified

Historical cases indicate that ignoring early warnings can lead to systemic failures. Whistleblower protections are therefore essential to maintaining both operational safety and organizational accountability in rapidly scaling AI systems (OECD, 2019; NIST, 2023).

CONCLUSION

Summary next steps in AI system security can be structured across near-term, mid-term, and long-term horizons. These steps support a transition from reactive defenses to sustained, lifecycle-based AI security. Immediate operational actions in the coming days focus on visibility and control. Tactical Short-term actions over the coming months focus on robustness and monitoring. Strategic Long-term actions over the coming years focus on governance and resilience.

Operational Efforts:

- Establish continuous logging for inputs, outputs, and model decisions.
- Baseline model performance using current production data.
- Audit data pipelines for access control and integrity checks.
- Define incident response procedures for model misuse or failure.

Tactical Efforts:

- Deploy automated drift detection for data, labels, and concepts.

- Introduce adversarial testing and red teaming for high-risk models.
- Implement model versioning and secure retraining workflows.
- Align security controls with organizational risk management policies.

Strategic Efforts:

- Integrate AI security into enterprise-wide cybersecurity frameworks.
- Develop adaptive and resilient models that support continuous learning under constraints.
- Establish formal AI governance structures with accountability and auditability.
- Contribute to and adopt industry standards for secure and trustworthy AI systems.

In addition to these applied strategies summarized earlier, additional research is needed to advance the research efforts holistically. Research is needed to unify data drift, label drift, concept drift, and adversarial behavior detection within a single monitoring framework because current approaches treat these risks independently which is not very effective. Another area of research is empirical research of public, reproducible benchmarks reflecting realistic attack surfaces and operational constraints since currently we do not have enough data which limits our ability to use acquired knowledge from experiences. We also need to research and confirm the effectiveness of technical controls. Research must connect technical controls with policy, compliance, and audit requirements.

REFERENCES

Baena-Garcıa, M., del Campo-Ávila, J., Fidalgo, R., Bifet, A., Gavalda, R., & Morales-Bueno, R. (2006, September). Early drift detection method. In *Fourth international workshop on knowledge discovery from data streams* (Vol. 6, pp. 77-86).

Biggio, B., & Roli, F. (2018). Wild patterns. Ten years after the rise of adversarial machine learning. Pattern Recognition, 84, 317 to 331. https://doi.org/DOI: 10.1016/j.patcog.2018.07.023

Brundage, M., Avin, S., Clark, J., Toner, H., Eckersley, P., Garfinkel, B., Dafoe, A., Scharre, P., Zeitzoff, T., Filar, B., Anderson, H., Roff, H., Allen, G., Steinhardt, J., Flynn, C., Beard, S., Belfield, H., Farquhar, S., Lyle, C., & Amodei, D. (2018). The malicious use of artificial intelligence. Forecasting, prevention, and mitigation. arXiv. https://arxiv.org/abs/1802.07228

Carlini, N., & Wagner, D. (2017). Towards evaluating the robustness of neural networks. Proceedings of the IEEE Symposium on Security and Privacy, 39 to 57. DOI: 10.1109/SP.2017.49

Cloud Security Alliance. (2023). AI security guidance for critical infrastructure. https://cloudsecurityalliance.org/artifacts/ai-security-guidance

Coalition for Content Provenance and Authenticity. (n.d.). C2PA specification. Content authenticity and provenance. https://c2pa.org/specifications/

European Union Agency for Cybersecurity. (2021). Threat landscape for artificial intelligence. https://www.enisa.europa.eu/publications/artificial-intelligence-threat-landscape

Fredrikson, M., Jha, S., & Ristenpart, T. (2015). Model inversion attacks that exploit confidence information. *Proceedings of the ACM Conference on Computer and Communications Security*

Gama, J., Žliobaitė, I., Bifet, A., Pechenizkiy, M., & Bouchachia, A. (2014). A survey on concept drift adaptation. ACM computing surveys (CSUR), 46(4), 1-37. 1322 to 1333. https://doi.org/DOI: 10.1145/2810103.2813677

Goodfellow, I., Shlens, J., & Szegedy, C. (2015). Explaining and harnessing adversarial examples. *International Conference on Learning Representations*. https://arxiv.org/abs/1412.6572

Microsoft. (2022). Responsible AI standard v2. https://www.microsoft.com/ai/responsible-ai

MITRE Corporation. (n.d.). MITRE ATLAS. Adversarial threat landscape for artificial intelligence systems. https://atlas.mitre.org/

National Institute of Standards and Technology. (2020). Adversarial machine learning. A taxonomy and terminology of attacks and mitigations (NIST IR 8269). U.S. Department of Commerce. https://nvlpubs.nist.gov/nistpubs/ir/2020/NIST.IR.8269.pdf

National Institute of Standards and Technology. (2023). AI risk management framework 1.0. U.S. Department of Commerce. https://www.nist.gov/itl/ai-risk-management-framework

Open, A. I. (2023). GPT 4 system card and safety evaluations. https://openai.com/research/gpt-4

Organisation for Economic Co operation and Development. (2019). OECD principles on artificial intelligence. https://oecd.ai/en/ai-principles

Papernot, N., McDaniel, P., Sinha, A., & Wellman, M. (2018). SoK. Security and privacy in machine learning. Proceedings of the IEEE European Symposium on Security and Privacy, 399 to 414. DOI: 10.1109/EuroSP.2018.00031

Shokri, R., Stronati, M., Song, C., & Shmatikov, V. (2017). Membership inference attacks against machine learning models. Proceedings of the IEEE Symposium on Security and Privacy, 3 to 18. https://doi.org/DOI: 10.1109/SP.2017.41

Tramèr, F., Zhang, F., Juels, A., Reiter, M. K., & Ristenpart, T. (2016). Stealing machine learning models via prediction APIs. Proceedings of the USENIX Security Symposium, 601 to 618. https://www.usenix.org/conference/usenixsecurity16/technical-sessions/presentation/tramer

Tsymbal, A. (2004). The problem of concept drift: Definitions and related work. Computer Science Department. *Trinity College Dublin*, *106*(2), 58.

U.S. White House. (2023). Executive order on the safe, secure, and trustworthy development and use of artificial intelligence. https://www.whitehouse.gov/briefing-room/presidential-actions/2023/10/30/executive-order-on-the-safe-secure-and-trustworthy-development-and-use-of-artificial-intelligence/

Widmer, G., & Kubat, M. (1996). Learning in the presence of concept drift and hidden contexts. *Machine Learning*, *23*(1), 69–101. DOI: 10.1023/A:1018046501280

Chapter 4
Communicating the Rationale Behind AI Decisions (Explainability)

Silvio Andrae
https://orcid.org/0000-0002-8586-7812
Independent Researcher, Germany

ABSTRACT

As Artificial Intelligence (AI) systems become increasingly prevalent in decision-relevant and high-risk domains, the exclusive focus on algorithmic performance is encountering normative and organizational constraints. Predictive accuracy alone is insufficient; there is a growing demand for decisions that are justifiable, verifiable, and accountable. This chapter examines explainability not merely as a technical property of models, but as a communicative and governance-oriented practice that structures interactions among humans, systems, and institutions. The methodology integrates a conceptual analysis of the Explainable AI (XAI) literature with perspectives from human–AI interaction, metacognition research, and governance theory. The findings indicate that explanations primarily influence decision-making by calibrating trust and responsibility through metacognitive processes, rather than by enhancing understanding of model internals. Building on these insights, the chapter introduces the Explainability Assurance Pipeline, a lifecycle-oriented framework for governing explainability.

WHY EXPLAINABILITY MATTERS

As learning systems become increasingly prevalent in high-risk domains such as finance, healthcare, and public administration, the discourse surrounding artificial

DOI: 10.4018/979-8-3373-6935-8.ch004

intelligence has undergone a fundamental shift. Whereas initial debates focused primarily on the performance of algorithmic systems, current discussions prioritize the justification of automated decisions. In these settings, high predictive accuracy is necessary but insufficient for the responsible deployment of AI. When decisions significantly impact individual rights, life trajectories, or physical integrity, there is a justified demand for comprehensible rationales.

In this context, explainability should be regarded not as a technical end in itself or an aesthetic attribute of contemporary models, but as a functional and normative requirement (Mersha et al., 2024; Vilone & Longo, 2020). Explainability facilitates accountability, underpins governance structures, and is essential for calibrating trust. Explanations render automated decisions verifiable, enable the allocation of responsibility between humans and systems, and create opportunities for correction, objection, or institutional oversight. In the absence of explanatory components, AI systems risk being perceived as authoritative yet opaque decision-makers whose legitimacy rests solely on empirical performance (Lipton, 2018).

The demand for explanations arises less from epistemic curiosity regarding model structures and more from the situational risks inherent in specific decisions. As the potential consequences of a decision become more severe, the requirements for its justification correspondingly increase. This rationale underpins critiques of the exclusive reliance on performance-oriented black-box models in sensitive application areas (Rudin, 2019). Mistakes in lending, medical diagnostics, or risk assessments are not simply technical errors; they are socially consequential events with legal, economic, and ethical implications. Explainability serves as a bridge between statistical inference and social legitimacy.

Explanations should not be viewed merely as descriptive artifacts that summarize or visualize model behavior. Instead, they constitute communicative acts situated within institutional contexts. As Hoffman et al. (2018) note, 'explanation' is not an inherent property of an output but a relational process between a system and its users. The adequacy of an explanation depends on the recipient, the intended purpose, and the specific decision-making context. For example, a data scientist investigating model instabilities, a loan officer evaluating a borderline case, and a data subject seeking to understand or contest an adverse decision each require distinct forms of explanation, despite referencing the same model output.

This communicative aspect distinguishes explainability from related concepts such as transparency, interpretability, and trustworthiness. Transparency typically denotes openness about data sources or system architectures, interpretability refers to the fundamental comprehensibility of model structures (Doshi-Velez & Kim, 2017), and trustworthiness concerns the subjective confidence that a system will function correctly or appropriately (Fritz-Morgenthal et al., 2022; Ali et al., 2023). While explainability intersects with these concepts, it remains distinct. A system may be transparent yet incomprehensible to non-experts, interpretable but irrelevant to specific decisions, or considered trustworthy even when its decisions lack justifiable grounds. The unique value of explainability lies in connecting automated decisions to reasons that can be assessed and acted upon.

This distinction is particularly evident in the use of standard post-hoc methods such as LIME or SHAP (Ribeiro et al., 2016; Lundberg & Lee, 2017). These techniques have greatly expanded the technical toolkit for analyzing complex models, yet they are frequently misconstrued as providing objective explanations for model decisions. In reality, they offer only approximations whose stability, fidelity, and context dependence require critical scrutiny. Empirical studies demonstrate that such explanations can be manipulated or foster a misleading sense of understanding, leading users to believe they comprehend a decision while engaging only with a plausible narrative surface (Adebayo et al., 2018; Molnar, 2022). In high-risk settings, this 'illusion of understanding' constitutes a significant risk.

In numerous high-risk application areas, the principal danger posed by AI systems with limited explainability is not merely a lack of transparency, but rather the miscalibration of human confidence. Users frequently base delegation and oversight decisions on implicit evaluations of their own competence, which plausible yet misunderstood explanations can further skew. It suggests that the impact of explainability extends beyond model comprehension to influence self-assessment and decision-making processes. Consequently, explainability addresses both epistemic and cognitive prerequisites for responsible decision-making.

Accordingly, this chapter proposes that explainability should be conceptualized as a governance capability. Explanations not only enhance individual understanding but also institutionalize safeguards within decision-making processes. They facilitate internal oversight, external accountability, and organizational learning over time. Moreover, explanations are essential for enabling practical mechanisms for objection and correction: only those who comprehend the rationale behind a decision can meaningfully challenge it or propose alternative actions (Wachter et al., 2017). Explainability thus establishes the infrastructural foundations for accountability without necessitating the full disclosure of proprietary or security-sensitive information.

Chapter Contributions

In light of these considerations, this chapter offers three principal contributions to the ongoing discourse on explainable AI. First, it advances a communication-oriented perspective on explainability, framing explanations as context-dependent justification practices within decision-making processes rather than mere technical analyses. Second, it systematically integrates state-of-the-art technical XAI methods with human-centered design principles and evaluation strategies, thereby bridging the gap between algorithmic analysis and practical application. Third, the chapter introduces the Explainability Assurance Pipeline, an integrated framework that embeds explainability across the entire AI lifecycle, encompassing model selection, user interaction, monitoring, and organizational responsibility. Thus, the chapter aims to provide a conceptual foundation for the development of explainable, verifiable, and socially acceptable AI decision-making systems, rather than serving as a mere survey of individual XAI techniques.

Chapter Structure

The remainder of the chapter is organized as follows. Section 8.2 clarifies foundational concepts by systematically distinguishing interpretability from explainability and relating them to adjacent terms. Section 8.3 addresses the human-centered design of explanations, examining how different target groups and roles require specific forms of explanation. Section 8.4 surveys key technical approaches to explainability, discussing their strengths, limitations, and risks. Section 8.5 explores explainable AI in selected high-risk domains, identifying domain-specific requirements. Section 8.6 considers methods for evaluating the quality of explanations. Section 8.7 situates explainability within the broader context of governance and organizational accountability. Section 8.8 integrates these elements in the Explainability Assurance Pipeline, and Section 8.9 concludes with a summary and outlook.

INTERPRETABILITY AND EXPLAINABILITY

Discussions regarding explainable artificial intelligence have long been marked by conceptual ambiguity. Specifically, the terms interpretability and explainability are frequently used interchangeably in research, regulation, and practice, even though they address distinct analytical levels. This conceptual confusion extends beyond mere terminology and has tangible consequences: it complicates the selection of appropriate methods, fosters unrealistic expectations of technical procedures, and contributes to misunderstandings about the capabilities and limitations of algorithmic systems in specific decision-making contexts.

Interpretability, in a narrow sense, denotes a structural property of a model. A model is considered interpretable if a human can directly understand its functioning, parameters, or decision-making logic. Classic linear models, shallow decision trees, and simple rule-based systems are often considered interpretable because their internal structures are immediately transparent (Doshi-Velez & Kim, 2017; Molnar, 2022). Interpretability is therefore primarily passive, indicating the degree to which a model permits understanding without actively providing explanations.

In contrast, explainability constitutes an active process. It encompasses all procedures, methods, and artifacts employed to render a model's results or behavior comprehensible to particular audiences. Explainability does not require the underlying model to be interpretable. Even highly complex and intrinsically opaque models can be rendered explainable if appropriate mechanisms are available to justify their decisions in a manner suited to the context. Whereas interpretability pertains to model structure, explainability concerns the communication of decision rationales.

The distinction between interpretability and explainability is increasingly highlighted in the literature, although it is not always consistently upheld. Lipton (2018) notes that interpretability is frequently conflated with post-hoc narratives, which may appear plausible yet fail to offer reliable insight into a model's actual decision-making mechanisms. Similarly, Miller (2019) differentiates between intrinsic interpretability and post-hoc explanation, emphasizing that these approaches serve distinct objectives and are subject to different quality standards.

A further noteworthy distinction relates to the scope of explanations. The literature commonly differentiates between global and local explanations. Global explanations seek to characterize a model's overall decision-making behavior across multiple cases, for instance, by employing feature importance measures or summary rules. In contrast, local explanations pertain to individual decisions or predictions and address why a specific output was produced in a particular instance (Ribeiro et al., 2016). These perspectives serve distinct purposes: global explanations facilitate model understanding, governance, and quality control, whereas local explanations are essential for reviewing individual decisions, enabling appeals, or inClosely associated with the scope of explanations is the distinction between ex ante and ex post explanatory approaches. Ex ante approaches integrate explainability during model development, for example, by selecting simple or structurally constrained models.

In contrast, ex post approaches retrospectively analyze a trained model without altering its internal structure. Each strategy entails specific trade-offs. Ex ante approaches typically provide greater structural traceability but may encounter performance limitations in complex application domains. Ex post approaches offer greater flexibility but may produce unstable or misleading explanations (Adebayo et al., 2018).

A further standard categorization differentiates among white-box, gray-box, and black-box models. White-box models are inherently transparent and interpretable; black-box models exhibit high complexity and limited structural transparency; gray-box approaches combine aspects of both, such as through hybrid architectures or explainable surrogate models (Molnar, 2022). While this classification is analytically functional, it should not be conflated with explainability. A white-box model does not inherently provide audience-specific justifications, nor is a black-box model necessarily incapable of being explained.

It is essential to distinguish explainability from causality. Explanations within the context of explainable artificial intelligence (XAI) typically do not constitute causal statements in the strict scientific sense. They describe associations, contributions, or sensitivities within a model, rather than causes defined by counterfactual scenarios (Pearl & Mackenzie, 2018). Equating model contributions with causal effects is problematic and may result in erroneous conclusions, particularly in regulated or liability-sensitive contexts. Although explainable models can inform causal hypotheses, they do not replace rigorous causal analysis.

Explainability should also be distinguished from trust. In numerous application domains, explainability is implemented to enhance confidence in AI systems. However, empirical research indicates that explanations can foster both overconfidence and underconfidence (Poursabzi-Sangdeh et al., 2021). A system that is well-explained yet error-prone may be accepted too readily, whereas a reliable system with inadequate explanations may be dismissed. Thus, explainability does not guarantee appropriate trust; rather, it serves as a mechanism. These considerations support a broader understanding of explainability: it is not primarily an inherent property of models, but rather a relational and context-dependent quality of decision-making systems. Explainability emerges from the interplay among the model, the explanation method, the intended audience, the institutional context, and the decision's consequences. An explanation is adequate if it is sufficiently comprehensible, verifiable, and actionable for a given purpose. This perspective underpins the subsequent sections of the chapter, which analyze explainability as a practical design challenge rather than an abstract concept.

HUMAN-CENTERED EXPLANATIONS AND METACOGNITION

Explainability as a Metacognitive Intervention

Human-centered approaches to explainable AI are frequently driven by the expectation that explanations will improve understanding, trust, or acceptance of algorithmic decisions. Although these objectives are essential, they may neglect a more fundamental cognitive function of explanations: shaping users' awareness of their own epistemic limitations when engaging with complex AI systems. From a metacognitive perspective, explanations primarily influence how users conceptualize system capabilities, uncertainty, and appropriate reliance, rather than simply revealing the mechanics of internal models (Hoffman et al., 2018).

This influence occurs through the development of mental models. Explanations shape users' internal representations of an AI system's capabilities, the contexts in which its outputs are trustworthy, and the circumstances where human judgment remains essential. Notably, empirical research indicates that enhanced subjective understanding does not necessarily lead to improved decision quality or oversight. In fact, explanations may increase user confidence without improving error detection or task performance, especially in complex or adaptive systems (Poursabzi-Sangdeh et al., 2021). Recent studies further support this metacognitive perspective by showing that highly plausible explanations can systematically increase perceived understanding and confidence while leaving actual decision accuracy unchanged (Haque et al., 2023; von Zahn et al., 2025).

Explainability should therefore be conceptualized as a metacognitive intervention that alters how users assess both the system and their own judgment. Its effects depend not only on informational completeness, but also on context, task structure, and institutional setting. This reframing shifts the focus from explanation as mere transparency to explanation as a mechanism that structures human reflection, responsibility, and awareness of limitations.

Mental Models, Trust Calibration, and the Boundaries of Transparency

Examining explainability from a metacognitive perspective clarifies why transparency alone is an insufficient design objective. The XAI literature emphasizes that explanations serve multiple purposes: epistemic, functional, and normative. These purposes should be analytically distinguished, even though they often overlap in practice (Doshi-Velez & Kim, 2017). An explanation that meets epistemic intelligibility or normative transparency requirements may still fail to support appropriate human oversight or may even worsen miscalibrated trust.

From a human-centered perspective, the central issue is not whether explanations increase trust, but whether they support calibrated reliance. Explanations stabilize mental models that guide expectations regarding system competence, uncertainty, and responsibility. When these models overestimate system reliability or minimize contextual limitations, explanations may decrease vigilance and critical engagement. Empirical evidence indicates that exceptionally fluent and intuitive explanations can reinforce such overestimation by conveying a sense of coherence and control that surpasses the system's actual robustness (von Zahn et al., 2025).

These dynamics reveal the limitations of simplified 'human-in-the-loop' oversight models. Human involvement does not inherently mitigate risk if users lack the metacognitive resources to interpret system outputs effectively. Explainability that is misaligned with cognitive capacities, task demands, or institutional roles may therefore undermine, rather than enhance, human agency, even when formal transparency criteria are satisfied.

Implications for the Design and Governance of Explainability

The metacognitive perspective outlined here has direct implications for the design, evaluation, and governance of explainability. Explanations should be assessed not only for correctness or completeness, but also for their impact on users' mental models, decision strategies, and perceptions of responsibility over time. It necessitates systematic testing under realistic usage conditions and attention to interaction effects, including the stability and robustness of explanations as models or data evolve (Adebayo et al., 2018).

These concerns are especially pronounced in the context of generative AI systems. In these systems, explanations are often generated using the exact mechanisms as primary outputs, which blurs the distinction between decision logic, justification, and narrative framing. Recent research demonstrates that fluent, context-sensitive rationales can obscure epistemic uncertainty and responsibility attribution, creating new governance risks that go beyond traditional model-centric explainability issues (Dhar et al., 2025). In this context, persuasive explanations may simultaneously increase user trust and diminish accountability.

Therefore, explainability should be regarded as a dynamic, lifecycle-dependent property rather than a static feature or mere communication. Shifts in data distributions, deployment contexts, or organizational practices can gradually erode the reliability or interpretability of explanations, resulting in governance risks that cannot be mitigated through one-time validation (Raji et al., 2020). This perspective establishes a direct conceptual link to the Explainability Assurance Pipeline discussed in the following section. By integrating metacognitive considerations into design, release, monitoring, and update processes, the pipeline treats explainability as an ongoing organizational capability rather than a symbolic compliance measure.

Human-centered explainability thus emerges not only as a cognitive or ethical requirement, but as a governance-relevant practice designed to maintain appropriate human agency, responsibility, and awareness of limitations within socio-technical AI systems.

TECHNICAL APPROACHES TO EXPLAINABILITY

Having established explainability as a communicative and human-centered practice in previous sections, it is necessary to consider which technical approaches can effectively support this practice. The literature on explainable artificial intelligence (XAI) presents a diverse array of methods, each differing significantly in objectives, significance, and suitability for various application contexts. A central challenge is to evaluate these methods not in isolation, but as tools with distinct strengths, limitations, and associated risks.

Technical approaches to explainability can be categorized along two primary axes: whether explainability is achieved intrinsically by the model or ex post through supplementary analysis, and whether explanations are global (cross-model) or local (decision-specific) (Doshi-Velez & Kim, 2017; Molnar, 2022). These distinctions facilitate a realistic assessment of individual methods' performance claims and help prevent misuse.

Intrinsically interpretable models embed explainability into their design. These include linear models, rule-based systems, shallow decision trees, and generalized additive models. Their advantage lies in their structural traceability, which requires no additional explanation. Relationships between input variables and model output can be derived directly from the model structure, making these approaches particularly attractive for governance, validation, and audit contexts (Rudin, 2019). However, intrinsically interpretable models often reach their performance limits in high-dimensional or highly nonlinear problem spaces. In practice, they are therefore increasingly being used deliberately in situations where justifiability takes precedence over maximum predictive accuracy.

In contrast, post-hoc explanation methods are applied to already trained, often complex models. Notable examples include local surrogate models, such as LIME (Ribeiro et al., 2016), and contribution-based methods, such as SHAP (Lundberg & Lee, 2017). These methods seek to approximate a model's decision-making behavior for individual predictions or across multiple cases. Their principal advantage is model-agnosticism, enabling explanations even when intrinsic interpretability is absent.

However, post-hoc methods present systematic limitations. They do not offer direct insights into the model itself; instead, they reconstruct its behavior based on specific assumptions. Empirical studies indicate that these explanations can be sensitive to minor changes in input data or model parameters, leading to unstable or inconsistent outcomes (Adebayo et al., 2018). In high-risk contexts, this raises concerns regarding the adequacy of approximate explanations as a foundation for justification and accountability.

Beyond feature-based approaches, additional forms of explanation have gained prominence. Counterfactual explanations seek to identify minimal input changes that would result in different decision outcomes (Wachter et al., 2017). Their value lies in their action orientation, as they translate model decisions into potentially controllable factors, thereby supporting objection and adjustment processes. However, these explanations are only meaningful if the proposed changes are realistic, permissible, and feasible to implement—criteria that are often challenging to satisfy in practice.

Concept-based approaches, such as testing with concept activation vectors (Kim et al., 2018), seek to connect abstract model representations to concepts comprehensible to humans. These methods are particularly valuable in domains where expert knowledge is essential, such as medical image analysis. Similarly, example- or prototype-based explanations facilitate plausible decisions by referencing comparative cases. While these approaches align more closely with human explanatory practices, they introduce new concerns regarding representativeness and potential bias.

Large language models represent a significant development in the explainability discourse, as they can generate linguistically coherent, context-sensitive explanations at scale without relying on accessible or causally interpretable internal representations (Mavrepis et al., 2024; Hsieh et al., 2024; Mumuni & Mumuni, 2025). LLMs primarily function as communicative interfaces that structure, translate, or personalize explanations, rather than serving as guarantors of epistemic transparency. This characteristic renders them metacognitively ambivalent: while they enhance comprehensibility and acceptance, they also increase the risk of overconfidence and uncritical delegation. Consequently, LLM-based explainability necessitates rigorous governance to maintain the distinction between linguistic plausibility and genuine knowledge acquisition.

Regardless of the specific procedure, every explanation method must contain implicit value assumptions. The selection of relevant features, the definition of 'minimal' changes, or the delimitation of aspects worthy of explanation are not neutral technical decisions. They structure what becomes visible—and what does not. Explainability is, therefore, always also a form of selection. This insight is central to understanding explanations not as objective windows into model logic, but as designed perspectives on algorithmic decisions.

These selection mechanisms introduce specific risks. One significant issue is the potential for explanations to be manipulated. Research demonstrates that models can be modified to produce plausible yet misleading explanations without materially affecting predictive accuracy (Slack et al., 2020). In such instances, explainability may merely simulate trust rather than provide genuine insight. Additionally, data protection risks arise when explanations inadvertently disclose sensitive information about training data or individuals, such as data memberships or feature distributions (Shokri et al., 2017).

Another risk involves the rationalization of decisions. Explanations can encourage retrospective legitimization of decisions rather than critical examination. This issue is particularly pronounced when explanations are presented as definitive justifications, even though they are only heuristic approximations. In such cases, they may undermine the accountability objectives they are intended to support.

In light of these considerations, an instrumental and context-sensitive approach to XAI methods is warranted. No single technique can deliver universally valid or comprehensive explanations. Instead, it is crucial to combine multiple approaches, tailored to decision consequences, user groups, and institutional requirements.

Technical explainability is a necessary but insufficient condition for explainable AI systems. Its effectiveness depends on integration with human-centered design, clear quality standards, and organizational embedding. These aspects will be examined in greater detail in the subsequent section, with reference to specific high-risk domains.

EXPLAINABILITY IN HIGH-RISK DOMAINS

The preceding discussion demonstrates that explainability should not be regarded as an abstract quality attribute or a universal technical solution. The institutional context and the potential consequences of decisions primarily determine their specific manifestation. It is especially apparent in high-risk domains, where algorithmically supported decisions significantly affect individuals and society. In these areas, explainability is a functional prerequisite for responsible decision-making rather than an optional feature. However, requirements differ substantially across domains, indicating that general XAI solutions are often insufficient.

A metacognitive perspective further reveals that the function of explainability in high-risk domains extends beyond supporting individual factual decisions. Explanations in these contexts significantly influence actors' confidence in their own judgment and the allocation of responsibility between human decision-makers and systems. In complex and consequential decision-making situations, risks arise not only from incorrect predictions but also from miscalibrations of human confidence, such as overconfidence or false self-assurance. Here, explainability primarily fosters responsibility by exposing metacognitive misconceptions and clarifying the boundaries of individual expertise.

Healthcare

In healthcare, AI systems operate within highly standardized professional practices and established structures of responsibility. Decisions related to diagnostics, triage, or therapy planning are seldom fully automated; instead, they are integrated into broader medical decision-making processes. In this context, explainability serves a primarily supportive and risk-mitigating role. For medical professionals, explanations are especially valuable when they facilitate the classification of algorithmic recommendations, identification of atypical cases, or recognition of uncertainties (Doshi-Velez et al., 2019; Mariappan, 2025). Thus, explanations not only assist with clinical plausibility assessments but also act as metacognitive cues, enabling physicians to discern when algorithmic recommendations align with their intuition and when they diverge, warranting closer scrutiny.

Nicolson et al. (2025) present an instructive empirical study examining the impact of explainable AI in a medical setting. In a three-stage reader study in which sonographers estimate gestational age, the authors demonstrate that AI predictions substantially enhance diagnostic accuracy. However, providing additional explanations does not consistently improve performance. Notably, participants' subjective confidence increases despite no systematic change in trust or reliance. The significant interindividual variability is particularly noteworthy: while some physicians benefit from explanations, others experience declines in both performance and engagement. These findings highlight that explainability in clinical contexts does not inherently improve decision-making, but instead functions as a metacognitive intervention that may either support or undermine individual self-calibration.

Differentiation according to the intended audience is crucial. Physicians require explanations that address pathophysiological contexts, relevant features, and model limitations, whereas patients prioritize comprehensibility, trust, and integration into their individual disease trajectories. Research indicates that patients find explanations most helpful when they avoid technical details and instead translate decisions into accessible, everyday narratives (Jacobs et al., 2021).

At the same time, dealing with uncertainty is central in the medical context. AI systems operate probabilistically, while clinical decisions often have clear implications for action. Explanations that conceal or downplay uncertainties can lead to overconfidence and undermine medical responsibility. Conversely, reflective communication of uncertainty can promote shared decision-making and strengthen AI's role as an assistive tool (Zhang et al., 2020).

Van Royen et al. (2026) provide a critical perspective on the prevailing call for comprehensive explainability, cautioning against overestimating the benefits of XAI in healthcare. The authors demonstrate that post-hoc explanations, such as SHAP, are prone to causal misinterpretation, potentially leading to unwarranted trust or premature dismissal of predictive models. A key concern is that even diligent medical professionals may struggle to avoid these interpretive errors. Thus, explainability in this context addresses metacognitive bias rather than a simple knowledge gap: the inclination to infer epistemic control from explanatory representations that merely reflect statistical correlation. The article concludes that explainability in medical settings should be employed judiciously, with careful attention to its cognitive side effects.

Finance and Risk Management

In finance, AI systems are primarily used to structure, evaluate, and predict economic risks. Applications range from credit decisions and fraud detection to portfolio and stress test scenarios. The close interplay among explainability, governance, control, and liability issues characterizes this area. Here, explanations serve less to convince individuals than to ensure institutional accountability (Andrae, 2024). In finance in particular, it is evident that explainable models exert their governance-relevant effect less through transparency in the narrow sense than through the reduction of unfounded decision-making certainty, for example, in borderline cases or rare events where human experience alone does not provide reliable guidance.

For internal stakeholders such as credit officers and risk controllers, explainable models facilitate plausibility assessments of algorithmic recommendations and their integration into established decision-making processes. In borderline cases or when confronted with unexpected model outputs, explanatory components are essential to prevent the uncritical delegation of responsibility to automated systems (Bussmann et al., 2021). Additionally, explanations must be consistent, reproducible, and well-documented to support subsequent review.

Fairness and equal treatment are particularly salient concerns in the financial sector. Credit and scoring decisions often impact structurally sensitive characteristics, making explanations vital for identifying potential discrimination. In this setting, explainability functions as an interface between model logic and normative standards, without entirely subsuming either. It is therefore essential that explanations not only justify individual decisions but also illuminate patterns at the portfolio level, thereby enabling the identification and remediation of systematic biases (Barocas et al., 2023).

Public Sector and Law Enforcement

Implementing explainable AI in the public sector poses distinct challenges, particularly in domains such as risk assessment, resource allocation, and rule-violation prediction. In these contexts, algorithmic decisions often involve power imbalances and limited avenues for appeal. Explainability thus becomes a fundamental requirement for legitimacy and adherence to constitutional principles, even if legal doctrine is not the primary focus here. In the public sector, explainability serves less as a tool for individual persuasion and more as a mechanism for metacognitive distancing from algorithmic recommendations, facilitating reflexive restraint and the verifiable assignment of responsibility.

A key problem is that prognostic systems in the public sector often work with socially biased data. Explanations must therefore not only make individual decisions plausible, but also reveal structural distortions without creating new risks of stigmatization (Selbst et al., 2019). In practice, purely local explanations are often insufficient here, as they ignore the broader context of algorithmic impact.

Stability and consistency are also critical quality requirements. Decisions that vary substantially under minimally altered conditions erode perceptions of fairness and equal treatment. Consequently, explainable systems must be able to delineate their own limitations and communicate uncertainties transparently. In the public sector, explainability is less concerned with exhaustive detail and more focused on facilitating review and contestation.

Domain-Specific Patterns and Limitations

Several common patterns emerge across high-risk domains. First, there is a shift from prioritizing technical sophistication to emphasizing functional appropriateness. Explanations need not be exhaustive or universally applicable; they must fulfill their intended purpose within specific decision-making contexts. Second, different stakeholder groups within the same domain often possess divergent explanatory needs. Third, explainability consistently interacts with other requirements, including data protection, safeguards against manipulation, and institutional efficiency.

These observations highlight that high-risk contexts are not amenable to uniform solutions. Instead, they necessitate domain-specific explanation strategies that integrate technical capabilities with professional standards, organizational practices, and societal expectations. Accordingly, explainability should be viewed not as a guarantee of correct decisions, but as a tool for reflection and control that renders responsibility visible and expands the scope. In this context, determining whether an explanation is 'good enough' cannot be resolved in abstract terms. It necessitates systematic evaluation criteria that consider both technical quality and the effects on human and institutional actors. The subsequent section addresses this evaluative dimension in detail.

WHEN IS AN EXPLANATION 'GOOD ENOUGH'?

As explainable AI becomes more widespread, the central question shifts from the mere provision of explanations to the assessment of their quality. The presence of an explanation alone provides limited insight into its suitability, reliability, or accountability. In high-risk domains, explanations that appear plausible but lack a robust foundation for verification, learning, or appeal are particularly problematic. Consequently, the evaluation of explainability emerges as a critical governance issue.

A key problem is that explanations cannot be evaluated independently of their purpose. A reason that is helpful for a data science team for model analysis may be incomprehensible or even misleading for affected individuals. Conversely, narratives that are understandable to laypeople are often unsuitable for audits or validation processes. The question of the 'quality' of an explanation is therefore inextricably linked to the question of the addressee, the decision-making context, and the objective (Doshi-Velez & Kim, 2017). Explainability is not an absolute quality feature, but a relational property.

Given this context, the quality of explanations cannot be assessed solely by their accuracy in representing model behavior or by their comprehensibility. From a metacognitive perspective, it is essential to consider how explanations affect human self-assessment, uncertainty evaluation, and control decisions. Technically correct and subjectively convincing explanations may still be problematic if they foster overconfidence or uncritical delegation. Conversely, explanations that initially induce uncertainty can ultimately enhance long-term decision-making.

Technical Quality Dimensions

At the technical level, several evaluation criteria address the relationship between the explanation and the underlying model. Fidelity, or faithfulness, is a primary criterion: an explanation is considered faithful if it accurately reflects the model's actual decision-making behavior. Explanations that present consistent or intuitive patterns without a close connection to the model may be misleading (Rudin, 2019).

Stability is another closely related criterion. Minor, irrelevant changes to input data should not yield significantly different explanations. Adebayo et al. (2018) found that many standard XAI methods only partially satisfy this requirement. Unstable explanations are especially problematic in legal or ethical contexts, as they may suggest arbitrary decision-making.

Additional technical criteria include sufficiency and parsimony. Sufficient explanations address aspects relevant to the decision while excluding irrelevant information. Parsimony seeks to ensure that explanations remain cognitively manageable. These criteria often conflict: comprehensive explanations are rarely simple, and straightforward explanations are seldom comprehensive. A high-quality explanation balances these competing goals within the given context (Molnar, 2022).

Human-Centered Evaluation

However, technical quality alone is not sufficient for using explainable AI responsibly in real-world decision-making. The decisive factor is how humans understand, use, and interpret explanations. Human-centered evaluation of explanations, therefore, focuses on questions of understanding, decision quality, and trust calibration. From a metacognitive perspective, it is thus important to ask not only whether users understand an explanation, but also whether they can realistically assess their own decision-making ability. A key evaluative question is whether explanations help people identify situations in which they themselves are highly likely to be wrong—and choose alternative control or delegation strategies accordingly.

A recent integrative analysis by Chiaburu et al. (2024) identifies uncertainty as a central yet underrepresented issue in XAI research. The authors contend that explanations failing to address their own uncertainty may either foster a false sense of security or unjustifiably undermine algorithmic recommendations. Notably, human users do not process uncertainty neutrally but incorporate it into existing heuristics of trust and control. In this context, explainability involves not only information provision but also metacognitive calibration in the face of uncertainty. Evaluation approaches that overlook this dimension are inherently incomplete.

Factual comprehensibility is an essential criterion. Empirical studies indicate that users frequently interpret explanations based on their existing knowledge structures rather than developers' intentions (Miller, 2019). Comprehension tests, qualitative interviews, and controlled user studies are therefore vital for accurately assessing the impact of explanations. It is imperative to determine whether users can identify errors or challenge inappropriate model outputs.

Another important criterion is the impact of explanations on decision quality. Explanations are problematic if they seem subjectively satisfactory but objectively result in poorer decisions. Poursabzi-Sangdeh et al. (2021) demonstrate that simplified or improperly calibrated explanations can lead to excessive acceptance of system outputs. Practical explanations are thus defined not by their persuasiveness, but by their capacity to foster appropriate skepticism.

It raises the question of trust calibration. The goal of explainable AI is not maximum trust, but appropriate trust. Explanations should help users assess when a system is reliable—and when it is not. This also includes making the system's limitations transparent. Studies on human-AI interaction research show that explicit references to uncertainties and the model's known weaknesses can improve long-term decision-making competence (Zhang et al., 2020).

Domain-Specific Evaluation Strategies

The preceding criteria demonstrate that a universal rating scale for explainability is unattainable. Instead, evaluation strategies must be tailored to specific domains. In medical contexts, an explanation is valuable if it improves diagnostic accuracy or reduces misjudgments. In finance, consistency, documentability, and fairness are prioritized. In the public sector, the effectiveness of explanations in supporting appeal and control processes must be assessed. In high-risk domains, evaluation strategies should explicitly account for metacognitive effects. Explanations are considered 'good enough' if they prompt appropriate restraint, inquiries, or escalations, rather than merely fostering acceptance. The metacognitive impact of explanations thus constitutes an independent quality criterion for XAI.

In light of these considerations, several authors recommend hybrid evaluation approaches that integrate technical metrics with user-centered evaluation procedures (Hoffman et al., 2018; Doshi-Velez et al., 2020). Such frameworks establish minimum standards for explainable AI while allowing for context-specific adaptation. A/B testing, pilot implementations, and ongoing monitoring are central components of these strategies.

In summary, an explanation is 'good enough' if it fulfills its intended purpose within the relevant context, rather than providing maximum transparency or detail. Explainability exists on a spectrum and requires ongoing evaluation. Assessing explanations is not solely a technical endeavor, but also an organizational and institutional responsibility. This process demands clear criteria, empirical validation, and accountability mechanisms to ensure explainability throughout the AI system's life cycle. The following section examines explainability within the broader framework of governance architectures.

EXPLAINABILITY, GOVERNANCE, AND ACCOUNTABILITY

Prior analysis demonstrates that explainability extends beyond technical methods or isolated user interactions. When AI systems are integrated into organizational decision-making, explainability becomes an issue of institutional design. Thus, explainable AI should be regarded not as a product feature, but as a governance capability established through defined roles, processes, and artifacts. Explanations achieve lasting impact only when embedded within organizational accountability structures.

Governance approaches to explainability emphasize practices that are recurring, verifiable, and documentable. Organizations must ensure that AI-supported decisions are not only explainable in specific instances but also systematically justified, verified, and accounted for. This requirement spans the development, operation, and application of models in decision-making. Explainability serves as a critical link between technical modeling, operational deployment, and institutional accountability.

A core governance principle is the assignability of responsibility. Although AI systems may operate autonomously, decisions retain social impact and must be attributable to individuals or organizational units. Explanations mediate this process by rendering decision-making transparent and clarifying responsibilities throughout the value chain, from data preparation and modeling to final decisions (Kroll et al., 2017). In the absence of documented explanations, responsibility may become diffuse, increasing the risk of unrecognized and unaddressed errors.

Auditability and reviewability of algorithmic decisions are closely related concerns. While many organizations have implemented control and audit mechanisms, these systems were initially designed for rule-based or statistical procedures. Explainable AI facilitates the integration of such mechanisms into learning systems by providing consistent justifications, temporal comparability, and traceable decision logic. The emphasis is not on full disclosure, but rather on enabling retrospective classification and evaluation of decisions (Raji et al., 2020).

Standardized explanatory artifacts are fundamental to effective governance structures. These artifacts, such as model descriptions, decision summaries, and ongoing protocols, provide essential descriptive information. They support internal communication between technical and domain-specific units, facilitate training and knowledge transfer, and serve as a foundation for external reviews. Additionally, they convert individual ad hoc explanations into consistent organizational practices (Mitchell et al., 2019) Explainability is also integral to organizational learning. Explanations reveal implicit assumptions, enable longitudinal comparisons of decisions, and help identify systematic biases or undesirable trends. In this context, explainable systems serve as instruments for reflecting on both individual choices and the overall quality of decision-making architecture. Organizations that prioritize explainability establish a foundation for continuous improvement rather than isolated control measures.

At the same time, governance through explainability should not be confused with complete transparency. Organizations must take legitimate protection interests into account, such as those relating to trade secrets, security, and personal data. Governance-oriented explainability, therefore, aims at appropriate disclosure: explanations should be designed to enable accountability without disproportionately jeopardizing other protected interests. This balance is not a purely technical one, but rather an organizational decision.

The precise delineation of responsibilities is increasingly critical in this context. Determining who decides which explanations are provided, who evaluates their quality, and who addresses explanation-based objections or feedback is essential.

Without defined roles, explainability may become merely symbolic, lacking substantive impact. Governance structures must therefore specify how explanations are incorporated into decision-making, control, and escalation processes (Raji & Buolamwini, 2019).

In summary, explainability is a critical instrument for responsible AI governance, though it does not guarantee success. Its effectiveness relies on its integration into stable organizational practices that support accountability, auditability, and learning. Only under these conditions can explainable AI be both understandable and institutionally viable. The systematic operationalization of these requirements throughout the AI system life cycle will be addressed in the concluding methodological framework.

THE EXPLAINABILITY ASSURANCE PIPELINE

Previous sections have examined explainability from conceptual, human-centered, technical, domain-specific, evaluative, and governance-oriented perspectives. Collectively, these analyses demonstrate that explainability cannot be achieved through isolated methods, ad hoc design choices, or post hoc documentation alone. Instead, explainability represents a cross-cutting quality that must be intentionally designed, assessed, and maintained throughout the entire lifecycle of an AI system. In this context, the Explainability Assurance Pipeline (EAP) is introduced as an integrative framework that connects technical development, human use, and organizational responsibility within a coherent governance architecture.

Practical experience across diverse application domains demonstrates the necessity of an integrative approach. In automated credit decision systems, explainability often serves to legitimize adverse outcomes for affected individuals and regulators. While post hoc explanations may accurately reference input features such as income stability or credit history, they can create an illusion of transparency by obscuring model uncertainty, proxy variables, or structural limitations. Consequently, such explanations may reinforce overconfidence in automated decisions and reduce the likelihood of contestation or human review. In clinical decision-support systems, explainability is expected to foster trust and informed oversight by medical professionals. However, empirical research indicates that plausible explanations can amplify automation bias, causing clinicians to overweight algorithmic recommendations even when these conflict with professional judgment, particularly in time-critical environments. In public-sector contexts, explainability often fulfills a dual role: supporting individual understanding and meeting institutional accountability requirements. Standardized explanations designed primarily for legal compliance may sacrifice meaningful intelligibility and become disconnected from actual decision logic or responsibility structures. Collectively, these examples indicate that explainability failures rarely result from missing techniques alone, but rather from misalignments between technical design, human interpretation, and organizational use. The Explainability Assurance Pipeline is designed to address these gaps precisely.

The EAP conceptualizes explainability not as a discrete step, but as a continuous, lifecycle-spanning process. In doing so, it addresses a central limitation of the existing XAI literature, which often either prioritizes methodological innovation or formulates abstract principles without systematically accounting for institutional implementation (Hoffman et al., 2018; Doshi-Velez et al., 2020). The pipeline complements these approaches by specifying when, where, and by whom explainability must be ensured across development, deployment, and use.

A foundational principle of the EAP is designing for explainability. Explainability begins not after model training, but with early architectural and modeling decisions. Choices regarding model classes, constraints, feature representations, and system boundaries are not solely technical optimizations; they are governance-relevant decisions that determine which forms of explanation are possible and which stakeholder groups can be meaningfully addressed. As Rudin (2019) notes, these upstream design choices fundamentally delimit the scope and fidelity of subsequent explanation. Building on this foundation, the EAP emphasizes systematic evidence generation and quality assurance. Explanations must be both produced and evaluated for their fidelity to the underlying model, stability over time and across contexts, and suitability for specific decision-making purposes. This process includes technical testing procedures and user-oriented evaluations. Importantly, these checks are not one-time validation exercises, but recurring safeguards that become increasingly important as data distributions, models, or usage conditions evolve (Adebayo et al., 2018). 2018).

Human-centered validation is another core component of the pipeline. As previously discussed, explanations are practical only when interacting with specific actors. The EAP, therefore, requires systematic testing of explanations with relevant user groups, assessing factors such as comprehensibility, capacity to act, and impact on decision quality. This feedback is intended not to optimize communication aesthetics, but to ensure that explanations fulfill their functional role and do not produce unintended effects such as overtrust or disengagement (Poursabzi-Sangdeh et al., 2021).

To operationalize these principles, the EAP is structured as a workflow encompassing four interrelated phases: design, deployment, monitoring, and update. In the design phase, explainability requirements are specified alongside functional and performance objectives, influencing model selection, architectural constraints, and explanation methods based on intended users and decision contexts. During deployment, explainability serves as an explicit release criterion rather than a retrospective justification. Explanations are validated against predefined quality standards, aligned with organizational roles, and integrated into interfaces and workflows to support informed use rather than overreliance. Deployment thus serves as a governance checkpoint, where responsibility for explainability shifts from development teams to operational ownership.

In the monitoring phase, explainability is regarded as a dynamic system property. Changes in data distributions, user behavior, or organizational practices can gradually undermine the validity, stability, or interpretability of explanations. Continuous observation of explanatory behavior, alongside performance and fairness metrics, enables organizations to detect explanation decay, emerging misinterpretations, or interaction effects that present governance risks (Raji et al., 2020). The update phase completes the cycle by incorporating insights from monitoring into model adaptation, interface redesign, or revised governance measures. Through this iterative process, the EAP treats explainability as a maintained organizational capability that evolves with system use and contextual change, rather than as a static compliance artifact. The emergence of generative AI systems, such as large language models, further highlights the necessity of this approach. Generative systems produce fluent, context-sensitive narratives that may seem inherently explanatory, yet often conflate plausibility with faithfulness. Explanations generated by these models can be linguistically convincing while lacking grounding in actual decision logic or internal model states, resulting in hallucinated explanations.

Additionally, explanatory behavior in generative systems is highly sensitive to prompts, interaction history, and context, leading to explanation decay as models are updated or deployed in new settings. Within the EAP, these challenges underscore the importance of assessing not only plausibility but also the stability, consistency, and functional role of explanations across deployment contexts. Effective explainability governance for generative AI requires close integration of technical validation, interaction design, and organizational oversight, acknowledging that persuasive explanations may increase trust while simultaneously obscuring uncertainty and accountability.

At the organizational level, the EAP bridges technical practice and institutional responsibility. Through standardized artifacts, documented testing procedures, and clearly defined handover points, it establishes a shared reference framework for developers, domain experts, management, and oversight functions. As a result, explainability transitions from an individual expert skill to an institutionalized capability embedded within governance processes.

The distinctive contribution of the Explainability Assurance Pipeline is its integrative perspective. It combines technical methods, human use, and organizational embedding without reducing these levels to a single logic. Explainability is presented not as a universal solution, but as a quality-assured process that requires active maintenance. In this respect, the EAP serves less as a rigid model and more as an orientation framework adaptable to various domains, organizational capacities, and risk profiles. This approach concludes the chapter's argument by translating normative demands for explainable decisions into a concrete, implementable governance architecture, thereby setting the stage for the discussion of open research questions and future directions in explainable AI.

CONCLUSIONS AND OUTLOOK

The chapter begins with the fundamental observation that integrating AI into decision-relevant contexts significantly alters the requirements for justifiability, accountability, and comprehensibility. Explainability is conceptualized not merely as a technical property of models, but as a social, organizational, and communicative practice that manifests through interactions among systems, individuals, and institutions. Predictions alone are insufficient; they must be translated into context-sensitive reasons that are verifiable, contestable, and actionable.

A key contribution of the chapter is its consistent use of terminology. By clearly distinguishing between interpretability and explainability, the chapter demonstrates that many misunderstandings in the explainable AI (XAI) debate stem from unclear objectives rather than a lack of methods. Explainability primarily concerns the communicative justification of model decisions, rather than their internal mechanisms. This perspective enables a realistic classification of technical procedures and facilitates transparent articulation of their scope and limitations.

Building on this foundation, the chapter examines the human-centered design of explanations. Explanations are inherently contextual, relating to specific roles, knowledge levels, and capacities for action. The analysis demonstrates that explainability is meaningful only when it addresses diverse target groups, discloses uncertainties, and mitigates overconfidence. Thus, explainability is characterized as a design challenge at the interface between humans and machines, rather than a mere optimization problem.

The analysis of technical approaches shows that the diversity of XAI methods should not lead to a universal solution or increased arbitrariness. Intrinsically interpretable models, post-hoc explanations, counterfactual approaches, and example-based explanations each serve distinct functions. Their value emerges when applied reflectively within specific decision-making and organizational contexts. The chapter emphasizes the importance of systematically addressing risks such as instability, manipulability, and rationalization, rather than relegating them to marginal concerns.

Domain-specific analysis of high-risk areas shows that explainability cannot be standardized across domains. Medical decisions, financial risk assessments, and algorithmic applications in the public sector each impose distinct requirements on the content, form, and depth of explanations. In these contexts, explainability does not guarantee correct decisions; rather, it serves as an infrastructure for control, learning, and accountability. It enables verification of decision-making systems while preserving the complexity of underlying processes.

Another significant contribution of the chapter is its systematic approach to evaluating explanations. The discussion clarifies that explainability should not be viewed in binary terms. An answer is considered sufficient if it is fit for purpose and supports responsible decision-making under specific conditions. Integrating technical quality criteria with human-centered evaluation methods establishes a necessary foundation and shifts the emphasis from formal transparency to functional appropriateness. The Explainability Assurance Pipeline (EAP) proposed an integrative framework that anchors explainability across the entire lifecycle of AI systems. The EAP combines design decisions, quality assurance, user interaction, operational approvals, and continuous monitoring into a coherent governance practice. Its contribution lies less in introducing new methods than in structuring existing elements into an organizationally manageable overall approach. Explainability thus becomes an institutionally secured capability rather than an individually generated property.

A key insight of the chapter addresses the metacognitive dimension of explainable AI. The analysis indicates that explainability primarily exerts its social impact by enhancing individuals' understanding of algorithmic models rather than improving their self-assessment of decision-making abilities. Explanations function less as epistemic tools for knowledge transfer and more as cognitive interventions that limit overconfidence, expose uncertainty, and facilitate responsible delegation.

This metacognitive perspective enables a reinterpretation of apparent contradictions in empirical XAI research. Explanations that prompt caution or restraint in the short term are not necessarily deficient; instead, they may contribute to improved control, escalation, and responsibility decisions over time. Consequently, explainability emerges as a foundational component of contemporary decision-making architectures, where the relationship between human and machine competence is dynamically negotiated.

Despite these advances, several challenges remain. Open research questions include the relationship between explanatory and causal analysis, the design of interactive explanation and recourse systems, and the long-term stability of explanations amid evolving data and usage contexts. Empirical investigation into the social impact of explanations, such as their role in attributing responsibility or legitimizing decisions, is still in its early stages.

In summary, the chapter demonstrates that explainable AI is a central element of responsible digital decision-making architectures, rather than a peripheral technical concern. Explainability does not supplant human judgment or institutional responsibility, but it renders them visible and verifiable. As automated decision-making becomes more prevalent, this visibility is essential to ensure that AI systems remain both practical and socially acceptable.

REFERENCES

Adebayo, J., Gilmer, J., Muelly, M., Goodfellow, I., Hardt, M., & Kim, B. (2018). Sanity checks for saliency maps. Advances in Neural Information Processing Systems, 31, 9505–9515. https://papers.nips.cc/paper_files/paper/2018/file/294a8ed24b1a d22ec2e7efea049b8737-Paper.pdf

Ali, S., Abuhmed, T., El-Sappagh, S., Muhammad, K., Alonso-Moral, J. M., Confalonieri, R., Guidotti, R., Del Ser, J., Díaz-Rodríguez, N., & Herrera, F. (2023). Explainable Artificial Intelligence (XAI): What we know and what is left to attain Trustworthy Artificial Intelligence. *Information Fusion*, *99*, 101805. DOI: 10.1016/j.inffus.2023.101805

Andrae, S. (2024). Explainable Artificial Intelligence in risk management: A framework. In Corazza, M., Shah Khan, F., Torre, D. La, & Masri, H. (eds.). *Artificial intelligence and beyond for finance*. World Scientific Publishing, 149–206. DOI: 10.1142/9781800615212_0004

Barocas, S., Hardt, M., & Narayanan, A. (2023). *Fairness and machine learning: Limitations and opportunities*. MIT Press.

Bussmann, N., Giudici, P., Marinelli, D., & Papenbrock, J. (2021). Explainable machine learning in credit risk management. *Computational Economics*, *57*(1), 203–216. DOI: 10.1007/s10614-020-10042-0

Chiaburu, T., Haußer, F., & Bießmann, F. (2024). Uncertainty in XAI: Human perception and modeling approaches. *Machine Learning & Knowledge Extraction*, *6*(2), 1170–1192. DOI: 10.3390/make6020055

Dhar, R., Brandl, S., Oldenburg, N., & Søgaard, A. (2025). Beyond technocratic XAI: The who, what & how in explanation design. *arXiv*. https://doi.org//arXiv .2508.09231DOI: 10.48550

Doshi-Velez, F., & Kim, B. (2017). Towards a rigorous science of interpretable machine learning. *arXiv*. https://doi.org//arXiv.1702.08608DOI: 10.48550

Doshi-Velez, F., Rudin, C., Schieber, S., Bavitz, C., Gershman, S., O'Brien, D., ... (2019). Accountability of AI under the law: The role of explanation. *arXiv*. https://doi.org//arXiv.1711.01134DOI: 10.48550

Fritz-Morgenthal, S., Hein, B., & Papenbrock, J. (2022). Financial risk management and explainable, trustworthy, responsible AI. *Frontiers in Artificial Intelligence*, *5*, 779799. DOI: 10.3389/frai.2022.779799 PMID: 35295866

Haque, A. K. M. B., Islam, N., & Mikalef, P. (2023). Explainable Artificial Intelligence (XAI) from a user perspective: A synthesis of prior literature and problematizing avenues for future research. *Technological Forecasting and Social Change, 186. Technological Forecasting and Social Change*, *122120*, 122120. Advance online publication. DOI: 10.1016/j.techfore.2022.122120

Hoffman, R. R., Klein, G., Mueller, S. T., & Litman, J. (2018). Explaining explanation for 'Explainable Ai'. *Proceedings of the Human Factors and Ergonomics Society Annual Meeting*, *62*(1), 197–201. DOI: 10.1177/1541931218621047

Hsieh, W., Bi, Z., Jiang, C., Liu, J., Peng, B., Zhang, S., ... (2024). A comprehensive guide to Explainable AI: From classical models to LLMs. *arXiv*. https://doi.org//arXiv.2412.00800DOI: 10.48550

Jacobs, M., Pradier, M. F., McCoy, T. H., Doshi-Velez, F., & Gajos, K. Z. (2021). How machine-learning recommendations influence clinician treatment selections. *Translational Psychiatry*, *11*(1), 108. DOI: 10.1038/s41398-021-01224-x PMID: 33542191

Kim, B., Wattenberg, M., Gilmer, J., Cai, C., Wexler, J., Viegas, F., ... (2018). Interpretability beyond feature attribution: Quantitative testing with concept activation vectors (TCAV). *arXiv*. https://doi.org//arXiv.1711.11279DOI: 10.48550

Kroll, J. A., Huey, J., Barocas, S., Felten, E. W., Reidenberg, J. R., & Robinson, D. G.. (2017). Accountable algorithms. *University of Pennsylvania Law Review*, *165*(3), 633–705. https://scholarship.law.upenn.edu/penn_law_review/vol165/iss3/3

Lipton, Z. C. (2018). The mythos of model interpretability. *ACM Queue; Tomorrow's Computing Today*, *16*(3), 31–57. DOI: 10.1145/3236386.3241340

Lundberg, S. M., & Lee, S.-I. (2017). A unified approach to interpreting model predictions. *arXiv*. https://doi.org//arXiv.1705.07874DOI: 10.48550

Mariappan, R. (2025). Extensive review of literature on Explainable AI (XAI) in healthcare applications. *Recent Advances in Computer Science and Communications*, *18*(1), e200324228159. Advance online publication. DOI: 10.2174/0126662558296699240314055348

Mavrepis, P., Makridis, G., Fatouros, G., Koukos, V., Separdani, M. M., & Kyriazis, D. (2024). *arXiv*. https://doi.org//arXiv.2401.13110DOI: 10.48550

Mersha, M., Lam, K., Wood, J., AlShami, A., & Kalita, J. (2024). Explainable Artificial Intelligence: A survey of needs, techniques, applications, and future direction. *Neurocomputing*, *599*, 128111. DOI: 10.1016/j.neucom.2024.128111

Miller, T. (2019). Explanation in Artificial Intelligence: Insights from the social sciences. *Artificial Intelligence*, *267*, 1–38. DOI: 10.1016/j.artint.2018.07.007

Mitchell, M., Wu, S., Zaldivar, A., Barnes, P., Vasserman, L., & Hutchinson, B.. (2019). Model cards for model reporting. *Proceedings of the Conference on Fairness, Accountability, and Transparency*, 220–229. DOI: 10.1145/3287560.3287596

Molnar, C. (2022). Interpretable machine learning (2nd ed.). Lulu.com. https://christophm.github.io/interpretable-ml-book/

Mumuni, F., & Mumuni, A. (2025). Explainable artificial intelligence (XAI): From inherent explainability to large language models. *arXiv*. https://doi.org//arXiv.2501.09967DOI: 10.48550

Nicolson, A., Bradburn, E., Gal, Y., Papageorghiou, A. T., & Noble, J. A. (2025). The human factor in Explainable Artificial Intelligence: Clinician variability in trust, reliance, and performance. *npj. Digital Medicine*, *8*(1), 658. DOI: 10.1038/s41746-025-02023-0 PMID: 41238825

Pearl, J., & Mackenzie, D. (2018). *The book of why: The new science of cause and effect*. Basic Books.

Poursabzi-Sangdeh, F., Goldstein, D. G., Hofman, J. M., Wortman Vaughan, J., & Wallach, H. (2021). Manipulating and measuring model interpretability. *Proceedings of the 2021 CHI Conference on Human Factors in Computing Systems*, 1–15. DOI: 10.1145/3411764.3445315

Raji, I. D., & Buolamwini, J. (2019). Actionable auditing: Investigating the impact of publicly naming biased performance results of commercial AI products. Proceedings of the AAAI/ACM Conference on AI, Ethics, and Society, 429–435. https://dam-prod.media.mit.edu/x/2019/01/24/AIES-19_paper_223.pdf

Raji, I. D., Smart, A., White, R. N., Mitchell, M., Gebru, T., & Hutchinson, B.. (2020). Closing the AI accountability gap: Defining an end-to-end framework for internal algorithmic auditing. *Proceedings of the Conference on Fairness, Accountability, and Transparency*, 33–44. DOI: 10.1145/3351095.3372873

Ribeiro, M. T., Singh, S., & Guestrin, C. (2016). 'Why should I trust you?' Explaining the predictions of any classifier. Proceedings of the 22nd ACM SIGKDD International Conference on Knowledge Discovery and Data Mining, 1135–1144. DOI: 10.1145/2939672.2939778

Rudin, C. (2019). Stop explaining black box machine learning models for high stakes decisions and use interpretable models instead. *Nature Machine Intelligence*, *1*(5), 206–215. DOI: 10.1038/s42256-019-0048-x PMID: 35603010

Selbst, A. D., Boyd, D., Friedler, S. A., Venkatasubramanian, S., & Vertesi, J. (2019). Fairness and abstraction in sociotechnical systems. *Proceedings of the Conference on Fairness, Accountability, and Transparency*, 59–68. DOI: 10.1145/3287560.3287598

Shokri, R., Stronati, M., Song, C., & Shmatikov, V. (2017). Membership inference attacks against machine learning models. *2017 IEEE Symposium on Security and Privacy*, 3–18. DOI: 10.1109/SP.2017.41

Slack, D., Hilgard, S., Jia, E., Singh, S., & Lakkaraju, H. (2020). Fooling LIME and SHAP: Adversarial attacks on post hoc explanation methods. *Proceedings of the AAAI Conference on Artificial Intelligence*, *34*(04), 180–187. DOI: 10.1145/3375627.3375830

Vilone, G., & Longo, L. (2020). Explainable Artificial Intelligence: A systematic review. *arXiv*. https://doi.org//arXiv.2006.00093DOI: 10.48550

von Zahn, M., Liebich, L., Jussupow, E., Hinz, O., & Bauer, K. (2025). Knowing (not) to know: Explainable Artificial Intelligence and human metacognition. *Information Systems Research*, ●●●, 1–23. DOI: 10.1287/isre.2024.1431

Wachter, S., Mittelstadt, B., & Floridi, L. (2017). Counterfactual explanations without opening the black box: Automated decisions and the GDPR. *SSRN*, *31*(2), 841–887. https://jolt.law.harvard.edu/assets/articlePDFs/v31/Counterfactual-Explanations-without-Opening-the-Black-Box-Sandra-Wachter-et-al.pdf. DOI: 10.2139/ssrn.3063289

Zhang, Y., Liao, Q. V., & Bellamy, R. K. E. (2020). Effect of confidence and explanation on accuracy and trust calibration in AI-assisted decision making. *Proceedings of the 2020 Conference on Fairness, Accountability, and Transparency*, 295–305. DOI: 10.1145/3351095.3372852

Chapter 5
Making AI Models Intelligible to Experts (Interpretability):
Interpretable AI Methods for Safety-Critical Systems

Shashank Parmar
http://orcid.org/0000-0003-4369-3647
VISA Inc., India

ABSTRACT

Artificial intelligence (AI) faces a critical "black box" problem, especially in safety-sensitive domains like healthcare and finance, where transparency is essential. This chapter provides a comprehensive exploration of interpretability, distinguishing it from post-hoc explainability. It covers methods from classical linear models and decision trees to modern techniques like GAMs, EBMs, and deep learning interpretation (saliency maps, Grad-CAM, LRP). The discussion extends to inherently interpretable architectures such as prototype-based, neuro-symbolic, and causal models, and situates interpretability within governance, using case studies and tools like Model Cards. We conclude that interpretability is a multidisciplinary imperative for building powerful, transparent, and human-aligned AI.

1. DEFINING INTERPRETABILITY IN AI RESEARCH: THEORETICAL FOUNDATIONS AND EVOLVING DEFINITIONS

The terms "interpretability" and "explainability" are often used interchangeably, but scholars have made valuable distinctions. We'll focus on two seminal views.

DOI: 10.4018/979-8-3373-6935-8.ch005

1. Zachary Lipton's View: The Mythos of Model Interpretability

Interpretability shouldn't be claimed abstractly; it should be tied to why it's needed. Lipton (Lipton, 2016) identifies key motivations: building trust in predictions (especially in high-stakes domains like medicine), uncovering causal relationships, ensuring fairness and ethical decision-making, and enabling safety, debugging, and error correction. He also distinguishes between transparency, which means understanding the model's internal workings, and post-hoc interpretation, which involves explaining a model's decisions after the fact, often for otherwise opaque (black-box) models.

2. Doshi-Velez & Kim's View: A Rigorous Science

In Doshi-Velez and Kim's 2017 paper (Doshi-Velez & Kim, 2017) defines interpretability as the ability of a model to explain itself in terms understandable to a human, stressing that interpretability is fundamentally driven by the human task at hand. They argue that sometimes explanations only need to be convincing enough for a person to trust a model's output, while in other cases explanations should help a human understand the model's behavior in order to analyze or improve it. In the most demanding settings, interpretability must go further by allowing humans to anticipate when a model will fail and to intervene or manage it effectively.

The Levels of Transparency (Peeling the Onion)

If interpretability is about understanding, we can break it down into levels. This framework helps us categorize *what* part of the model we are trying to understand.

1. Simulatability

Simulatability refers to whether a human can mentally execute a model, given its parameters and an input, and arrive at the same output within a reasonable amount of time. For example, a simple linear model with a small number of features can be simulated by a human, whereas a deep neural network with millions of parameters cannot. This makes simulatability the strongest and most demanding form of model transparency.

2. Decomposability

Decomposability refers to whether every part of a model can be understood in an intuitive way, including its inputs, parameters, and calculations. Each input feature should have a clear real-world meaning, each parameter should be interpretable in terms of how it influences the output, and each step of the computation should be simple enough to follow. A small decision tree typically satisfies these conditions and is therefore decomposable, whereas large or ensemble models generally are not.

3. Algorithmic Transparency

Algorithmic transparency refers to how well we can understand the learning process of a model itself and whether the behavior of the algorithm is theoretically well understood. For example, linear regression is algorithmically transparent because it has a closed-form solution and clear guarantees about how it converges to optimal weights given the data. In contrast, deep neural networks rely on non-convex and stochastic training processes, which makes their learning dynamics and outcomes far less transparent.

The Radical Argument: Stop Explaining Black Boxes!

Now, let's challenge everything. In her provocative 2019 paper, "Stop Explaining Black Box Models for High-Stakes Decisions," Professor Cynthia Rudin makes a powerful argument (Rudin, 2018).

Her Thesis: We should not use post-hoc explanations for black-box models in high-stakes scenarios. Instead, we should use models that are inherently interpretable by design.

Her main arguments are:

1. **Post-hoc Explanations are Not Faithful:** They are approximations of the model's behavior, not the truth. They can be misleading and create a false sense of security.
2. **The "Rashomon Effect":** There can often be multiple, equally accurate models that make predictions for different reasons. A post-hoc explanation might not reveal the true logic of your specific model.
3. **A Wrong Solution to the Right Problem:** Instead of building an uninterpretable model and then struggling to explain it, we should invest that effort into creating models that are both accurate and transparent from the start (like rule-based models, sparse linear models, or small decision trees).
4. **The "Right to an Explanation":** Regulations like the GDPR suggest a "right to an explanation" for automated decisions. Rudin argues that a post-hoc explanation for a black box does not satisfy this right; only a model whose entire reasoning process is clear does.

For high-stakes decisions, her argument is compelling: If you need to understand the decision, the model itself must be understandable.

Table 1. Summarizing Concepts in Interpretable AI

Concept	Core Idea	Key Thinker
Interpretability	Intrinsic understanding of the model's mechanics (a glass box).	Lipton, Doshi-Velez & Kim
Explainability	Post-hoc explanations for a black box's predictions.	Doshi-Velez & Kim
Transparency	Broken down into Simulatability, Decomposability, Algorithmic Transparency.	Lipton
Human-Centered Criteria	Explanations should be judged by Fidelity, Stability, Completeness, Parsimony.	Doshi-Velez & Kim
Inherently Interpretable Models	For high-stakes decisions, avoid post-hoc explanations; use interpretable models by design.	Rudin

2. MATHEMATICAL AND STATISTICAL INTERPRETABILITY: FEATURE IMPORTANCE, DECISION BOUNDARIES, SURROGATE MODELS, AND INTERPRETABLE-BY-DESIGN MODELS

The Classics: Intrinsically Interpretable Models

We begin with models that are interpretable by their very design. As Rudin would advocate, these should be your first choice when possible.

1. Linear & Logistic Regression

Linear and logistic regression are based on a weighted sum of input features (Chung, 2020; Kuchibhotla et al., 2019), producing a continuous output for linear regression and a probability for classification in logistic regression. Their interpretability comes from decomposability, since each coefficient represents the effect of a one-unit change in a feature on the prediction while holding all other features constant. In linear regression, this means a one-year increase in age corresponds to an increase of $\beta_{(age)}$ in the predicted outcome, while in logistic regression it corresponds to a multiplicative change of $\exp(\beta_{(age)})$ in the odds of the positive class. However, these models assume linear relationships and their interpretations can become unreliable when features are highly correlated, as multicollinearity can destabilize coefficient estimates.

2. Decision Trees

Decision trees (Quinlan, 1986) model predictions as a hierarchy of if-then-else rules that split the data into increasingly specific groups. Their interpretability comes from both simulatability and decomposability, since a human can follow the exact path taken for a single prediction from the root to a leaf, yielding a clear, rule-based explanation such as "if age is greater than 50 and blood pressure is above 120, then the risk is high." Features that appear near the top of the tree are generally the most important for making broad decisions across the dataset. However, single decision trees can be unstable because small changes in the data may lead to very different structures, they often perform worse than more complex models, and large trees lose the simplicity that makes them easy to interpret.

3. Rule-Based Learners (e.g., RIPPER, OneR)

Rule-based learners such as RIPPER and OneR (Hinton et al., 2015; Margot & Luta, 2021) produce models in the form of discrete, human-readable if-then rules, for example stating that if blood pressure and cholesterol are both high, then the patient is high risk. Their interpretability comes from simulatability, since the model itself acts as the explanation and can be followed like a checklist. However, these methods can grow complex as more rules are added and often struggle to capture subtle or highly non-linear relationships compared to more flexible models.

The Modern Powerhouses: GAMs and EBMs

What if we need more predictive power than a linear model but more interpretability than a black box? Enter Generalized Additive Models.

1. Generalized Additive Models (GAMs)

Generalized Additive Models, introduced by Lou et al. (2012) (Lou et al., 2012), extend linear models by relaxing the assumption of strict linearity while preserving interpretability. Instead of modeling the outcome as a weighted sum of features, a GAM expresses the prediction through a link function applied to the sum of smooth, non-linear functions of each feature. Its interpretability comes from decomposability, because each feature contributes independently through its own function. The key advantage of the additive structure is that each function can be visualized, allowing us to directly see the shape of the relationship between a single feature and the output while holding all others constant. This makes it possible to say, for example, that the effect of age on medical risk follows a specific non-linear curve rather than increasing at a constant rate. In a healthcare setting, a GAM can model disease risk as the sum of smooth functions of age, BMI, and cholesterol, capturing realistic non-linear effects while still allowing each variable's influence to be isolated and interpreted.

2. Explainable Boosting Machines (EBMs) - The Best of Both Worlds

Explainable Boosting Machines, introduced by Caruana et al. (2015) (Nori et al., 2021), are a modern, high-performance extension of generalized additive models that use boosting to carefully learn each feature's contribution. Their key innovation is cyclic boosting, where the model updates one feature function at a time using very small tree stumps and low learning rates, cycling repeatedly through features. This controlled process allows EBMs to capture limited, interpretable interactions between features while preserving the additive structure. As a result, EBMs retain all the interpretability benefits of GAMs while achieving accuracy comparable to models like random forests or gradient boosting machines. Each feature's global effect can be visualized, and individual predictions can be explained locally by summing the contributions from each feature and any learned interaction terms. In practice, an EBM predicting heart disease risk might learn distinct, plottable patterns for age, BMI, cholesterol, and smoking status, and also reveal interpretable interactions such as older smokers facing disproportionately higher risk, shown through a simple two-dimensional heatmap.

Explaining Black Boxes: Surrogates and Feature Importance

Sometimes, you *must* use a black box. For those cases, we have post-hoc explanation tools.

1. Global Surrogate Models
    - **The Idea:** Global surrogate models aim to explain black-box predictors by training a simpler, interpretable model such as a decision tree or a GAM to mimic the black box's behavior (Hassija, Chamola, & Mahapatra, 2024; Longo et al., 2023). The approach works by first generating predictions from the black-box model on a dataset and then training the interpretable model to predict those outputs rather than the true labels. Interpretation is performed on the surrogate, with the understanding that it provides an approximate picture of how the original

model makes decisions. A key limitation is that the surrogate's fidelity may be limited, meaning it can fail to capture the black box's true reasoning in complex or highly non-linear regions. In practice, banks often use global surrogate models for credit scoring, combining accurate but opaque ensembles with simpler surrogate trees to give regulators and managers a high-level understanding of model behavior..

- **Example:** Here's an example of using a global surrogate model for interpretability. First, a black-box model—a Random Forest—is trained on the Pima Indians Diabetes dataset, which includes features like glucose level, BMI, and age. Next, the Random Forest is used to generate predicted probabilities of diabetes for each patient, and these predictions are saved. These outputs, not the original labels, become the target for the surrogate. Finally, a decision tree is trained on the same input features, but its goal is to predict the Random Forest's outputs. The resulting decision tree approximates the behavior of the black box, allowing humans to interpret how the Random Forest makes its predictions in an understandable, rule-based form.

2. Feature Importance

Feature importance methods aim to measure how much each input feature contributes to a model's overall predictive performance. Common approaches include permutation importance, which assesses importance by shuffling a feature's values and observing how much the model's accuracy drops, making it a robust and model-agnostic technique, and tree-based importance, which relies on how much a feature reduces impurity across decision trees in ensembles. These methods support global interpretations such as identifying which features matter most on average for the model's performance. However, feature importance does not explain individual predictions, nor does it reveal the mechanism behind a feature's influence, and it can be biased toward features with many distinct values.

Visualization: Seeing the Decision

A picture is worth a thousand words, especially in interpretability.

Visualizing Decision Boundaries

Visualization is a powerful tool for interpretability, especially when examining decision boundaries. For models with one or two features, you can plot how the model partitions the input space by creating a dense grid of points across the feature ranges, computing the model's prediction at each point, and coloring the points according to the predicted class or value. This shows, for example, that linear or logistic regression produces a straight line or smooth S-curve, decision trees create axis-aligned rectangles reflecting hierarchical splits, and more complex models like SVMs or neural networks generate highly non-linear boundaries. Such visualizations make the model's behavior intuitive, but they become impractical when dealing with more than two or three features.

Table 2. Summarizing Mathematical and Statistically Interpretable Models

Model/Method	Core Idea	Interpretability Source
Linear/Logistic Reg.	Weighted sum of features.	Coefficient values.
Decision Trees	Hierarchical if-then rules.	Simulatable prediction paths.
GAMs	Sum of smooth, non-linear functions.	Plottable shape functions f_j(x_j).
EBMs	High-accuracy GAM with controlled interactions.	Plottable functions + additive local scores.
Surrogate Models	Train a simple model to mimic a black box.	Interpret the surrogate.
Feature Importance	Measure performance drop without a feature.	Global ranking of feature relevance.

While classical interpretability work centered around pre-2019 foundations, recent years have seen significant expansion in both the scope and technical sophistication of XAI. Surveys by Samek et al. (Saarela & Jauhiainen, 2021), Vilone & Longo (Ewald et al., 2024), and Miller (Breiman, 2001) highlight new dimensions such as cognitive-grounded explanations, human–AI collaboration, and domain-specific explainability requirements. More recent XAI frameworks incorporate robustness testing, explanation stability evaluation, fairness-aware explainers, and causal interpretability mechanisms.

A second wave of research focuses on scalable interpretability, especially for deep networks and transformer architectures. Methods such as Shapley value extensions, causal SHAP, and dataset attribution techniques help bridge gaps in transparency for large-scale systems. These contemporary frameworks provide deeper insight into model behavior and align interpretability with practical governance needs.

3. TRADE-OFFS WITH PERFORMANCE: EXPLORING ACCURACY–INTERPRETABILITY DILEMMAS IN MODEL SELECTION

The Fundamental Trade-Off: Accuracy vs. Interpretability

At the heart of this topic is a seeming contradiction: the models that are easiest to understand are often not the most accurate, and vice-versa.

Why Do Complex Models Often Outperform Simpler Ones?

This was the central argument of Leo Breiman's seminal 2001 paper, "Statistical Modeling: The Two Cultures." Breiman identified two competing paradigms in statistics (Breiman, 2001):

1. **The Data Modeling Culture:** Assumes that data is generated by a given stochastic model (e.g., a linear model with Gaussian noise). The goal is to fit the parameters of this model. This culture prizes simplicity and interpretability.
2. **The Algorithmic Modeling Culture:** Treats the data mechanism as unknown and uses flexible, complex algorithms to find a function f(X) that predicts the response variable Y. This culture prizes predictive accuracy.

Breiman argued forcefully that the algorithmic modeling culture (which includes Random Forests, Boosted Trees, and Neural Networks) was vastly more powerful for prediction because it does not make strong, and often incorrect, *a priori* assumptions about the world

Let's break this down:

- **Simple/Interpretable Models (e.g., Linear Regression):** Assume the world is, well, linear. They have high bias. If the true underlying relationship in your data is complex and non-linear, a linear model is fundamentally incapable of capturing it, no matter how much data you have. It will be inaccurate but interpretable.
- **Complex/Black-Box Models (e.g., Deep Neural Networks):** Make very few assumptions about the data's structure. They are highly flexible, with low bias. They can learn incredibly complex, non-linear, and interactive patterns. This allows them to achieve high accuracy, but at the cost of opacity.

Empirical Evidence: Challenging the Dogma

The conventional wisdom is "black boxes are more accurate." But is this always true? A growing body of empirical evidence, often in high-stakes domains, challenges this.

Case Study: Healthcare (The Caruana et al. Pneumonia Risk Story)

A famous healthcare case study by Caruana et al. illustrates the importance of interpretability. The goal was to predict pneumonia mortality risk to guide hospitalization decisions. A complex neural network achieved high accuracy, but an interpretable GAM revealed a dangerous flaw: the model assigned lower risk to patients with asthma. This happened because, historically, asthma patients in the training data were immediately admitted to the ICU and received excellent care, so their outcomes were better. The neural network learned the correlation "asthma → lower risk" without understanding the causal reality. By using an interpretable GAM, doctors could see and correct this issue, ensuring asthma was correctly treated as a high-risk factor. This case shows that black-box models can exploit spurious correlations or biases in the data, whereas interpretable models allow human oversight, aligning predictions with domain knowledge and producing safer, more trustworthy outcomes.

Techniques for Balancing the Trade-off

So, what do you do when you face this tension? You have several strategic options.

1. The "Interpretable First" Strategy

This is the Rudin/Caruana philosophy. Your default should be to try the most interpretable model that can solve the problem (e.g., a GAM/EBM). Only move to a black box if you can empirically demonstrate a significant and necessary performance gain that justifies the loss of interpretability. Often, you'll find the interpretable model is "good enough" and sometimes even better (Rudin, 2019; Rudin et al., 2022).

2. The Ensemble Strategy: Hybrid Models

Why choose one? You can combine them.

- **Concept:** Use a black-box model for its raw predictive power, but use an interpretable model to "clean up" or explain its results (Hassija, Chamola, & Mahapatra, 2024).
- **Example:** Use a high-performance gradient boosting machine for 95% of your predictions. However, for the most critical or uncertain predictions (e.g., the top 5% of risk scores), have a human expert apply a simple, vetted rule set or use a surrogate model to generate a trustworthy explanation before acting.

3. Knowledge Distillation for Interpretable Surrogates

This is a more advanced technique for when you *must* use a black box for training but need an interpretable model for deployment (Biehler et al., 2022; Plumb et al., 2019).

- **The Idea:** Instead of training a surrogate model on the original data, you train it on the *predictions* of the black-box model. The goal is to "distill" the knowledge of the large, accurate "teacher" model (the black box) into a small, interpretable "student" model (e.g., a shallow decision tree).
- **The Process:**

1. Train your high-accuracy black-box teacher model.
2. Generate a large, potentially synthetic dataset and get the teacher's predictions for it.
3. Train your interpretable student model to mimic the teacher's predictions on this new dataset.

The Hope: The student model will learn the key patterns discovered by the teacher, achieving higher accuracy than if it were trained on the original data, while remaining interpretable.

The Caveat: This is still a surrogate model! You are trading some fidelity for interpretability. The student may not capture all the teacher's nuances.

Table 3. Summarizing Predictability and Interpretability tradeoffs

Strategy	Core Idea	When to Use
Interpretable First	Start with GAMs/EBMs; only use black boxes if necessary.	Default for high-stakes decisions. Aligns with Rudin's argument.
Empirical Validation	Test if the black box's accuracy gain is real and meaningful.	Always. The "trade-off" may be an illusion, as in the pneumonia case.
Hybrid Ensembles	Use a black box for bulk predictions, interpretable models for edge/critical cases.	When you need high overall accuracy but must explain specific high-stakes decisions.
Knowledge Distillation	Train an interpretable model to mimic a pre-trained black box.	When a black box is the only way to achieve accuracy, but deployment requires an interpretable model.

4. INTERPRETING DEEP NEURAL NETWORKS: SALIENCY MAPS, GRAD-CAM, INTEGRATED GRADIENTS, LRP, ATTENTION MECHANISMS, FEATURE VISUALIZATION, AND CONCEPT ACTIVATION VECTORS

The phenomenal performance of Deep Neural Networks (DNNs) comes at a cost: their inherent complexity and non-linearity make them "black boxes." Unlike linear models or decision trees, the reasoning behind a DNN's prediction is not directly accessible. The field of interpretability aims to open this box, not by creating simplified, post-hoc explanations (explainability), but by developing methods to understand the internal mechanisms and representations of the models themselves. This section explores key techniques for interpreting DNNs, which can be broadly categorized into methods that attribute importance to input features and those that probe the model's internal concepts.

A useful framework for understanding these methods is to see them as answering different questions about the model's decision:

1. **What parts of the input were most influential?** (Input Feature Attribution)
2. **What internal features or concepts did the model use?** (Representation Analysis)

4.1 Interpreting via Input Feature Attribution

These methods assign an "importance score" to each feature of the input (e.g., each pixel in an image), creating a heatmap that highlights regions most critical for the model's specific prediction.

A) Saliency Maps

One of the earliest and simplest approaches, Saliency Maps compute the gradient of the output score (e.g., the score for "German Shepherd") with respect to the input image (Chmiel et al., 2023; Sigut et al., 2024; Simonyan et al., 2013; Zhang et al., 2023). The absolute values of these gradients are interpreted as importance scores; pixels whose small changes would most impact the output are deemed salient. While intuitive, vanilla saliency maps are often noisy and susceptible to gradient saturation, where a feature is critical but has a zero gradient.

Sample Execution:

We'll use a 2D input and a binary classifier.

- Input: a 2D vector (x_1,x_2).
- Output: probability of class 1 vs. class 0.

Imagine a classifier that distinguishes "points above vs. below a line".
A 1-hidden-layer network:

$$h = \text{ReLU}(W_1 x + b_1)$$

$$\hat{y} = \sigma(W_2 h + b_2)$$

Where:
$x= [x_1,x_2]$ is our input.
$\hat{y}$ is the predicted probability for "Class 1".
σ is the sigmoid.
Saliency for input pixel (or feature, here just x_1,x_2) is:

$$S = \left| \frac{\partial \hat{y}}{\partial x} \right|$$

Let's pick specific weights:

$$W_1 = \begin{bmatrix} 1 & -1 \\ -0.5 & 2 \end{bmatrix}, \quad b_1 = [0,0]$$

$$W_2 = [1,1], \quad b_2 = 0$$

So the hidden layer:

$$h_1 = \text{ReLU}(x_1 - x_2), \quad h_2 = \text{ReLU}(-0.5x_1 + 2x_2)$$

Final output:

$$\hat{y} = \sigma(h_1 + h_2)$$

Say our input is:

x= [2,1]

Compute forward pass:

$$h_1 = \text{ReLU}(2 - 1) = 1$$

$$h_2 = \text{ReLU}(-1 + 2) = 1$$

$$\hat{y} = \sigma(2) \approx 0.88$$

Prediction = Class 1 (high confidence).
We compute:

$$\frac{\partial \hat{y}}{\partial x}$$

First, derivative of sigmoid:

$$\frac{\partial \hat{y}}{\partial z} = \hat{y}(1 - \hat{y}) = 0.88 \times 0.12 \approx 0.105$$

Now chain rule:

$$z = h_1 + h_2$$

$$\frac{\partial z}{\partial x} = \frac{\partial h_1}{\partial x} + \frac{\partial h_2}{\partial x}$$

For $h_1 = \text{ReLU}(x_1 - x_2)$:
Gradient = [1, -1] since inside is positive.
For $h_2 = \text{ReLU}(-0.5x_1 + 2x_2)$:
Gradient = [-0.5, 2] since inside is positive.
So total gradient:

$$\frac{\partial z}{\partial x} = [1 - 0.5, -1 + 2] = [0.5, 1]$$

Now multiply by sigmoid derivative (0.105):

$$\frac{\partial \hat{y}}{\partial x} = 0.105 \cdot [0.5, 1] = [0.0525, 0.105]$$

Take absolute values:

$$S = [0.0525, 0.105]$$

This means: Feature x_2 is twice as important as x_1 for this prediction. If we slightly change x_2, the model output shifts more strongly.

Key Takeaways: Saliency maps are computed as the gradients of a model's output with respect to its input. In simple examples, this can be done step by step, and in images, the same principle is applied to every pixel to produce a heatmap showing which parts of the input most influence the output.

B) Grad-CAM (Gradient-weighted Class Activation Mapping):

Grad-CAM addresses the coarseness of saliency maps by leveraging the convolutional layers that naturally preserve spatial information (Selvaraju et al., 2017). It computes the gradients of the target class flowing into the final convolutional layer, and uses them to weight the corresponding feature maps. The result is a coarse heatmap that highlights the class-discriminative regions in the image. Its strength lies in its clarity, often showing where the model is looking (e.g., the head of a dog), but its resolution is limited by the size of the final convolutional feature maps.

Sample Execution:

Suppose we train a CNN to classify small grayscale images (say 4×4 pixels) into two classes:

Class 0: mostly dark

Class 1: bright spot in the top-left

Input = 4×4 image.

Model = 1 convolution layer → ReLU → global average pooling → classifier.

Unlike saliency maps (which look at pixel-level gradients), Grad-CAM works at the feature map level:

1. Pick a convolutional layer (say the last one).
2. Compute the gradient of the class score w.r.t. the feature maps.

3. Average the gradients across spatial positions → get an importance weight per channel.
4. Weight the feature maps by these importance values.
5. Sum → Class Activation Map (CAM).
6. Upsample to input size → heatmap over the original image.

This highlights which regions of the image influenced the prediction.
Say our conv layer has 2 filters producing 2 feature maps of size 2×2.
Example input image (class 1 candidate):

$$X = \begin{bmatrix} 1 & 0 & 0 & 0 \\ 0 & 0 & 0 & 0 \\ 0 & 0 & 0 & 0 \\ 0 & 0 & 0 & 0 \end{bmatrix}$$

- Feature maps after conv+ReLU:

$$A^1 = \begin{bmatrix} 1 & 0 \\ 0 & 0 \end{bmatrix}, A^2 = \begin{bmatrix} 0.5 & 0 \\ 0 & 0 \end{bmatrix}$$

- Class score for Class 1:

$$y^c = w_1 \cdot \mathrm{GAP}(A^1) + w_2 \cdot \mathrm{GAP}(A^2)$$

Suppose:

$$\mathrm{GAP}(A^1) = 0.25, \ \mathrm{GAP}(A^2) = 0.125.$$

Weights: w_1=2, w_2=1.
Then:

$$y^c = 2(0.25) + 1(0.125) = 0.625$$

We compute: Backward Pass (Gradients)

$$\alpha_k^c = \frac{1}{Z}\sum_i m \sum_j n \frac{\partial y^c}{\partial A_{ij}^k}$$

Where:
A^k= feature map k.
Z= number of spatial locations (here 4).

α_k^c= importance of feature map k.

For our toy example:

$\alpha_1^c = 2$ (strongly influences output).

$\alpha_2^c = 0.5.$

Grad-CAM map before ReLU:

$$L^c = \mathrm{ReLU}\left(\alpha_1^c A^1 + \alpha_2^c A^2\right)$$

$$L^c = \mathrm{ReLU}\left(2\begin{bmatrix}1 & 0\\0 & 0\end{bmatrix}+0.5\begin{bmatrix}0.5 & 0\\0 & 0\end{bmatrix}\right)$$

$$L^c = \begin{bmatrix}2.25 & 0\\0 & 0\end{bmatrix}$$

Upsample to Input Size

Resize 2×2 → 4×4→ heatmap highlighting the top-left corner, exactly where the bright spot was.

That's Grad-CAM: instead of noisy per-pixel gradients, we get structured regions of importance.

Key Differences from Saliency:

Attention differs from saliency-based explanations in several ways. Saliency maps measure per-pixel sensitivity, which often results in noisy and hard-to-interpret visualizations. Grad-CAM improves on this by computing importance at the feature-map level, producing smoother, more localized, and class-discriminative maps. Both methods output heatmaps over the input image, showing where the network focused, but attention weights are inherently part of the model's computation, whereas saliency and Grad-CAM are post-hoc analyses.

C) Integrated Gradients

This method tackles the gradient saturation problem directly. Instead of using the gradient at a single input, Integrated Gradients computes the average gradient along a path from a baseline input (e.g., a black image) to the actual input (Moraliyage et al., 2025; Wang et al., 2024). By integrating these gradients, it attributes the prediction fairly to each input feature, fulfilling desirable axioms like Completeness (the attributions sum to the difference between the output at the input and the baseline). It provides a principled and often less noisy attribution map.

Sample Execution:

Vanilla gradients can vanish or be misleading (gradient saturation). Integrated Gradients solve this by considering not just one gradient at the input, but the average gradient along the path from a baseline input to the actual input.

Mathematically, for input x, baseline x', model F:

$$\mathrm{IG}_i(x) = (x_i - x_i') \cdot \int_{\alpha=0}^{1} \cdot \frac{\partial F(x' + \alpha(x - x'))}{\partial x_i} d\alpha$$

x= actual input

x'= baseline (e.g., black image, or zero vector)

IG = cumulative sensitivity from baseline → input

Completeness: $\sum_i . IG_i(x) = F(x) - F(x')$

Recall the network:

$$h_1 = \mathrm{ReLU}(x_1 - x_2), h_2 = \mathrm{ReLU}(-0.5x_1 + 2x_2)$$

$$\hat{y} = \sigma(h_1 + h_2)$$

Input: x= [2,1]

Baseline: $x' = [0,0]$

The straight-line interpolation:

$$x(a) = x' + \alpha(x - x') = [2\alpha, 1\alpha]$$

for $\alpha \in [0,1]$.

We need $\frac{\partial \hat{y}}{\partial x}$ at various α.

Forward pass:

$$h_1 = \mathrm{ReLU}(2\alpha - \alpha) = \mathrm{ReLU}(\alpha) = \alpha$$

$$h_2 = \mathrm{ReLU}(-0.5(2\alpha) + 2(\alpha)) = \mathrm{ReLU}(-\alpha + 2\alpha) = \alpha$$

$$z = h_1 + h_2 = 2\alpha$$

$$\hat{y}(\alpha) = \sigma(2\alpha)$$

Derivative wrt z:

$$\frac{\partial \hat{y}}{\partial z} = \hat{y}(1 - \hat{y})$$

Gradients wrt input:
$\frac{\partial z}{\partial x} = [0.5, 1]$ (from earlier computation)
So:

$$\frac{\partial \hat{y}}{\partial x} = \hat{y}(1 - \hat{y}) \cdot [0.5, 1]$$

IG requires:

$$IG(x) = (x - x') \cdot \int_0^1 \cdot \frac{\partial \hat{y}(x(\alpha))}{\partial x} d\alpha$$

Here: $x - x' = [2, 1]$.
So for each component:

$$IG_i(x) = \left(x_i - x_i^{'}\right) \cdot \int_0^1 \cdot \frac{\partial \hat{y}}{\partial x_i}(\alpha)\, d\alpha$$

We can approximate by summing gradients at a few points (say 3 points $\alpha=$ 0.25, 0.5, 0.75).
At $\alpha=$ 0.25:

$$z = 0.5,\ \hat{y} = \sigma(0.5) \approx 0.62,$$

derivative wrt z = 0.235

Gradient = [0.118, 0.235]
At $\alpha=$ 0.5:

$$z = 1.0,\ \hat{y} = 0.73,$$

derivative = 0.197

Gradient = [0.099, 0.197]
At $\alpha=$ 0.75:

$$z = 1.5,\ \hat{y} = 0.82,$$

derivative = 0.149

Gradient = [0.074, 0.149]

Average gradient ≈ [0.097, 0.194].

Now apply formula:

$$IG = (x - x') \odot \text{AvgGradient}$$

$$IG = [2,1] \odot [0.097, 0.194] = [0.194, 0.194]$$

Baseline output: $\hat{y}(0) = \sigma(0) = 0.5$

Input output: $\hat{y}(2,1) = 0.88$

Difference = 0.88–0.5= 0.38.

Sum of attributions = 0.194+0.194= 0.388 (close, small error due to approximation).

D) Layer-wise Relevance Propagation (LRP)

LRP operates on a different principle than gradient-based methods. It treats the model's prediction as a value to be "distributed" backward through the network, from the output back to the input layer, using a set of conservation rules (Binder et al., 2016; Samek et al., 2019). At each layer, the relevance received from the layer above is redistributed to the neurons in the current layer based on their contribution. Different LRP rules allow for tailoring the propagation to the network's architecture (e.g., handling positive and negative contributions separately), offering a flexible and theoretically grounded approach.

Gradient-based methods (Saliency, IG, Grad-CAM) look at derivatives of the output w.r.t. inputs. LRP instead takes the output score itself (say $F(x)$) and redistributes it backward through the network until it's assigned to each input feature.

Sample Execution:

The key principle: Relevance conservation

$$\sum_i . R_i^{(l)} = \sum_j . R_j^{(l+1)}$$

Meaning the total relevance at one layer equals the total relevance at the previous layer i.e., the "credit" is preserved.

Same setup as before for consistency:

$$h_1 = \text{ReLU}(x_1 - x_2), h_2 = \text{ReLU}(-0.5x_1 + 2x_2)$$

$$\hat{y} = \sigma(h_1 + h_2)$$

Take input x= [2,1].
Forward pass:

$$h_1 = 1,\ h_2 = 1,\ z = 2,\ \hat{y} \approx 0.88.$$

We want to distribute this prediction score back to $[x_1,x_2]$.
The simplest LRP rule is the LRP-ε or LRP-0 rule:
For neuron jat layer lwith inputs i:

$$R_i = \sum_j \cdot \frac{x_i w_{ij}}{\sum_{i'} \cdot x_{i'} w_{i'j} + \epsilon} R_j$$

Rj= relevance of neuron j.
Numerator = contribution of input ito neuron j.
Denominator = total input to neuron j.
Ensures conservation.

Step A: From Output to Hidden

Start with relevance at output: $R^{(out)} = \hat{y} = 0.88$.
We split relevance between h_1 and h_2.
Since $\hat{y} = \sigma(z)$, one common way:
First unwrap the sigmoid by attributing relevance to the pre-activation score z= h_1+h_2= 2.
Then distribute R_z= 0.88 to h_1,h_2 proportionally to their activations:

$$R_{h_1} = \frac{h_1}{h_1 + h_2} R_z = \frac{1}{2} \cdot 0.88 = 0.44$$

$$R_{h_2} = \frac{h_2}{h_1 + h_2} R_z = 0.44$$

Step B: From Hidden to Inputs

Now distribute R_{h_1}, R_{h_2} to x_1,x_2.
For h_1= ReLU(x_1–x_2):
Contribution from x_1: 2×1= 2.
Contribution from x_2: 1×(-1)= -1.
Denominator = 2–1= 1.
So:

$$R_{x_1}^{(h_1)} = \frac{2}{1} \cdot 0.44 = 0.88$$

$$R_{x_2}^{(h_1)} = \frac{-1}{1} \cdot 0.44 = -0.44$$

For $h_2 = \text{ReLU}(-0.5x_1 + 2x_2)$:
Contribution from x_1: 2× -0.5= -1.
Contribution from x_2: 1×2= 2.
Denominator = -1+2= 1.
So:

$$R_{x_1}^{(h_2)} = \frac{-1}{1} \cdot 0.44 = -0.44$$

$$R_{x_2}^{(h_2)} = \frac{2}{1} \cdot 0.44 = 0.88$$

Now sum over all paths:

$$R_{x_1} = 0.88 - 0.44 = 0.44$$

$$R_{x_2} = -0.44 + 0.88 = 0.44$$

Total relevance at inputs: 0.44+0.44= 0.88.
This equals the output score.

Key Insights:

Layer-wise Relevance Propagation (LRP) works by redistributing the actual output of a neural network backward through the layers, rather than relying on gradients. It assigns “credit” to each neuron layer by layer, proportionally to their contribution to the final output. Unlike methods such as Integrated Gradients or basic saliency maps, LRP can explicitly account for negative contributions depending on the rule used. Its conservation principle ensures that the total relevance is preserved as it flows backward, which provides a clear, interpretable decomposition of the model’s prediction.

4.2 Interpreting via Representation Analysis

While attribution methods tell us *where*, representation analysis methods aim to tell us *what* the model has learned—what concepts, patterns, and features populate its internal layers.

A) Attention Mechanisms

Originally designed to improve model performance on tasks like machine translation, attention mechanisms are inherently interpretable (Vaswani et al., 2017). They allow the model to dynamically "focus" on different parts of the input sequence when producing an output. By visualizing the attention weights, we can see which input tokens (e.g., words in a sentence) the model considered most important at each step. This provides a direct, human-readable rationale for the model's sequential decision-making process.

Given an input sequence $x= [x_1,x_2,\ldots,x_n]$, when predicting an output (say, a translated word), the model computes attention weights over the inputs:

$$\alpha_i = \frac{\exp(e_i)}{\sum_j \cdot \exp(e_j)}$$

where e_i= compatibility score between the current decoding state and input token i.

Then the context vector is:

$$c = \sum_i \cdot \alpha_i h_i$$

hi= hidden representation of token i.

α_i= attention weight (importance).

Sample Execution:

Imagine we're translating from French → English:

Input: ["le", "chien", "court"]

Target translation: "the dog runs"

Suppose at the moment of predicting "dog", the model computes:

Attention scores → Softmax → weights:

- "le": 0.1
- "chien": 0.8
- "court": 0.1

So the model's context vector cis mostly influenced by "chien".

Interpretation: when predicting "dog", the model looked at "chien".

Why Attention is Naturally Interpretable:

Attention is often considered naturally interpretable because the attention weights are normalized probabilities over input tokens, making them easy to visualize and understand. They indicate which parts of the input the model focuses on when producing each output. Unlike gradient-based methods, this information comes directly from the model's forward pass, so no post-hoc approximation or analysis is needed.

B) Feature Visualization

This technique answers the question: "What kind of input would maximally activate a specific neuron, channel, or even an entire layer?" By starting from random noise and performing gradient ascent to maximize the activation of a chosen unit, we can visualize the patterns that the model is "looking for." This can reveal everything from simple edges and textures in early layers to complex, object-like features in higher layers, providing a stunning window into the hierarchical feature detectors the network has built.

For a neuron $f(u)$ at some layer (say, neuron #5 in Conv2), we want an input image x^* that maximizes its activation.

Mathematically:

$$x^* = \arg\max_x f(x)$$

Since $f(x)$ is differentiable, we can use gradient ascent:

$$x \leftarrow x + \eta \frac{\partial f(x)}{\partial x}$$

Start with random noise.

Iteratively update the input in the direction that increases activation.

After many steps, the image reveals what the neuron "likes".

Sample Execution:

Let's imagine a super simple neuron:

$$f(x_1, x_2) = \text{ReLU}(2x_1 - x_2)$$

What input maximizes this neuron?

The gradient wrt x_1= 2, wrt x_2= -1 (when inside ReLU > 0).

So during gradient ascent:

x_1 keeps increasing.
x_2 keeps decreasing.

The neuron "likes" big positive x_1, small negative x_2.

If this were an image neuron, it would correspond to a "feature" like a bright pixel on the left and dark pixel on the right.

C) Concept Activation Vectors (TCAV)

TCAV takes a more human-centered approach to representation analysis. Instead of showing what the model could see, it tests for the presence of user-defined concepts. For example, one can define the concept of "striped" by providing a set of striped images. TCAV then learns a direction in the model's activation space corresponding to this concept. By measuring the sensitivity of a prediction (e.g., "zebra") to this direction, it can quantitatively answer: "How important was the concept 'striped' for the 'zebra' classification?" This allows for testing high-level, abstract human ideas against the model's internal representation (Kim et al., 2018).

Most interpretability techniques (saliency, Grad-CAM, feature visualization) tell us *where* the model looks or *what features* a neuron prefers.

But TCAV asks:

"How much does this specific human concept matter for the model's prediction?"

For example:

Does the model's "zebra" classification depend on the concept of stripes?

Does "doctor" prediction depend on the concept of gender (male vs female cues)?

The Concept Activation Vector (CAV) methodology provides a way to quantify how much a human-understandable concept influences a neural network's predictions. First, a set of images representing a concept—like 50 images of stripes—is collected along with a random counterexample set. A target internal layer of the neural network, such as a layer in Inception-v3, is chosen, and activations for both sets of images are extracted. A simple linear classifier is trained on these activations, producing a separating hyperplane whose normal vector defines the Concept Activation Vector (CAV). Sensitivity analysis is then performed for a target class, such as "zebra," by computing the directional derivative of the network's output in the CAV direction, $\nabla f(x) \cdot v\_concept$. This measures how much moving in the "striped" direction would increase or decrease the "zebra" score. By repeating this across many images of zebras and calculating the fraction where the sensitivity is positive, the method produces the TCAV score, representing the percentage of predictions for that class that are positively influenced by the concept.

4.3 Interpreting Large Language Models and Generative AI

The rapid rise of foundation models and large language models (LLMs) such as GPT-4, Llama 3, and Claude has fundamentally reshaped interpretability. Traditional methods like saliency maps are often insufficient for models with billions of parameters. As a result, new research directions focus on mechanistic interpretability, where researchers reverse-engineer model components to understand algorithmic circuits (e.g., induction heads, composition heads, and steering vectors inside transformer blocks).

Key modern techniques include:

a) **Sparse autoencoders** for decomposing activations into human-understandable features.
b) **Activation patching**, which identifies which components of the model are responsible for specific behaviors.
c) **Dataset attribution** methods that trace which training examples most influenced a specific output.
d) **Model editing methods** such as ROME and MEMIT, which reveal how factual knowledge is stored and can be safely modified.

These tools help diagnose hallucinations, detect bias, analyze emergent reasoning, and ensure safer deployment of generative models. As AI ecosystems shift toward general-purpose models, interpretability becomes a central pillar of modern AI safety.

5 EXPLAINABLE AI ARCHITECTURES AND HYBRID METHODS: PROTOTYPE-BASED NETWORKS, NEURO-SYMBOLIC MODELS, CAPSULE NETWORKS, CAUSAL INFERENCE APPROACHES, AND GLASS-BOX DEEP LEARNING ARCHITECTURES

While post-hoc interpretation methods are applied *after* a model makes a prediction, a more foundational approach to transparency is to design models that are inherently explainable by their very architecture. This shifts the paradigm from "explaining the black box" to "building the glass box." These architectures often integrate mechanistic structures, symbolic reasoning, or causal principles directly into the learning process, resulting in models whose decision-making logic is more accessible, trustworthy, and aligned with human reasoning.

This section explores key architectural innovations and hybrid paradigms that aim to make explainability a first-class citizen in AI system design.

5.1 Prototype-Based Networks: Learning by Comparison

Prototype-based networks, such as Prototypical Part Networks (ProtoPNet), introduce a fundamentally different reasoning process into deep learning (Carmichael et al., 2023; De Santi et al., 2024; Singh, 2023; Ukai et al., 2023). Instead of a final, opaque fully connected layer making a classification, these models learn to compare parts of a new input to "prototypical parts" it has seen during training.

1. **Mechanism:** A ProtoPNet achieves interpretability through two main components. First, the prototype layer stores a set of latent prototypes i.e., vector representations of distinctive parts of the training data, such as a specific bird wing pattern or a type of car headlight. Second, the reasoning process works by comparing parts of a new image to these learned prototypes and computing similarity scores. The final classification is determined by a weighted combination of these scores, making it clear which prototypes contributed to the decision.
2. **Explainability Value:** The explanation is naturally generated: "This is a 'German Shepherd' because certain parts of the input image closely match these prototypical German Shepherd features (e.g., a pointed ear prototype, a fur texture prototype)." The model can visually show *which* part of the input activated *which* prototype, providing a "this looks like that" justification that is highly intuitive.

Figure 1. Overview of ProtoPNet

Sample Execution:
We'll use a simple 2D shape dataset with just two classes:
Class A: Circles
Class B: Triangles
Dataset (tiny)

- Training images:
    - o 10 black-and-white circles
    - o 10 black-and-white triangles

- Each image: 28×28 pixels

ProtoPNet Architecture (Simplified)

ProtoPNet is a prototype-based network that combines a CNN backbone with a prototype layer for interpretable classification. The backbone CNN extracts latent features from the input, producing a feature map (e.g., 8×8×16). The prototype layer stores a small set of learned prototypes, such as circle edges, filled circular interiors, triangle corners, or triangle edges. During training, the network learns which latent features make good prototypes and forces each prototype to align with an actual training patch—for example, one prototype might capture the arc of a circle while another captures a triangle corner. During inference, a new input image is processed through the backbone, and each prototype is compared with patches of the latent features. A test circle image, for instance, would match strongly with the circle-related prototypes and weakly with triangle prototypes. The similarity scores are then aggregated in the classification layer, leading the network to correctly predict "Circle." This design makes the model inherently interpretable, as each decision can be traced back to specific, human-understandable prototype matches.

ProtoPNet's decision is interpretable: "This looks like a Circle because part of the input (edge region) is similar to Prototype 1 (circle edge from training), and another part matches Prototype 2 (circle interior). It does not look like triangle prototypes." The model can visually show heatmaps of where the input matched each prototype.

5.2 Neuro-Symbolic Models: Integrating Logic and Learning

Neuro-symbolic AI seeks to combine the robust pattern recognition of neural networks (the "neuro" component) with the explicit, logical reasoning of symbolic AI (the "symbolic" component) (Nawaz et al., 2025; Susskind et al., 2021; Yan et al., 2022).

- **Mechanism:** These models use neural networks to perceive the world—for instance, extracting objects and their relationships from an image. The outputs of these networks are then mapped to a symbolic representation (e.g., logical facts like OnTopOf(box, table)). A symbolic reasoner (e.g., a knowledge base or logic engine) then applies rules to derive a conclusion.
- **Explainability Value:** The explanation takes the form of a logical deduction trace. The model can provide a step-by-step rationale: "I classified this as a 'dining scene' because I detected a plate, fork, and wine glass (neural perception), and my knowledge base states that Plate ∧ Fork ∧ WineGlass

→ DiningScene (symbolic reasoning)." This offers a transparent, auditable chain of logic that is absent in purely sub-symbolic neural networks.

Figure 2. Overview of Neuro Symbolic AI

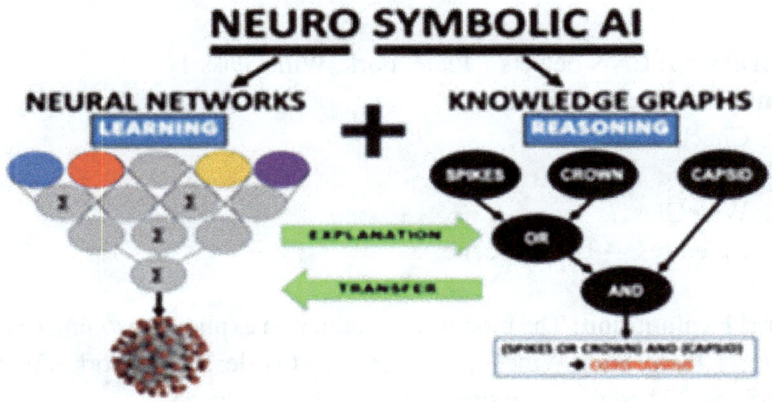

Sample Execution: Dining Scene Detection
Dataset

- Images containing simple objects (icons, synthetic data, or even MNIST-like sketches):
  - o Plates
  - o Forks
  - o Wine glasses
  - o Random background items (chair, book, etc.)

Model Architecture
Two parts:

(a) Neural Perception

A small CNN detects objects in the image.
Output: set of symbolic facts (like object labels).
Example: { Plate, Fork, WineGlass }

(b) Symbolic Reasoner

Rules stored in a knowledge base:

Plate ∧ Fork ∧ WineGlass → DiningScene
Book ∧ DeskLamp → StudyScene
Sofa ∧ TV → LivingRoomScene

Inference Example
Input image: a dinner table with plate, fork, and wine glass.

- **Neural step:** CNN detects { Plate, Fork, WineGlass }.
- **Symbolic step:** Apply rules:
  - o Check: Plate?
  - o Fork?
  - o WineGlass?
  - o Rule fires → DiningScene.

Natural Explanation: The model can produce an explicit reasoning trace: "Detected objects: Plate, Fork, WineGlass. According to rule: Plate ∧ Fork ∧ WineGlass → DiningScene. Therefore, classified scene as DiningScene."

Key Difference vs. ProtoPNet

ProtoPNet explanation: "This *looks like* that" (visual similarity).

Neuro-Symbolic explanation: "This *implies* that" (logical deduction).

5.3 Capsule Networks: Encoding Hierarchical Poses

Capsule Networks (CapsNets) were proposed to address a key limitation of standard Convolutional Neural Networks (CNNs): their inability to encode spatial hierarchies and relationships between features robustly (Haq et al., 2023; Patrick et al., 2019).

- **Mechanism:** Where CNNs output scalar activations, CapsNets output "capsules"—vectors whose length represents the probability of an entity's presence and whose orientation represents its instantiation parameters (e.g., pose, scale, rotation). Higher-level capsules agree to activate through a dynamic routing mechanism, which prioritizes consensus between lower-level features (e.g., a nose, mouth, eyes) and a higher-level concept (e.g., a face).
- **Explainability Value:** By explicitly representing part-whole relationships, CapsNets are more robust to viewpoint changes and can, in principle, explain their reasoning in terms of the presence and pose of object parts. If a prediction changes, one can trace which parts were misaligned or absent. This makes their internal representation more equivariant and their failures more diagnosable.

Figure 3. Overview of Capsule Networks

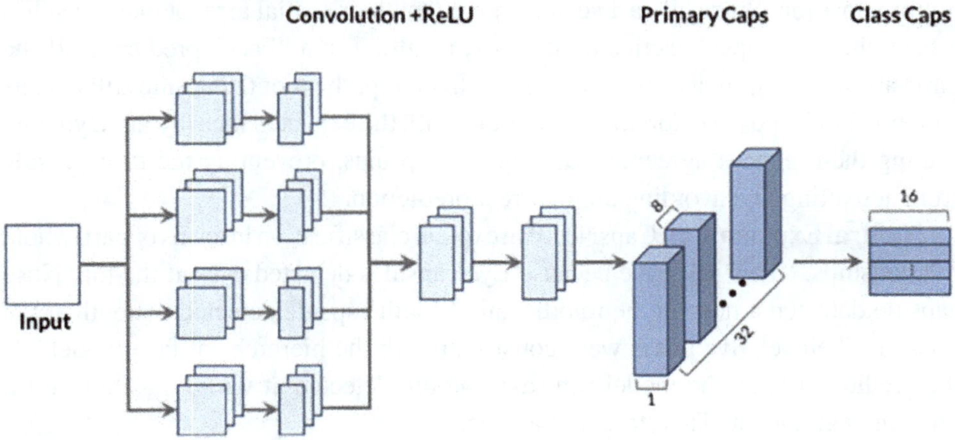

Sample Execution:

Dataset

- Very simple images with just a few shapes:
  - o **Eyes** = small circles
  - o **Nose** = triangle
  - o **Mouth** = half-circle
- A "Face" is defined as these parts in the right spatial arrangement.

Standard CNN Limitation

A CNN might learn to detect these parts individually (two circles, one triangle, one curve). But if you shuffle the parts (e.g., put the mouth above the eyes), CNN may still think "yes, that's a face," because it only cares about part presence, not arrangement.

Capsule Network Architecture (simplified)

- **Primary Capsules:** Encode low-level parts (e.g., eye capsule, nose capsule, mouth capsule). Each capsule outputs a vector: Length = probability part exists and Orientation = pose (location, rotation, scale).
- **Higher-Level Capsule:** A Face capsule receives votes from the part capsules. Uses dynamic routing to check if parts agree on forming a face.

Inference Example

In a CapsNet inference example, when given a properly aligned cartoon face, the eye capsules activate with vectors representing their top-left and top-right positions, the nose capsule encodes the center position, and the mouth capsule encodes the bottom position. Since all part vectors agree that their spatial arrangement matches a face, the face capsule activates strongly, resulting in a "Face" prediction. If the parts are shuffled, such as placing the mouth on top, the mouth capsule still detects a mouth, but its pose vector no longer aligns with the expected face layout. Dynamic routing then reduces agreement among the capsules, preventing the face capsule from activating and avoiding an incorrect prediction.

Natural Explanation: CapsNets can explain classification in terms of part-whole relationships: "This is a Face because Eye capsules detected eyes at the top, Nose capsule detected a nose in the middle, and Mouth capsule detected a mouth at the bottom. Their relative poses were consistent with the hierarchical face model." If the prediction fails, the model can say: "Mouth detected at wrong position (top), breaking agreement. Therefore, not a Face."

Key Takeaway: Convolutional Neural Networks (CNNs) typically recognize objects by detecting parts like eyes, nose, and mouth, concluding "this is a face" whenever those features appear. Capsule Networks (CapsNets), in contrast, not only detect these parts but also consider their spatial arrangement, asking "are the eyes, nose, and mouth positioned correctly?" Only if the arrangement makes sense does the model classify it as a face. This hierarchical, pose-aware reasoning gives CapsNets greater interpretability and robustness compared to standard CNNs.

5.4 Causal Inference Approaches: Moving Beyond Correlation

Perhaps the most significant leap towards robust and trustworthy AI is the integration of causal reasoning. Most deep learning models are masters of finding correlations, but causality is necessary for understanding interventions ("What happens *if I do X*?") and counterfactuals ("What would have happened *if I had not done Y*?").

- **Mechanism:** Causal models incorporate a representation of the data-generating process, often as a Structural Causal Model (SCM) or a causal graph. Techniques like double machine learning or causal forests are then used to estimate causal effects from observational data, controlling for confounders (Chen et al., 2023; Cinquini et al., 2024; Wu et al., 2024).
- **Explainability Value:** The explanation provided by a causal model is fundamentally different and more powerful. Instead of "Features A and B were important," a causal model can state: "Variable X has a direct causal effect on outcome Y, with an estimated magnitude of Z, even when controlling for confounders W." This allows for explanations that are stable across environments and support responsible decision-making in high-stakes fields like medicine and economics.

Figure 4. Causal Graphs

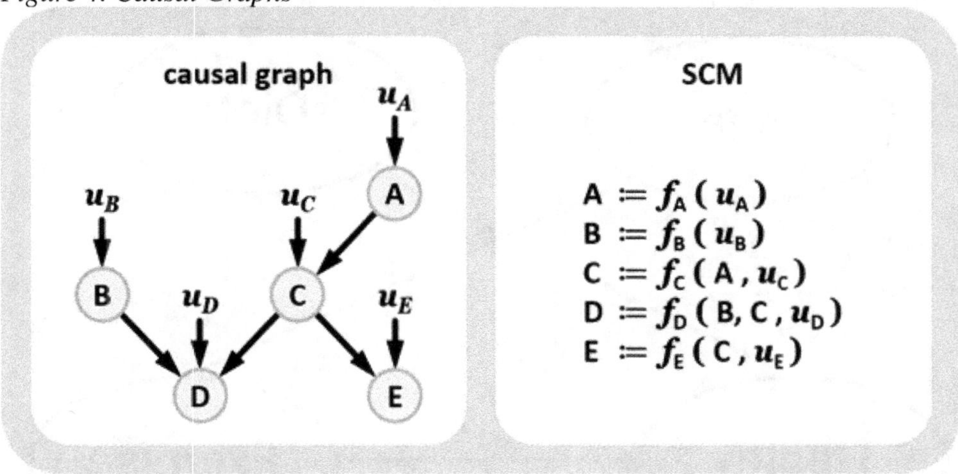

Sample Execution:

Studying Effect of Exercise on Health

We want to know: "*Does daily exercise causally improve health score (Y)?*"

But there are confounders like diet quality and age, which affect both exercise habits and health.

Correlation Trap (What deep learning would do)

A standard ML model might say: People who exercise more also have higher health scores. Therefore: *Exercise causes health.*

But this could just be correlation — maybe people who exercise also eat healthier, and diet is the real cause.

We represent the data-generating process as a causal graph:

Figure 5. Causal Graph for Studying Effect of Exercise on Health

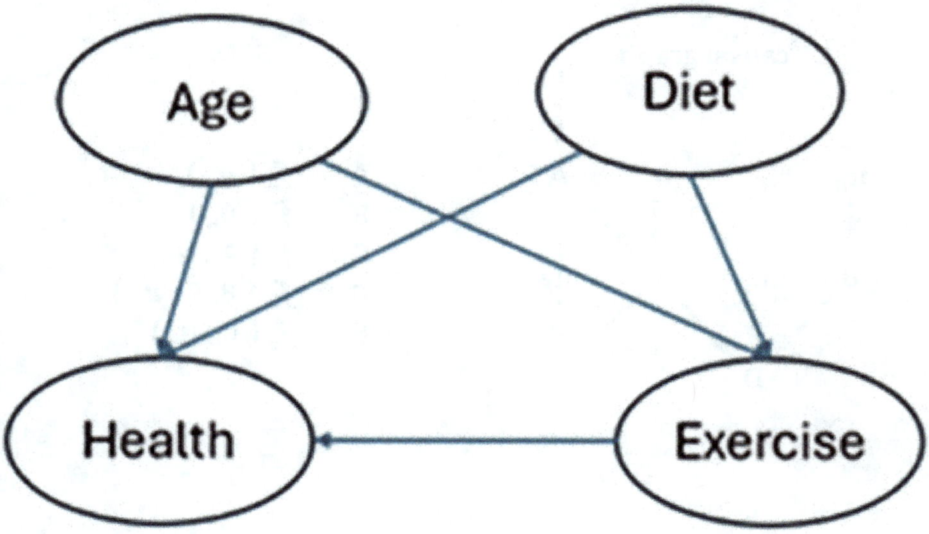

Age influences both exercise and health. Diet influences both exercise and health. Exercise directly influences health.

Estimating Causal Effect

Causal effects can be estimated using methods that account for confounding and isolate the impact of a specific treatment. Techniques include backdoor adjustment, which controls for confounders like age and diet; Double Machine Learning (DML), which models both the outcome and the treatment and then residualizes to estimate effects; and Causal Forests, which capture heterogeneous treatment effects across individuals. Using DML in this scenario, we might estimate that each hour of daily exercise causally improves health by +5 points, after properly adjusting for age and diet.

Inference Example

In this causal inference example, two patients are compared: Patient A, who exercises an hour a day, and Patient B, who does not, while both have the same age and diet. The causal model predicts that Patient A's health score is 80 and Patient B's is 75, indicating that exercising contributes a causal effect of +5 on health. This illustrates how causal AI isolates the effect of a single intervention, independent of other factors.

Key Takeaway: The key distinction is that correlation-based AI identifies associations—like noticing that exercise is linked to better health, which might actually reflect confounding factors such as diet—whereas causal AI estimates the direct effect of an action, such as exercise improving health by five points regardless of other variables. This causal framework enables counterfactual reasoning: we can predict what would happen if a patient started or stopped exercising, allowing the AI to answer "what-if" questions with actionable, individualized insights.

6. SUMMARY, CONCLUSION, AND NEXT STEPS

This chapter has journeyed through the intricate landscape of interpretability in AI, arguing that it is a fundamental and non-negotiable pillar of responsible AI development. We began by establishing a crucial distinction: while *explainability* often involves creating post-hoc, approximate rationales for a model's behavior, *interpretability* seeks to understand the intrinsic properties, mechanisms, and representations of the model itself. This deeper understanding is not merely an academic exercise; it is a prerequisite for trust, safety, and accountability in real-world systems.

Interpretability stands at the core of AI safety because it enables error detection, bias mitigation, and robust auditing across the system lifecycle. It empowers practitioners, regulators, and decision-makers to understand model behavior, verify compliance with policy constraints, and diagnose failures before they cause harm. In safety-critical systems, interpretability functions as a safeguard that transforms opaque models into accountable and trustworthy components of larger socio-technical environments.

Our exploration covered the technical arsenal available to practitioners. We detailed post-hoc interpretation methods like saliency maps, Grad-CAM, and Integrated Gradients, which act as diagnostic tools to reverse-engineer the reasoning behind specific predictions. We then examined a new generation of inherently interpretable architectures, such as prototype-based networks and neuro-symbolic models, which build explainability directly into their fabric. Finally, we placed these technical capabilities within the critical context of regulation and governance, demonstrating how interpretability is the enabling technology for compliance, auditing, and ethical deployment in high-stakes domains like healthcare and finance.

The overarching conclusion is that the field is maturing from a reactive pursuit—trying to explain black boxes after the fact—to a proactive one, designing transparent and well-understood systems from the outset. The future of AI lies not in creating ever-larger inscrutable models, but in advancing a holistic discipline where performance, robustness, and interpretability are co-equal design goals.

Future Research Directions and Open Challenges

Despite significant progress, the field of interpretability is dynamic and faces several profound challenges that chart the course for future research.

1. **The Faithfulness vs. Understandability Trade-off:** A central tension persists. The most *faithful* explanations, which accurately represent the model's true computational process, can be highly complex and difficult for humans to understand (e.g., precise neuron-by-neuron analyses). Conversely, the most *understandable* explanations for humans (e.g., "the model saw a ear shape") may be simplified, post-hoc approximations that lose fidelity. Future work must strive to bridge this gap, developing new methods that are both perfectly faithful and intuitively understandable.
2. **Scalability to Foundation and Large Language Models (LLMs):** Current interpretability methods, designed for vision models or smaller networks, struggle to scale to the massive parameter spaces and complex behaviors of foundation models and LLMs. How can we meaningfully interpret a model with hundreds of billions of parameters? Research into scalable techniques, such as sparse autoencoders for decomposing activations and efficient methods for tracing the influence of training data, is a critical frontier.
3. **Quantitative Evaluation and Benchmarking**: There is still no universally accepted suite of metrics to answer the question, "Is this a good explanation?" While qualitative assessment by humans is essential, the field needs robust, quantitative benchmarks to compare different interpretability methods objectively. This requires standardized datasets with ground-truth explanations and well-defined metrics for faithfulness, stability, and robustness.
4. **Causal Interpretability**: Most current methods are correlational—they highlight what features were associated with a prediction. The next leap will be towards causal interpretability, which seeks to uncover the true cause-effect relationships within the model and between the model and the world. This would allow us to answer counterfactual questions like, "Would the model have made the same decision if this specific feature were absent?"
5. **Human-Centered and Interactive Interpretability**: Interpretability is not a one-way street. Future systems will need to be interactive, allowing users to ask follow-up questions, probe hypothetical scenarios, and receive explanations tailored to their specific background and task. This moves us from static

explanation-generating systems to dynamic AI partners that can engage in a dialogue about their reasoning.

6. **Standardization and Regulation-Driven Development**: As regulations like the EU AI Act come into force, the demand for certified, auditable interpretability will grow. This will drive research into standardized interpretability protocols, formal verification of model behavior, and the development of "interpretability APIs" that can reliably generate explanations meeting specific legal or ethical standards.

In conclusion, interpretability is the key that unlocks the vast potential of AI while mitigating its risks. The path forward requires a collaborative effort among computer scientists, social scientists, ethicists, and regulators. By continuing to advance both the science and the practice of interpretability, we can ensure that the AI systems of the future are not only powerful but also transparent, trustworthy, and aligned with human values. The journey from black box to glass box is one of the most important and exciting endeavors in modern AI.

REFERENCES

Biehler, M., Guermazi, M., & Starck, C. (2022). Using Knowledge Distillation to improve interpretable models in a retail banking context. *arXiv (Cornell University)*. 2209.15496

Binder, A., Montavon, G., Bach, S., Müller, K., & Samek, W. (2016). Layer-wise Relevance Propagation for Neural Networks with Local Renormalization Layers. *arXiv (Cornell University)*. 1604.00825

Breiman, L. (2001). Statistical Modeling: The Two Cultures (with comments and a rejoinder by the author). *Statistical Science*, *16*(3). Advance online publication. DOI: 10.1214/ss/1009213726

Carmichael, Z., Lohit, S., Cherian, A., Jones, M., & Scheirer, W. (2023). Pixel-Grounded prototypical part networks. *arXiv (Cornell University)*. 2309.14531

Chen, X., Sun, R., Saluz, U., Schiavon, S., & Geyer, P. (2023). Using causal inference to avoid fallouts in data-driven parametric analysis: A case study in the architecture, engineering, and construction industry. *Developments in the Built Environment*, *17*, 100296. DOI: 10.1016/j.dibe.2023.100296

Chmiel, W., Kwiecień, J., & Motyka, K. (2023). Saliency Map and Deep Learning in Binary Classification of Brain Tumours. *Sensors (Basel)*, *23*(9), 4543. DOI: 10.3390/s23094543

Chung, M. K. (2020). Introduction to logistic regression. *arXiv (Cornell University)*. 2008.13567

Cinquini, M., Beretta, I., Ruggieri, S., & Valera, I. (2024). A Practical Approach to Causal Inference over Time. *arXiv (Cornell University)*. 2410.10502

De Santi, L. A., Piparo, F. I., Bargagna, F., Santarelli, M. F., Celi, S., & Positano, V. (2024). Part-Prototype Models in Medical Imaging: Applications and Current Challenges. *BioMedInformatics*, *4*(4), 2149–2172. DOI: 10.3390/biomedinformatics4040115

Doshi-Velez, F., & Kim, B. (2017). Towards a rigorous science of interpretable machine learning. *arXiv (Cornell University)*. 1702.08608

Ewald, F. K., Bothmann, L., Wright, M. N., Bischl, B., Casalicchio, G., & König, G. (2024). A guide to feature importance methods for scientific inference. *arXiv (Cornell University)*. 2404.12862

Haq, M. U., Sethi, M. A. J., & Rehman, A. U. (2023). Capsule Network with Its Limitation, Modification, and Applications—A Survey. *Machine Learning and Knowledge Extraction, 5*(3), 891–921. DOI: 10.3390/make5030047

Hassija, V., Chamola, V., & Mahapatra, A. (2024). Interpreting Black-Box Models: A Review on Explainable Artificial Intelligence. *Cognitive Computation, 16*, 45–74. DOI: 10.1007/s12559-023-10179-8

Hinton, G. E., Vinyals, O., & Dean, J. (2015). Distilling the knowledge in a neural network. *arXiv (Cornell University)*. 1503.02531

Kim, B., Wattenberg, M., Gilmer, J., Cai, C., Wexler, J., Viegas, F. & sayres, R. (2018). Interpretability Beyond Feature Attribution: Quantitative Testing with Concept Activation Vectors (TCAV). Proceedings of the 35th International Conference on Machine Learning, in Proceedings of Machine Learning Research 80:2668-2677 Available from https://proceedings.mlr.press/v80/kim18d.html

Kuchibhotla, A. K., Brown, L. D., Buja, A., & Cai, J. (2019). All of linear regression. *arXiv (Cornell University)*. 1910.06386

Lipton, Z. C. (2016). The mythos of model interpretability. *arXiv (Cornell University)*. 1606.03490

Lou, Y., Caruana, R., & Gehrke, J. (2012). Intelligible models for classification and regression. *Proceedings of the 18th ACM SIGKDD International Conference on Knowledge Discovery and Data Mining*, 150–158.

Margot, V., & Luta, G. (2021). A New Method to Compare the Interpretability of Rule-Based Algorithms. *AI, 2*(4), 621–635. DOI: 10.3390/ai2040037

Moraliyage, H., Kulawardana, G., De Silva, D., Issadeen, Z., Manic, M., & Katsura, S. (2025). Explainable Artificial Intelligence with Integrated Gradients for the Detection of Adversarial Attacks on Text Classifiers. *Applied System Innovation, 8*(1), 17. DOI: 10.3390/asi8010017

Nawaz, U., Anees-Ur-Rahaman, M., & Saeed, Z. (2025). A review of Neuro-Symbolic AI integrating reasoning and learning for advanced cognitive systems. *Intelligent Systems with Applications, 200541*. Advance online publication. DOI: 10.1016/j.iswa.2025.200541

Nori, H., Caruana, R., Bu, Z., Shen, J. H., & Kulkarni, J. (2021). Accuracy, interpretability, and differential privacy via explainable boosting. *arXiv (Cornell University)*. 2106.09680

Patrick, M. K., Adekoya, A. F., Mighty, A. A., & Edward, B. Y. (2019). Capsule Networks – A survey. *Journal of King Saud University. Computer and Information Sciences*, *34*(1), 1295–1310. DOI: 10.1016/j.jksuci.2019.09.014

Plumb, G., Al-Shedivat, M., Cabrera, A. A., Perer, A., Xing, E., & Talwalkar, A. (2019). Regularizing black-box models for improved interpretability. *arXiv (Cornell University)*. 1902.06787

Quinlan, J. R. (1986). Induction of decision trees. *Machine Learning*, *1*(1), 81–106. DOI: 10.1007/bf00116251

Rudin, C. (2018). Stop explaining black box machine learning models for high stakes decisions and use interpretable models instead. *arXiv (Cornell University)*. 1811.10154

Rudin, C. (2019). Stop explaining black box machine learning models for high stakes decisions and use interpretable models instead. *Nature Machine Intelligence*, *1*, 206–215. DOI: 10.1038/s42256-019-0048-x

Rudin, C., Chen, C., Chen, Z., Huang, H., Semenova, L., & Zhong, C. (2022). Interpretable machine learning: Fundamental principles and 10 grand challenges. *Statistics Surveys, 16*. DOI: 10.1214/21-ss133

Saarela, M., & Jauhiainen, S. (2021). Comparison of feature importance measures as explanations for classification models. *SN Applied Sciences*, *3*, 272. DOI: 10.1007/s42452-021-04148-9

Selvaraju, R. R., Cogswell, M., Das, A., Vedantam, R., Parikh, D., & Batra, D. (2017). Grad-CAM: Visual Explanations from Deep Networks via Gradient-Based Localization. *2017 IEEE International Conference on Computer Vision (ICCV)*, 618-626. DOI: 10.1109/ICCV.2017.74

Sigut, J., Fumero, F., Estévez, J., Alayón, S., & Díaz-Alemán, T. (2024). In-Depth Evaluation of Saliency Maps for Interpreting Convolutional Neural Network Decisions in the Diagnosis of Glaucoma Based on Fundus Imaging. *Sensors (Basel)*, *24*(1), 239. DOI: 10.3390/s24010239

Simonyan, K., Vedaldi, A., & Zisserman, A. (2013). Deep inside convolutional networks: visualising image classification models and saliency maps. *arXiv (Cornell University)*. 1312.6034

Singh, G. (2023). One and one make eleven: An interpretable neural network for image recognition. *Knowledge-Based Systems*, *279*, 110926. DOI: 10.1016/j.knosys.2023.110926

Susskind, Z., Arden, B., John, L. K., Stockton, P., & John, E. B. (2021). Neuro-Symbolic AI: An Emerging Class of AI Workloads and their Characterization. *arXiv (Cornell University)*. 2109.06133

Ukai, Y., Hirakawa, T., Yamashita, T., & Fujiyoshi, H. (2023). Toward prototypical part interpretable similarity learning with ProtoMetric. *IEEE Access : Practical Innovations, Open Solutions*, *11*, 62986–62997. DOI: 10.1109/access.2023.3287638

Vaswani, A., Shazeer, N., Parmar, N., Uszkoreit, J., Jones, L., Gomez, A. N., Kaiser, L., & Polosukhin, I. (2017). Attention is all you need. *arXiv (Cornell University)*. 1706.03762

Wang, Y., Zhang, T., Guo, X., & Shen, Z. (2024). Gradient based Feature Attribution in Explainable AI: A Technical Review. *arXiv (Cornell University)*. 2403.10415

Wu, X., Peng, S., & Li, J. (2024). Causal inference in the medical domain: A survey. *Applied Intelligence*, *54*, 4911–4934. DOI: 10.1007/s10489-024-05338-9

Yan, R., Ma, T., Fokoue, A., Chang, M., & Julius, A. (2022). Neuro-symbolic Models for Interpretable Time Series Classification using Temporal Logic Description. *arXiv (Cornell University)*. 2209.09114

Zhang, H., Torres, F., Sicre, R., Avrithis, Y., & Ayache, S. (2023). Opti-CAM: Optimizing saliency maps for interpretability. *arXiv (Cornell University)*. 2301.07002

Chapter 6 Safeguarding Data in Artificial Intelligence Systems: Privacy-Preserving Frameworks, Risks, and Future Directions (Privacy)

Nivetha Baskar
https://orcid.org/0000-0003-2091-7767
Kingston Engineering College, India

Vivek Menon U.
University of Modena and Reggio Emilia, Italy

Sridhar Venkatesan
Vellore Institute of Technology, India

ABSTRACT

Artificial Intelligence (AI) is becoming deeply integrated into everyday life, powering applications from healthcare diagnostics and financial decision-making and autonomous vehicles. While these advancements bring efficiency and innovation, which is central to building and maintaining public trust in AI. Unlike traditional data-driven systems that can operate with limited exposure, AI relies on vast and often sensitive datasets to achieve accuracy and reliability. This dependence on large-scale data introduces risks such as leakage, re-identification, and unauthorized access, which, if left unaddressed, could undermine both user confidence and regulatory compliance. Safeguarding privacy in AI adherence to ethical principles and legal

DOI: 10.4018/979-8-3373-6935-8.ch006

frameworks that ensure data is handled responsibly. This proposal explores the principles of privacy in AI, the risks of privacy-preserving technologies, the impact of global legal frameworks, and the challenge of balancing data utility with privacy protections, before outlining steps toward resilient, privacy-conscious AI systems.

1 INTRODUCTION

The foundation of privacy in AI lies in a set of guiding principles designed to minimize harm and promote transparency. Among these, data minimization ensures that systems collect only necessary to achieve their purpose, avoiding unnecessary accumulation of sensitive information that could later be misused. Consent plays a critical role by empowering individuals to make informed decisions about how their data will be used, ensuring that collection and processing occur under conditions of fairness and autonomy Chau et al. (2025). Purpose limitation adds another safeguard by restricting data use strictly to the objectives for which it was originally collected, thereby preventing secondary uses that may violate expectations or rights. Collectively, these principles form the ethical baseline for AI systems, embedding respect for individual privacy into the design and deployment of technology rather than treating it as an afterthought.

Even when these principles are followed, risks of data leakage and re-identification remain significant. Data leakage occurs when information escapes from secure environments, either through intentional breaches, insider threats, or inadvertent disclosure. For AI systems that handle highly sensitive information, such as medical records, financial histories, or biometric identifiers, even small leaks can have severe consequences. Re-identification presents an even more subtle risk. Though data can be anonymized before being used in AI models, advances in data analytics and cross-referencing techniques often allow adversaries to trace supposedly anonymous data back to individuals Demelius et al. (2025). For example, combining anonymized medical records with publicly available demographic data can make it possible to re-identify patients, exposing personal health details. This demonstrates the inherent tension between the promise of data-driven AI and the vulnerability of individuals whose information fuels its development. Addressing these risks requires both robust technical defenses and regulatory oversight.

Privacy-preserving machine learning has therefore emerged as a vital field, offering technical solutions to mitigate risks while still enabling valuable insights from data. Differential privacy is one such technique, designed to obscure the contribution of individual data points by injecting carefully calibrated noise into datasets or model outputs. This ensures that the inclusion or exclusion of any single individuals data has negligible impact on results, making it extremely difficult for adversaries to extract personal information. Federated learning offers another promising approach by enabling models to be trained directly on distributed devices without requiring centralized data collection. In this model, only the learning updates are shared with the central system, while raw data remains securely on users devices. This architecture significantly reduces exposure and enhances privacy. Homomorphic encryption extends these protections further by allowing computations to be performed on encrypted data, ensuring that even during processing, sensitive information remains hidden Feretzakis et al. (2024). These technologies represent critical building blocks for trustworthy AI, enabling organizations to leverage data while reducing privacy risks.

In parallel with technological innovations, legal frameworks provide essential safeguards to ensure responsible handling of personal data. The General Data Protection Regulation (GDPR) in the European Union sets a global benchmark by enforcing strict requirements for transparency, consent, data minimization, and the right to be forgotten. Similarly, the California Consumer Privacy Act (CCPA) grants individuals greater control over how their data is collected and shared, reflecting growing recognition of digital rights. The Health Insurance Portability and Accountability Act (HIPAA) in the United States introduces additional protections for medical data, emphasizing confidentiality in healthcare-related AI applications. These frameworks not only regulate organizational behavior but also signal the societal value placed on privacy as a human right. However, cross-border issues complicate compliance, as AI systems often rely on datasets aggregated across jurisdictions with differing privacy standards Jones et al. (2018). This creates challenges for global AI development and underscores the need for harmonization of international privacy regulations.

Balancing privacy with data utility presents one of the most difficult challenges in AI security. On the one hand, stringent privacy protections are essential to prevent misuse, re-identification, or discrimination; on the other hand, excessively restricting access to data may compromise model performance and hinder innovation Apicella et al. (2025). For example, in healthcare, overly aggressive anonymization of patient records might strip out details crucial for accurate diagnosis, reducing the effectiveness of AI systems designed to save lives. Achieving balance requires nuanced approaches that preserve the richness of data while protecting individual identities. Differential privacy allows for this balance by injecting statistical noise in ways that preserve overall trends while shielding individuals, while federated learning enables collaborative insights without centralizing sensitive information. Successful strategies will depend on carefully aligning privacy-preserving methods with the performance goals of specific AI applications, ensuring that privacy protections do not come at the expense of societal benefits.

The path forward requires integrating privacy as a fundamental design principle in AI development. Organizations must move beyond reactive compliance and adopt proactive strategies that embed privacy protections into every stage of the AI lifecycle, from data collection and preprocessing to model training, deployment, and monitoring. This involves building systems that respect user consent, investing in technologies such as differential privacy and federated learning, and ensuring alignment with global regulations Naresh and Thamarai (2023). Equally important is cultivating transparency through explainable AI, allowing stakeholders to understand how data is being used and what safeguards are in place. Collaboration across industries, governments, and academia is also critical to establish best practices, create cross-industry benchmarks, and harmonize privacy standards internationally.

1.1 Organization of the Chapter

This chapter presents a systematic discussion of privacy concerns in artificial intelligence systems. It begins by establishing privacy as a core ethical, legal, and societal requirement in AI development. Fundamental privacy principles, including data minimization, informed consent, and purpose limitation, are introduced. The chapter then analyzes key privacy threats such as data leakage and re-identification across the AI lifecycle. Distinct privacy risks associated with generative AI and large foundation models are examined. These include memorization of sensitive data, prompt-based data leakage, and unintended reproduction of training data. Subsequently, the chapter reviews major privacy-preserving machine learning techniques. Approaches such as differential privacy, federated learning, and homomorphic encryption are discussed. The role of legal and regulatory frameworks in governing AI privacy is outlined. Finally, the chapter emphasizes embedding Privacy by Design throughout the AI lifecycle to enable trustworthy AI.

2 PRIVACY PRINCIPLES IN AI

The basis of privacy in AI is built upon a framework of guiding principles that are developed with the objective of minimizing harm and boosting transparency. This framework comprises key guiding principles, including data minimization, informed consent, and purpose limitations. The underlying concepts related to these principles are elaborated upon in the discourse that follows.

2.1 Data Minimization

The underlying notion of the data minimization approach is that it gathers and retains only the data strictly essential to the stated objectives, thereby mitigating the risk of accumulating sensitive data that could be susceptible to misuse or breaches in the near future by Goldsteen et al. (2021). That is, the principle of data minimization points to the fundamental notion that the collection of personal data must be commensurate with necessity; specifically, data should be adequate, relevant, and confined to the extent necessary to fulfil the intended purpose by Staab et al. (2024).

Furthermore, it is crucial to embed the data minimization principle from the outset or the initial stages of AI system design. This proactive integration is essential for reinforcing the tenets of trust and accountability within the development framework. Although integrating data minimization with AI systems presents noteworthy advantages, it also poses some challenges. One of the crucial challenges is that the humongous volume and diversity of data needed for training AI models often conflict with the requirement to gather only strictly necessary data. Additionally, the black box nature of complex AI models, such as deep learning and large language models, makes it challenging to determine which data is truly essential. However, these challenges can be overcome through privacy-preserving approaches such as federated learning, differential privacy, and the use of synthetic data, which will be elaborated on in section 10. 4.

The work in Ganesh et al. (2025) formalizes the principle of data minimization from privacy law into a bilevel optimization framework for Machine Learning (ML), balancing utility and information reduction. This work also presents algorithms that selectively mask redundant features while preserving model accuracy. The empirical results across datasets exhibit considerable data reduction with minimal performance loss, but indicate that even the minimized datasets still risk privacy leakage. This highlights a misalignment between regulatory intent and actual privacy protection. Thus, this work provides a rigorous formulation and benchmark of data minimization in ML, offering insights for privacy-compliant model design. Then, the authors Bufi et al. (2025) analyzed the implications of the data minimization principle on the accuracy and fairness of recommender systems. Through empirical analysis, this work identified that minimizing data can increase fairness from the consumer's perspective but degrade the provider's fairness and accuracy. In addition, the authors concluded that, compared with traditional recommendation models, graph-based models achieve better data minimization. Furthermore, the importance of developing advanced data minimization strategies that balance privacy with fairness and accuracy while maintaining robustness under constrained data conditions is essential.

Later Park and A (2025) suggested a multi-layer encryption protocol, termed DtMin, combining attribute-based encryption with a hybrid, multi-layer encryption approach to operationalize data minimization in healthcare information sharing, was developed. The framework facilitates selective disclosure of medical information, contingent upon patient consent and the specificity of their requests, and is validated through established security models. This framework enhances operational efficiency, ensures regulatory compliance, and improves scalability, setting a foundation for secure medical data exchange in complex environments.

2.2 Consent

The crucial role of consent is that it enables individuals to make informed choices about the use of their data, ensuring that data collection and processing occur under conditions that prioritize fairness and individual autonomy. Thus, the principle of consent emphasizes the idea that individuals possess the right to autonomy and authority over their personal data Jones et al. (2018). Also, it is crucial to emphasize that the notion of informed consent is fundamentally grounded in the principle that individuals have independent, informed, and voluntary control over the collection, use, and interpretation of their personal data by AI systems Solaiman and I. Glenn Cohen (2024). Furthermore, there exist advanced consent models, such as layered consent frameworks and dynamic as well as continuous consent models, to name a few. A layered consent framework is characterized by a hierarchical organization of data, offering a succinct overview tailored for a general audience while granting experts access to in-depth technical or legal intricacies underlying the data Symons et al. (2022). Whereas in the dynamic and continuous consent model, rather than relying on a one-time agreement, users are periodically re-engaged, permitting consent to evolve alongside system updates or new data uses Lay et al. (2024).

In the rapidly evolving domain of healthcare and modern medicine, informed consent has emerged as a pivotal, ethical, and legal framework, particularly as AI becomes increasingly integrated into various practices. The work of Chau et al. (2025) analysed the constraints encountered by the present informed consent practices, such as the dearth in transparency, poor clinician training, and inadequate patient comprehension in AI-based healthcare diagnostics, and presented the need to redesign the framework of consent with the aid of simple as well as understandable language, visual tools, and continuous feedback mechanisms. Therefore, this work focuses on improving the patients trust and uphold ethical standards in the responsible implementation of AI technologies within the healthcare sector.

2.3 Purpose Limitation

The underlying principle of purpose limitation is that it provides an additional layer of data protection by ensuring that the personal data gathered is used exclusively for the objective for which it was initially collected. Fundamentally, it states that data acquired for a defined objective cannot be repurposed for other objectives without proper reassessment and often renewed consent or a new legal basis M and A. J (2021). Then, Rainer Mühlhoff and Ruschemeier (2024), the principle of purpose limitation is reconceptualized for the era of AI by transitioning the emphasis from data processing to the governance of trained models. It also highlights a regulatory gap present in the General Data Protection Regulation (GDPR) and the European Union's (EU) AI act, wherein the secondary use of anonymized models stays unregulated. This work also supports the establishment of "purpose limitation for models" to ensure that AI is used strictly for its declared purpose throughout the model's lifecycle. Thus, this approach seeks to address breaches of privacy, instances of discrimination, and the utilization of AI-generated outputs outside their intended applications. Eventually, it supports the establishment of systemic governance and accountability mechanisms designed to mitigate informational power imbalances in societies increasingly influenced by AI.

Faisal (2023) works systematically and studies the principle of purpose limitation within the framework of the EU's GDPR and explores its implications for managing personal data processing within the context of smart city initiatives. It also determines that compatibility assessment and purpose specification are fundamental mechanisms for ensuring the legal and proportional use of data. Moreover, through a detailed comparative case analysis, this work explains the necessity for both public and private sector stakeholders to harmonize the implementation of smart-city services with robust privacy protection measures. Therefore, this work contends that the principle of purpose limitation establishes a structured permission framework rather than enabling unrestricted data exploitation, thereby safeguarding individual rights.

In addition to these foundational guiding principles, the framework also includes other prominent tenets such as transparency, accountability, security, and fairness. Where transparency points to the notion that AI systems need to be understandable and open about the rationale for data collection and to delineate the intended use of such data. The flow chart in figure 1 illustrating the key privacy risks arising during data collection, processing, storage, and sharing within digital systems. Building on this, accountability necessitates that organizations involved in the development or deployment of AI systems bear the responsibility for safeguarding privacy. Thus, all these principles collectively establish an ethical framework for AI systems, prioritizing the unification of individual privacy considerations into the design and implementation of technology. Furthermore, these approaches ensure that privacy is not merely an afterthought but a fundamental element of the development process. Therefore, it can be concluded that the privacy principles in AI are guidelines that ensure AI systems operate ethically, transparently, and with consideration for personal data, shielding individuals from harm and fostering public trust in technology. Even with strict adherence to privacy principles in AI, the potential for data leakage and re-identification persists as a significant concern. The nuances of these risks, including their mechanisms and implications, are thoroughly discussed in the forthcoming section 10.3.

Figure 1. Overview of the privacy risk flow, showing how vulnerabilities emerge and propagate across different stages of the data lifecycle.

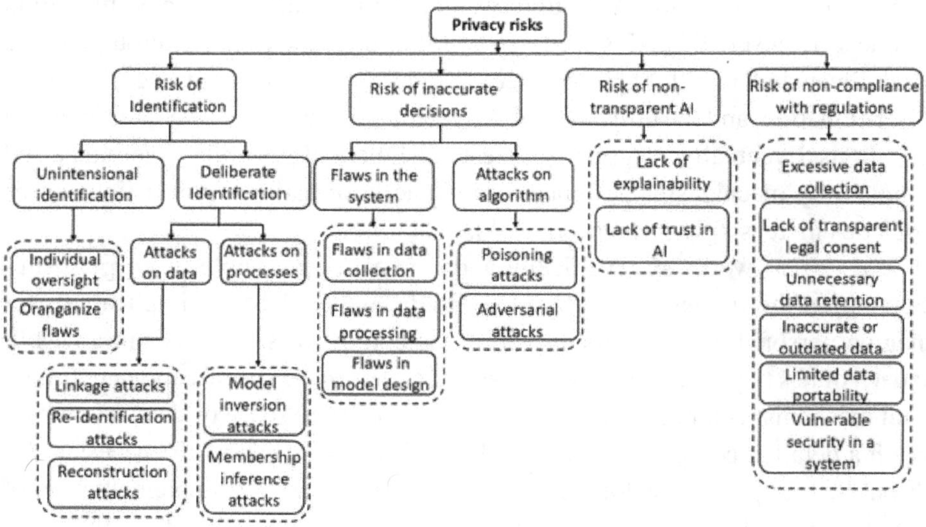

3 RISKS OF DATA LEAKAGE AND RE-IDENTIFICATION

In the current era of data-centric frameworks, notably those leveraging AI and extensive analytics, the threats associated with data leakage and re-identification are paramount. These threats pose a significant challenge to security, privacy, and adherence to regulations. Data leakage points to a situation in which the confidentiality of the data, considered a valuable asset to an organization, is breached or compromised by Domnik and Holland (2024). There exist numerous ways for the data leakage to occur, with primary factors including deliberate leakage of data by a malicious insider within the organization, leakage of data by an outside individual having gained temporary access to the resources of the affected organization, and inadvertent leakage by an authorized internal user or system administrator by M and M.J (2019). Furthermore, for AI systems that manage extremely sensitive data, like medical records, financial information, even minimal data leaks can lead to severe repercussions.

In ML, the issue of data leakage arises when the data that is not a part of the training dataset is utilized to build the model, and furthermore, this future data is not accessible to the model during the time of prediction, inadvertently affecting the training process Apicella et al. (2025). The underlying reasons for data leakage in ML stem from numerous factors, including unsuitable feature selection, flawed data preprocessing procedures, erroneous cross-validation strategies, external data contamination, and the incorporation of future data, among others. Consequently, in ML frameworks, the issue of data leakage can give rise to a range of adverse consequences, such as biased decision-making, deterioration of stakeholders' trust, inefficient use of resources, inflated performance metrics, and increased legal or regulatory exposure. Therefore, to overcome these adverse issues of data leakage in ML, the involved organizations need to engage in careful data handling and systematic evaluation.

The re-identification risk points to the potential for anonymized or de-identified data to be linked back to the specific individuals through correlation with auxiliary information or with external datasets Sondeck and Laurent (2025). Despite the removal of direct identifiers, residual attributes, patterns, or auxiliary datasets can enable third parties to reconstruct identities, thereby undermining the privacy protections originally intended. In essence, re-identification occurs when the identity of an individual or organization is inferred despite the removal of explicit identifiers. The risk of re-identification occurs either through direct or indirect mechanisms. In the direct approach, the anonymized datasets are mapped directly to the publicly available datasets, enabling straightforward linkage, whereas the indirect approach relies on statistical inference to derive associations based on distinct patterns or specific combinations of quasi-identifiers, allowing for identification without direct linkage.

The risk of re-identification poses a crucial challenge to the integrity of privacy-preserving data practices, as it exposes sensitive personal information that was presumed to be protected. The consequences arising from re-identification risk include privacy breaches, regulatory penalties, loss of trust, and significant damage to reputation. The strategies adopted to mitigate the re-identification risk include carrying out systematic risk evaluations, data minimization, implementing rigorous anonymization methodologies, ensuring precise categorization of sensitive data, and regularly revising the policies governing anonymization.

Compared to data leakage, re-identification presents an even more nuanced threat. Despite data anonymization prior to use in AI models, advancements in data analytics and cross-referencing techniques often enable adversaries to re-identify ostensibly anonymous datasets. For example, integrating anonymized medical records with publicly accessible demographic datasets poses a significant risk of patient re-identification, potentially exposing sensitive health information Ford et al. (2025). This scenario highlights the fundamental conflict between the potential benefits of data-driven AI technologies and the inherent vulnerabilities of individuals whose data underpins these advancements.

3.1 Privacy Risks in Generative AI and Large Foundation Models

The rapid adoption of generative AI and large foundation models has introduced a new class of privacy risks that extend beyond those associated with traditional machine learning systems. These models are typically trained on massive, heterogeneous datasets that may include sensitive, personal, or proprietary information, raising significant concerns regarding data protection and misuse. One prominent risk is memorization, where a model inadvertently retains and reproduces specific data points from its training corpus Liu et al. (2024). When training data contains personal or confidential information, such memorization can lead to direct privacy violations, especially when models output verbatim or near-verbatim content. This risk is amplified in large-scale models due to their capacity and extensive exposure to raw data.

Another critical issue is prompt-based data leakage. Carefully crafted prompts or adversarial queries can exploit a model's learned representations to extract sensitive information. Attackers may intentionally manipulate prompts to trigger the disclosure of private details, system instructions, or training data fragments, highlighting vulnerabilities in model alignment and access control mechanisms. Additionally, unintended reproduction of training data poses serious privacy and intellectual property concerns. Generative models may produce outputs that closely resemble copyrighted works, personal records, or proprietary datasets without explicit intent or authorization. Such outputs blur the line between generalization and replication, making it difficult to ensure compliance with privacy regulations and data usage agreements Feretzakis et al. (2024). These risks are central to modern AI privacy debates, particularly in high-stakes domains such as healthcare, finance, and governance. They challenge existing assumptions about anonymization, consent, and data minimization, as even de-identified data can be reconstructed or inferred through model outputs. Consequently, ensuring privacy in generative AI systems requires advanced safeguards, including privacy-preserving training techniques, rigorous evaluation for data leakage, and governance frameworks aligned with Privacy by Design principles.

On this basis, it signifies that the consequences of data leakage and re-identification extend far beyond isolated technical shortcomings; they fundamentally undermine individual privacy rights and diminish the foundational trust essential for the ethical operation of digital systems. Therefore, mitigating these risks needs a dual approach that combines strong technical safeguards alongside comprehensive regulatory frameworks to ensure data privacy and security. Building on this foundation, Section 10.4 that follows explains the various privacy-preserving ML techniques in detail.

4 PRIVACY-PRESERVING MACHINE LEARNING TECHNIQUES

The field of privacy-preserving ML approaches has become an important domain, capable of providing state-of-the-art methodologies to reduce risks due to privacy while still deriving insights that are meaningful from data. Differential privacy, federated learning, and homomorphic encryption are some of the privacy-preserving ML techniques that will be explored in depth.

4.1 Differential Privacy

The principle behind the approach of differential privacy is that it aims to protect or safeguard individual data points by carefully introducing calibrated noise into the datasets or model outputs Feretzakis et al. (2024). This technique confirms that the presence or absence of any particular individual's data does not significantly alter the overall outcomes. As a result, it becomes incredibly challenging for adversaries to derive personal information from the dataset. Also, this approach that is used for safeguarding data in ML models relies on the most common noise distributions, such as the Gaussian, Laplace, and exponential distributions. In addition to other well-known methods such as k-anonymity, t-closeness, and l-diversity, the prominent approach of differential privacy is also a prevalent method used in anonymization. The key advantages of differential privacy lie in its ability to provide quantifiable privacy guarantees while remaining resilient against both the specifics of the input and any supplementary data, including publicly accessible datasets or forthcoming information. Its composable nature, resilience to post-processing, and flexibility are other significant advantages. Here, the property of flexibility allows noise to be introduced at various stages of the data flow on the input data, the algorithm's output, or during the training phase. Furthermore, it has the capability to seamlessly unify with various other privacy-boosting technologies such as federated learning, secure multi-party computation (SMPC), and homomorphic encryption.

The Blanco-Justicia et al. (2022) works comprehensively analyzed the application of the differential privacy framework to safeguard privacy in ML contexts. Later Demelius et al. (2025), performed a comprehensive analysis of the current landscape of differentially private centralized deep learning, delving into its recent advancements, identifying key open challenges, and exploring prospective future directions in this evolving domain. Then, to overcome the privacy challenges in internet of things (IoT) - enabled critical infrastructure and to enhance its security, which existing privacy-preserving approaches fail to meet, was achieved by the method of differential privacy, and the M. A et al. (2021) work comprehensively analysed this aspect. Furthermore, this study delves into the deployment and operationalization of differential privacy across four key domains within IoT-enabled critical infrastructure. These domains include intelligent transportation systems, smart grid technologies Vivek and Poongundran Selvaprabhu (2022) Wen et al. (2022), industrial IoT applications, as well as healthcare and medical systems. Also, differential privacy has significant applications in various domains, particularly in cyber-physical systems and healthcare. In the healthcare sector, it is employed to generate synthetic patient data, ensuring that sensitive information remains protected from unauthorized access and disclosures.

4.2 Federated Learning

Federated learning facilitates the training of models directly on distributed devices, thereby eliminating the need for centralized data aggregation. Within this framework, only the updates associated with learning are communicated with the central server, while the raw data remains resident on the user devices. Thus, this decentralized approach significantly minimizes the risks associated with data exposure but also improves privacy and data sovereignty Goswami et al. (2025) Chen et al. (2024). Also, the privacy vulnerabilities linked to traditional ML frameworks, where data is collected in a centralized location, resulting in a single point that can fail and be susceptible to misuse or infringement, can be overcome by federated learning, which is characterized by its decentralized architecture. As a result, federated learning has surfaced as an innovative solution for privacy-preserving ML, enabling multiple clients to work together on model training while eliminating the need to share raw data. The two primary architectural methods linked to federated learning are centralized federated learning, which is the configuration most commonly used, and decentralized federated learning, which enhances the robustness; however, it introduces greater complexity to both communication and convergence. In the former approach, a centralized server manages the training process by disseminating the global model to participating clients and subsequently aggregating their local model updates to iteratively enhance overall performance.

In the latter, the central coordinator is eliminated, facilitating direct peer-to-peer communication and collaboration among clients for model training. Even though federated learning keeps data local, it remains vulnerable to privacy issues. Attackers can use information from data updates, known as gradients, to figure out sensitive details or determine whether someone's data was part of the training set. To reduce these risks, several privacy-protecting methods are added to federated learning systems. These include combining federated learning with techniques such as differential privacy, homomorphic encryption, and SMPC. Also, based on the distribution of data among the clients, federated learning is categorized into horizontal federated learning, vertical federated learning, and federated transfer learning.

The author Dembani et al. (2025) provides a detailed overview of the growing integration of federated learning within digital agriculture. This trend is driven by the rapid increase in data generated in the agriculture sector and the need to protect privacy during data analysis. Furthermore, the proposed federated learning approach enables multiple parties to collaborate on training models using sensitive agricultural data without sharing the actual data. This is crucial for modern agriculture because sharing data is key to improving crop yields, managing resources, and making sustainable choices. The survey also covers various applications of federated learning, including pest and disease detection, precision farming, resource management, and crop yield prediction, showing federated learning's role in supporting advanced data analysis while keeping data private among different users. Table 1 summarizes recent works on federated learning for privacy preservation across various emerging domains.

Table 1. Summary of works on federated learning for privacy preservation across various application domains

Author	Application Domain	Summary
Liu et al. (2025)	Healthcare	This work presents a novel framework for protecting data in federated learning, explicitly designed for psychological assessment scenarios characterized by high sensitivity and variability of data. While federated learning eliminates the need for data sharing, it is evident that model updates can still potentially disclose private information. Thus, to overcome this problem, an algorithm termed FL-PDP that combines personalized differential privacy with privacy-conscious aggregation methods that encompass both client and server phases has been presented in this work.
Shukla et al. (2025)	Healthcare	This work presents a hybrid approach that unifies federated learning with differential privacy, aiming to effectively optimize the trade-off between data privacy and the accuracy of models in breast cancer detection.
Yao et al. (2025)	Edge-based smart unmanned aerial vehicle	This work presents an enhanced privacy-preserving framework named FedShufde that combines federated learning with the shuffle model and differential privacy in IoT systems based on edge computing, using an unmanned aerial vehicle delivery system as a case study.
Tariq Alqubaysi et al. (2025)	Autonomous vehicle traffic management in intelligent transportation systems	The conventional traffic management systems disclose raw vehicular data, thereby introducing privacy threats and raising susceptibility to man-in-the-middle attacks. To overcome these challenges of conventional traffic management systems, this work presents a new system for managing traffic that uses federated learning to enhance service accessibility while ensuring data privacy for autonomous vehicles operating within intelligent transportation systems.
Ragab et al. (2025)	Smart city	This work presents a sophisticated artificial intelligence model integrated with a federated learning architecture, aiming to protect privacy while detecting cyber threats in smart city environments powered by internet of things.

4.3 Homomorphic Encryption

This approach permits computations to be carried out on data that is encrypted, thereby confirming that throughout the processing, the sensitive information remains hidden or protected Acar et al. (2018). More precisely, homomorphic encryption is a type of encryption that permits third parties to carry out some computations on encrypted data while guaranteeing that both the format of the encrypted information and the properties of the underlying functions remain intact. In this context, encryption refers to a fundamental approach developed for safeguarding the confidentiality of any sensitive data or information. Nevertheless, traditional encryption approaches do not directly permit working on encrypted data without decrypting it first, thereby compromising its privacy when utilizing third-party services. As these third-party service providers can store personally traceable information of users even after terminating their relationship with them, it is a crucial privacy concern for users. These issues of privacy concern associated with traditional encryption approaches can be overcome by the homomorphic encryption approach. Furthermore, key generation, encryption, decryption, and evaluation are the four essential operations involved in a homomorphic encryption scheme.

Homomorphic encryption is typically categorized into three main types: partially homomorphic, somewhat homomorphic, and fully homomorphic encryptions. The partially homomorphic encryption enables the execution of a single class of mathematical operations on the encrypted data, with no limit on the number of operations performed. Whereas, somewhat homomorphic encryption supports both addition and multiplication operations but restricts the total number of each operation that can be processed within a single encryption context. Finally, the fully homomorphic encryption allows for the execution of both addition and multiplication operations on encrypted data any number of times. Furthermore, the key benefits of homomorphic encryption include the ability to keep data encrypted throughout processing, which reduces the need for raw data sharing and facilitates secure collaboration for multi-party analyses by Shah et al. (2025). However, this technique is constrained by considerable computational overhead, a limited set of supported operations, and resource-intensive implementation requirements. Visualization of encrypted data processing under homomorphic encryption, highlighting the preservation of privacy during computation and the recovery of the final result via decryption are illustrated in figure 2.

The author Yang et al. (2023) presents a thorough review of cutting-edge homomorphic encryption methodologies, particularly within the biometric domain. It further explores the potential integration of homomorphic encryption with other state-of-the-art technologies in the realm of biometric systems. Additionally, this work addresses recent advancements in homomorphic encryption for biometrics and outlines current challenges and prospective research avenues in this domain. Later, in Lee et al. (2025), the authors performed an in-depth study of homomorphic encryption for safeguarding sensitive healthcare data. This study highlights the adaptability of homomorphic encryption across numerous medical applications, including the protection of electronic health records, secure handling of medical images, maintaining data confidentiality in clinical trials, and so on. Overall, this work reinforces the critical role of homomorphic encryption in ensuring the long-term security and resilience of healthcare infrastructures. In addition to these privacy-preserving ML approaches, there exist other privacy-preserving approaches, such as SMPC. The SMPC approach, which is widely employed in the financial industry, allows collaborative function evaluation by multiple parties while protecting the confidentiality of each party's input data Singh et al. (2025). Hybrid approaches merging federated learning with improved privacy-preserving ML techniques, mentioned above, are capable of transforming sectors that handle sensitive information.

Thus, these approaches are potent enough to improve data security while allowing for collaborative models, which in turn mould trust and support informed decision-making in those environments that are data-centric. Furthermore, recent advancements in privacy-preserving technologies have introduced a wide variety of cutting-edge methods such as quantum cryptography, blockchain implementations, and techniques like anonymization, obfuscation, and pseudonymization. Moreover, the use of synthetic data and deep learning-based privacy-preserving approaches is gaining traction Prabowo et al. (2025).

Figure 2. Schematic representation of homomorphic encrypted data processing, highlighting the transition from plaintext to ciphertext and the final decryption of computed results.

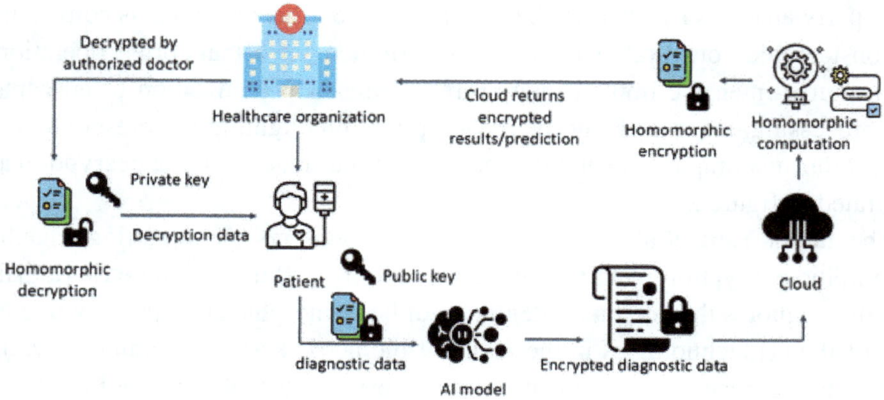

With the objective of safeguarding data privacy in the era of rapidly advancing technologies where the traditional encryption algorithms fail, arises the technology of quantum cryptography, which points to the numerous cybersecurity approaches adopted for encrypting and transmitting secure data that relies on the unique principle of quantum mechanics. Another key privacy-preserving approach that has gained importance is blockchain technology, which utilizes the mechanism of distributed ledgers for improving the privacy protection while upholding basic tenets of accountability and transparency Vinoth Kumar et al. (2024). Moreover, the approach of anonymization lowers the risks due to privacy by changing or removing those recognizable attributes from the dataset, thereby ensuring that the analytical utility is maintained. The technique of differential privacy mentioned above is an important anonymization method that safeguards the privacy of individuals while permitting advantageous assessment. Likewise, the technique of pseudonymization replaces those recognizable data with aliases or pseudonyms, thereby lowering re-identification risks while preserving the data's value for subsequent evaluation and processing. Also, to safeguard the privacy of users and to mitigate potential data misuse, the use of synthetic data, an alternative to real-time data in different sectors, plays a crucial role. The underlying notion of synthetic data involves generating artificial data through advanced generative models while maintaining the original dataset's statistical properties and underlying patterns as accurately as possible. Therefore, these privacy-preserving ML technologies constitute an important component for a trustworthy AI system. Their integration not only strengthens compliance with evolving regulatory frameworks but also fosters greater confidence among stakeholders, ensuring that advanced analytics and AI development proceed in a manner that is both ethically responsible and privacy-conscious. In parallel to these technological advancements, established legal and regulatory frameworks also play an important role in ensuring that the personal data is handled responsibly and further details on the various legal and regulatory frameworks are presented in section 10.5.

5. LEGAL AND REGULATORY FRAMEWORKS

Concurrent with technological advancements and in the current era of AI-powered frameworks that handle a huge amount of personal as well as sensitive data, the necessity of legal and regulatory frameworks is essential for establishing robust safeguards that govern the responsible management of this data. These legal and regulatory frameworks are categorized into three different levels: international, national, and local levels Lim and Oh (2025). At the international level, it consists of the GDPR, Convention 108, and the Universal Declaration of Human Rights (UDHR). Whereas at the national and local levels each countries have its own rules and regulatory frameworks, some of the most common ones are the CCPA, as well as the HIPAA associated with the United States. Similar to the United States, countries like China, Japan, South Korea, Canada, Singapore, Germany, and other developed as well as developing nations have their own legal and regulatory frameworks.

At the international level, the GDPR enforced by the European Union (EU) sets rules for safeguarding the personal data of EU citizens by putting strict restrictions on organizations that use this data. Furthermore, it establishes a global benchmark by imposing stringent mandates for transparency, consent, data minimization, and the right to be forgotten. Even though GDPR imposes strict rules for protecting personal data, it simultaneously presents compliance challenges for organizations owing to its inherent complexity Zaeem and Barber (2020). Another important international treaty established by the Council of Europe is the Convention 108. This treaty aims to safeguard individuals in the context of automatic personal data processing. It also establishes a comprehensive framework of guidelines and regulations aimed at securing the data, with the objective of standardizing data protection laws among member states. Then the UDHR, although not particularly addressing AI and privacy, incorporates those principles that are pertinent to the protection of data and individual privacy. Moreover, it underscores the rights associated with privacy and safeguards people from unjustified intrusions into their privacy, home, and family life.

At the national and local levels, while considering the case of the United States, there exist a number of legal and regulatory frameworks that affect AI and privacy, including the CCPA, HIPAA, and the Federal Trade Commission Act (FTC Act). The CCPA provides improved privacy and digital rights for those individuals residing in California by granting more significant authority regarding the gathering and dissemination of their personal data, signifying an increasing recognition of the importance of digital rights in today's data-centric landscape G. A., et al. (2025). Then, to increase the protection of medical data, the United States has introduced HIPAA, which contains critical regulations for the protection of medical data, thereby improving the requirements of confidentiality for AI applications present in the healthcare sector Schmidt Batista (2025). Also, the fraudulent and misleading practices related to data management are dealt with by the FTC Act. In addition to the GDPR, each of the member states in the EU has its own individual laws for safeguarding the data, and one such law was the Data Protection Act 2018 pertaining to the United Kingdom, which emphasizes the country's commitment to safeguarding personal information.

In Canada, the Personal Information Protection and Electronic Documents Act (PIPEDA) serves as the federal privacy legislative framework that regulates the handling of personal data by those organizations present in the private sector. Specifically, it sets rules that pertain to the collection, processing, and sharing of personal information. Similarly, the Personal Data Protection Act of Singapore and the Federal Data Protection Act (Bundesdatenschutzgesetz (BDSG)) of Germany are other regulatory frameworks that safeguard the data of users within their jurisdictions. Thus, all the above-mentioned frameworks not only govern organizational conduct but also reflect that society values privacy as a basic human right. In China, with the application of AI in the medical and healthcare fields, there is a growing concern about the security of the vast amount of data generated. Thus, to ensure the protection of data, the prevailing legal landscape in China has established a comprehensive framework consisting of ten principal laws, along with nine administrative regulations and five national standards He and Chen (2025), Menon U and Selvaprabhu (2024). These regulatory instruments collectively delineate the parameters for data protection within this sector. Out of these, the personal information protection law, along with the data security law, the civil code, and the network security law, collectively establish a coherent and comprehensive regulatory framework for the safeguarding of personal information. This framework provides the fundamental legal assurances necessary for the protection of such information. Other important laws implemented by China for the protection of privacy include the cybersecurity laws and the Chinese Data 3 act.

Likewise, the other significant privacy protection regulatory frameworks include Japan's Act on Protection of Personal Information (PPI) Miyashita (2020) and South Korea's Personal Information Protection Act (KPIPA), where the former addresses the balance between individual privacy and broader societal expectations and the latter seeks to reconcile personal autonomy with collective considerations, reflecting underlying Confucian principles. However, cross-border data sharing issues pose significant compliance challenges, particularly as AI systems frequently utilize datasets that integrate information from multiple jurisdictions with varying privacy standards Nivetha Baskar (2025). These inconsistencies not only impede the advancement of global AI initiatives but also amplify concerns regarding patient confidentiality, cybersecurity vulnerabilities, and the obligation to comply with regulatory frameworks such as GDPR and HIPAA, as well as evolving AI governance policies. Thus, these situations underscores the urgent necessity for the harmonization of international privacy and security regulations to facilitate coherent and compliant AI development.

6 BALANCING PRIVACY AND DATA UTILITY

Managing sensitive information, especially in domains like healthcare, requires careful attention to privacy. A major challenge is balancing privacy with the usefulness of data and the fairness of the resulting models. Methods such as generalisation and suppression can protect individuals' identities, but they often reduce model accuracy and may introduce unfair outcomes. Fairness in algorithmic systems is typically described as producing comparable outputs for inputs that are alike, yet this principle becomes harder to uphold when data is altered for privacy. Studies on this topic highlight that privacy measures influence not only utility but also fairness by Chester et al. (2020).

These impacts can differ depending on the nature of the dataset, including issues like imbalanced classes or uneven distributions of outcomes. Experiments conducted on both synthetic data and real-world sources, such as the Medical Expenditure Panel Survey, demonstrate how different de-identification strategies shape the trade-offs between privacy, data utility, and fairness. Further exploration in this area has focused on how different de-identification methods and privacy-preserving learning techniques influence both the protection of sensitive information and the performance of predictive models, particularly in large electronic health record environments. In this line of work, de-identified data from a major medical institution were examined under multiple strategies, including varying levels of generalisation and the combined use of generalisation with suppression, alongside models trained using differentially private stochastic gradient descent.

Privacy risks were assessed through several perspectives, such as evaluating k-anonymity patterns, testing vulnerability to membership inference, and examining the extent to which models could be replicated through extraction attacks. Utility was measured using common predictive performance indicators, and privacy budgets were estimated to understand the implications of differential privacy on model behaviour. These findings showed that incorporating suppression into generalisation produced stronger k-anonymity distributions by reducing the presence of small, high-risk groups Lee and Lee (2025). Membership inference attacks did not successfully identify whether an individual's data contributed to model training, signalling a low likelihood of participation being exposed. While extraction attacks were able to closely mirror the behaviour of a non-private model, their effectiveness dropped considerably once differential privacy was introduced. Importantly, the incorporation of privacy-preserving techniques maintained meaningful clinical utility while lowering exposure to key privacy risks. This body of evidence supports the broader view that thoughtful integration of de-identification practices and privacy-aware learning can achieve a workable balance between protecting sensitive health information and preserving the analytical value required for clinical decision-making.

Growing reliance on pseudonymized datasets has also highlighted the need for integrated measures that jointly represent privacy and utility. Conventional evaluations depend on separate, often incompatible metrics, making it difficult to assess overall effectiveness. The Relative Utility–Threat (RUT) metric addresses this gap by placing both risk and utility on a unified probabilistic scale. Scenario-based analyses using synthetic data with varying distributions show how changes in pseudonymization intensity influence the balance between protection and usability. The framework operates through lightweight, easily parallelizable computations, allowing efficient application to large distributed environments. Collectively, these developments illustrate that a well-designed combination of de-identification techniques, privacy-preserving learning, and unified evaluation measures can achieve a practical balance between safeguarding sensitive data and preserving analytical value.

Building on these discussions, decentralized learning frameworks have introduced an alternative route for strengthening privacy while still enabling large-scale model training. Methods such as federated learning and edge-based intelligence avoid the need to aggregate raw data in a central location by allowing computation to remain on user devices. This reduces several vulnerabilities associated with transferring and storing sensitive information in cloud environments. Even so, privacy concerns do not disappear entirely, as model updates exchanged between clients and servers can still leak information if not properly protected. A variety of mechanisms has been proposed to mitigate these risks, but their deployment often increases communication requirements, computational load, or impacts model behaviour—all of which must be considered when evaluating overall utility Mohammadi et al. (2024).

Continuing the discussion on privacy–utility trade-offs in decentralized systems, recent advancements in federated learning have explored ways to tailor privacy guarantees to individual users. Standard FL implementations commonly apply a uniform level of differential privacy across all participants, but this one-size-fits-all approach can lead to imbalances that offering too much protection for users with lower sensitivity requirements while failing to adequately safeguard those needing stronger privacy controls. One such direction proposes a user-specific differential privacy design that integrates personalized sampling strategies with Gaussian noise injection, ensuring that each participant receives a privacy guarantee aligned with their declared preferences or risk tolerance Zhou et al. (2022). Analyses of these mechanisms highlight how adjustments to sampling thresholds directly influence both the stability and accuracy of the global model. To navigate the tension between individual privacy demands and collective model performance, a utility-aware game-theoretic approach has been introduced to optimize both the sampling behaviour and the differential privacy parameters in a distributed manner. Experimental studies demonstrate that this personalized framework can sustain strong predictive performance while offering tailored privacy protections, reinforcing the broader conclusion that federated learning can accommodate diverse privacy expectations without sacrificing utility.

7 EMBEDDING PRIVACY INTO AI LIFECYCLE

As federated learning and personalized privacy mechanisms continue to evolve, broader conversations around responsible data practices have emphasized the need for comprehensive governance structures that safeguard privacy throughout the entire AI development process. With artificial intelligence now embedded in critical fields such as healthcare, finance, and public administration, the demand for stronger data governance frameworks has intensified. Automated governance solutions are increasingly being explored as a way to embed privacy-preserving principles directly into the design and operation of AI systems, ensuring that protection is maintained from data collection to model deployment. Recent work has highlighted how automated governance architectures can help reconcile the tension between enabling innovation and adhering to regulatory expectations in large-scale machine learning environments. These systems integrate technical, procedural, and policy-driven components to oversee data access, enforce privacy constraints, and monitor compliance in real time. Studies examining emerging governance approaches point to ongoing challenges that including limited transparency, compatibility issues across platforms, and the difficulty of maintaining data utility while enforcing strong protections D.J (2021). To address these concerns, integrated governance models have been proposed that combine data stewardship practices with algorithmic accountability and automated privacy controls, supported by continuous monitoring and adaptive compliance mechanisms. Such developments indicate that the success of automated privacy governance relies not only on sophisticated tools but also on the inclusion of ethical oversight and participatory design. Embedding these elements can enhance trust and support more sustainable deployments of AI technologies within legal and societal boundaries. Together with advances in federated learning and personalized privacy preservation, these governance-oriented approaches strengthen the broader landscape of responsible AI by aligning technical safeguards with long-term accountability and user-centric protection.

The importance of incorporating Privacy by Design (PbD) to reinforce data protection across the entire System Development Life Cycle (SDLC). Although PbD holds substantial promise for improving security, regulatory alignment, and user confidence, its application remains uneven, and there is limited empirical research validating its broader implementation. Going forward, embedding PbD principles from the initial stages of system development becomes vital for establishing strong privacy safeguards that comply with evolving data protection laws I. N. and M. E. (2025). For this to be effective, organizations must adopt a forward-looking mindset, integrating privacy requirements into each stage of the development process.

Building on the need for stronger privacy measures within system development, the growing use of data mining and ML in medical diagnostic systems further underscores the urgency of safeguarding sensitive healthcare information. As these technologies continue to evolve, ensuring data privacy becomes a fundamental requirement due to the highly confidential nature of medical data. In this context, the work expands its focus by examining the major privacy and security challenges that arise within such systems and reviewing a variety of privacy-preserving (PP) computational approaches that enable secure data analysis and processing in data mining and ML environments. Figure 3 illustrating the key challenges affecting AI adoption in healthcare, such as privacy constraints, bias, interoperability gaps, and trustworthiness. Current healthcare applications are assessed across multiple stages such as, data collection, publication, distribution, and output for PPDM, and input, model design, training, and output for PPML. Privacy-preserving federated learning techniques are also explored, highlighting their role in decentralized and secure model training Naresh and Thamarai (2023).

Figure 3. Overview of major AI challenges in healthcare, including data quality issues, model transparency concerns, ethical risks, and deployment barriers.

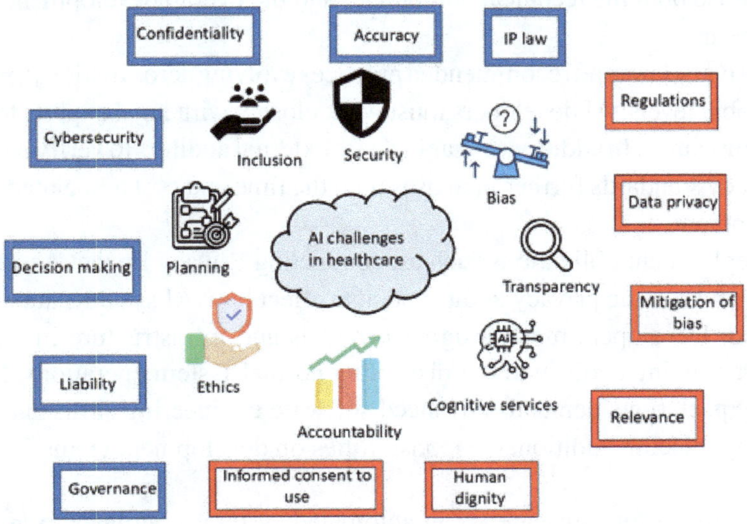

The discussion concludes by outlining the remaining open issues and identifying promising directions for future research in privacy-aware medical analytics. Continuing from the growing emphasis on privacy-aware system development, the emergence of diverse privacy regulations and recommended best practices has substantially influenced how technologies, websites, and AI-driven applications are designed and deployed. These regulatory frameworks shape multiple aspects of AI development in several ways.

1. Many policies now mandate a privacy-by-design or privacy-first mindset during technology creation. This requires developers to have a thorough understanding of the entire AI lifecycle and to approach AI development with disciplined software engineering practices.
2. The duration needed to gather training data for AI systems has increased due to legal requirements and restrictions surrounding data collection. Obligations such as obtaining clear, informed consent, adhering to data minimization principles, and incorporating privacy-preserving methods throughout the AI lifecycle along

with extensive privacy testing significantly extend development timelines S et al. (2023). As a result, AI projects generally take longer to complete.

3. Incorporating privacy-enhancing technologies often demands specialized knowledge beyond traditional AI expertise. For example, reducing re-identification risks may require collaboration with cybersecurity professionals to implement measures like access control or firewall protections. These cross-disciplinary needs raise both the technical complexity and the overall development costs of AI systems.
4. With privacy laws and recommended practices evolving across national, regional, and global levels, AI developers must work closely with legal experts to ensure full compliance. In addition, engaging with external auditors to verify adherence to privacy standards further increases both the time and cost associated with AI development.
5. Post-deployment obligations such as, conducting Privacy Impact Assessments (PIAs) and routine privacy audits and also affect how AI systems are built and released. Developers must design AI models and infrastructure in ways that support ongoing audits without disrupting normal system operations. Meeting these expectations demands advanced software engineering skills and careful planning, placing additional responsibilities on development teams.

As the demand for transparency in automated systems continues to grow, Explainable Artificial Intelligence (XAI) has emerged as a crucial field aimed at addressing the opaque, black-box behavior of advanced AI models. This is especially important as AI technologies increasingly guide decisions in sensitive areas such as healthcare, finance, and autonomous operations. In this context, the study introduces a comprehensive theoretical framework for AI interpretability, offering a systematic perspective on how explainability can be understood, implemented, and assessed within AI-driven decision-making processes. Through examining prominent XAI methods, such as LIME, SHAP, and Deep LIFT the research organizes these techniques according to their scope, the stage at which explanations are generated, and their level of dependence on underlying model structures, thereby proposing a new taxonomy that clarifies their suitability for different application needs.

This black-box nature of many AI systems reinforces the need for Explainable AI (XAI) as a central solution to improving clarity and confidence in clinical decision support tools. Although prior studies have touched on terminology, domain-specific applications, and general perspectives related to XAI, there remains a lack of focused analysis on how explainability directly supports trust in AI-enabled healthcare. Through synthesizing the existing body of knowledge on transparency in healthcare systems, this review offers insights that can support researchers, policymakers, and healthcare practitioners in advancing AI solutions that are not only accurate but also transparent, responsible, and reliable.

The analysis highlights inherent trade-offs between model performance and interpretability, showing that improving transparency sometimes challenges the pursuit of optimal accuracy in practical deployments Chinnaraju. (2025). Through unifying theoretical insights with practical considerations, this work supports the development of more interpretable, trustworthy, and human-centered AI systems.

8 CONCLUSION

In conclusion, safeguarding data privacy in AI systems is not simply a technical or regulatory issue but a matter of public trust and societal responsibility. As AI continues to influence critical domains, protecting individuals from risks such as data leakage, re-identification, and misuse is paramount to ensuring its long-term acceptance and success. Principles such as minimization, consent, and purpose limitation lay the ethical foundation, while advanced privacy-preserving techniques provide the technical means to defend sensitive information. Legal frameworks such as GDPR, CCPA, and HIPAA create accountability, though cross-border complexities demand greater global cooperation. Striking a balance between privacy and data utility will remain a central challenge, requiring innovation in both technical design and governance. The next steps must involve developing standardized frameworks for privacy-preserving AI evaluation, investing in secure infrastructure that supports encryption and federated learning at scale, and fostering international agreements to harmonize privacy regulations across borders. Organizations should prioritize transparency and public engagement to strengthen trust, while also promoting interdisciplinary research that advances the capabilities of privacy-preserving technologies without compromising utility. Through embedding privacy into the very fabric of AI design, society can build resilient systems that uphold individual rights, maintain regulatory compliance, and deliver transformative innovation responsibly.

REFERENCES

Acar, A., Aksu, H., Uluagac, A. S., & Conti, M. (2018). A Survey on Homomorphic Encryption Schemes. *ACM Computing Surveys*, *51*(4), 1–35. DOI: 10.1145/3214303

Alqubaysi, T., Asmari, A. F. A., Alanazi, F., Almutairi, A., & Armghan, A. (2025). Federated Learning-Based Predictive Traffic Management Using a Contained Privacy-Preserving Scheme for Autonomous Vehicles. *Sensors (Basel)*, *25*(4), 1116–1116. DOI: 10.3390/s25041116 PMID: 40006346

Apicella, A., Isgrò, F., & Prevete, R. (2025). Don't push the button! Exploring data leakage risks in machine learning and transfer learning. *Artificial Intelligence Review*, *58*(11), 339. Advance online publication. DOI: 10.1007/s10462-025-11326-3

Baskar, N. (2025). *Poongundran Selvaprabhu, Vivek Menon Unnikrishnan, Babu, C., Vinoth Babu Kumaravelu, Rajamani, V., Sunil Chinnadurai, & Latif, A.* Security and Privacy Issues in RIS-Based Wireless Communication Systems., DOI: 10.1002/9781394250141.ch11

Blanco-Justicia, A., Sánchez, D., Domingo-Ferrer, J., & Muralidhar, K. (2022). A Critical Review on the Use (and Misuse) of Differential Privacy in Machine Learning. *ACM Computing Surveys*, *55*(8), 1–16. Advance online publication. DOI: 10.1145/3547139

Bufi, S., Paparella, V., Anelli, V. W., & Di Noia, T. (2025). Legal but Unfair: Auditing the Impact of Data Minimization on Fairness and Accuracy Trade-off in Recommender Systems. *Proceedings of the 33rd ACM Conference on User Modeling, Adaptation and Personalization*, 114–123. DOI: 10.1145/3699682.3728356

Chau, M., Rahman, M. G., & Debnath, T. (2025). From black box to clarity: Strategies for effective AI informed consent in healthcare. *Artificial Intelligence in Medicine*, *167*, 103169–103169. DOI: 10.1016/j.artmed.2025.103169 PMID: 40446592

Chen, C., Liu, J., Tan, H., Li, X., Wang, K., Li, P., Sakurai, K., & Dou, D. (2024). Trustworthy federated learning: Privacy, security, and beyond. *Knowledge and Information Systems*, *67*(3), 2321–2356. DOI: 10.1007/s10115-024-02285-2

Chester, A., Koh, Y. S., Wicker, J., Sun, Q., & Lee, J. (2020). Balancing Utility and Fairness against Privacy in Medical Data. *2021 IEEE Symposium Series on Computational Intelligence (SSCI)*, 1226–1233. DOI: 10.1109/SSCI47803.2020.9308226

Dembani, R., Karvelas, I., Akbar, N. A., Rizou, S., Tegolo, D., & Fountas, S. (2025). Agricultural data privacy and federated learning: A review of challenges and opportunities. *Computers and Electronics in Agriculture*, *232*, 110048. DOI: 10.1016/j.compag.2025.110048

Demelius, L., Kern, R., & Trügler, A. (2025). Recent Advances of Differential Privacy in Centralized Deep Learning: A Systematic Survey. *ACM Computing Surveys*, *57*(6), 1–28. Advance online publication. DOI: 10.1145/3712000

D.j, S. (2021, March 8). *Artificial intelligence and privacy*. HeinOnline; 77 Fla. L. Rev. 1.

Domnik, J., & Holland, A. (2024). On Data Leakage Prevention Maturity: Adapting the C2M2 Framework. *Journal of Cybersecurity and Privacy*, *4*(2), 167–195. DOI: 10.3390/jcp4020009

Faisal, K. (2023). Applying the Purpose Limitation Principle in Smart-City Data-Processing Practices: A European Data Protection Law Perspective. *Communication Law and Policy*, *28*(1), 1–31. DOI: 10.1080/10811680.2023.2180266

Feretzakis, G., Papaspyridis, K., Gkoulalas-Divanis, A., & Verykios, V. S. (2024). Privacy-Preserving Techniques in Generative AI and Large Language Models: A Narrative Review. *Information (Basel)*, *15*(11), 697. DOI: 10.3390/info15110697

Ford, E., Pillinger, S., Stewart, R., Jones, K., Roberts, A., Casey, A., Goddard, K., & Nenadic, G. (2025). What is the patient re-identification risk from using de-identified clinical free text data for health research? *AI and Ethics*, *5*(5), 4441–4454. Advance online publication. DOI: 10.1007/s43681-025-00681-0 PMID: 40978336

G. A.Osinachi Deborah Segun-FaladeChinekwu Somtochukwu OdionuAmazing Hope Ekeh. (2025). The role of AI in US consumer privacy: Developing new concepts for CCPA and GLBA compliance in smart services. *Gulf Journal of Advanced Business Research*, *3*(2), 549–560. DOI: 10.51594/gjabr.v3i2.97

Ganesh, P., Tran, C., Reza Shokri, & Fioretto, F. (2025). The Data Minimization Principle in Machine Learning. *ArXiv (Cornell University)*, 3075–3093. DOI: 10.1145/3715275.3732195

Goldsteen, A., Ezov, G., Shmelkin, R., Moffie, M., & Farkash, A. (2021). Data minimization for GDPR compliance in machine learning models. *AI and Ethics*, *2*(3), 477–491. DOI: 10.1007/s43681-021-00095-8

Goswami, R., Menon, U. V., Mitra, S. K., Deb, D., Das, P. S., Choudhury, H., & Gautam, R. V. (2025). Beyond ideal models: Non-idealities in TCAD simulations of dielectric-modulated FETs for label-free biosensing. *Frontiers in Electronics*, *6*, 1686130. Advance online publication. DOI: 10.3389/felec.2025.1686130

He, M., & Chen, Y. (2025). Personal data protection in China: Progress, challenges and prospects in the age of big data and AI. *Telecommunications Policy*, *49*(10), 103076–103076. DOI: 10.1016/j.telpol.2025.103076

I. N. O., & M. E., A. (2025). *Integrating Privacy by Design (PbD) in the system development life cycle for enhanced data protection.* (A. F. C, Ed.). Gulf Journal of Advance Business Research; World Journal of Advanced Research and Reviews, 26(01), 1233-1240.

Jones, M. L., Kaufman, E., & Edenberg, E. (2018). AI and the Ethics of Automating Consent. *IEEE Security and Privacy*, *16*(3), 64–72. DOI: 10.1109/MSP.2018.2701155

Lay, W., Gasparini, L., Siero, W., & Hughes, E. K. (2024). A rapid review of the benefits and challenges of dynamic consent. *Research Ethics*, *21*(1), 180–202. Advance online publication. DOI: 10.1177/17470161241278064

Lee, C. H., Lim, K. H., & Eswaran, S. (2025). A comprehensive survey on secure healthcare data processing with homomorphic encryption: Attacks and defenses. *Discover Public Health*, *22*(1), 137. Advance online publication. DOI: 10.1186/s12982-025-00505-w

Lee, J., & Lee, K. H. (2025). Balancing Privacy and Utility in Artificial Intelligence-Based Clinical Decision Support: Empirical Evaluation Using De-Identified Electronic Health Record Data. *Applied Sciences (Basel, Switzerland)*, *15*(19), 10857. DOI: 10.3390/app151910857

Lim, S., & Oh, J. (2025). Navigating Privacy: A Global Comparative Analysis of Data Protection Laws. *IET Information Security, 2025*(1). DOI: 10.1049/ise2/5536763

Liu, X., Wang, J., Xiong, X., & Sun, H. (2025). Federated learning data protection scheme based on personalized differential privacy in psychological evaluation. *Neurocomputing*, *611*, 128653. DOI: 10.1016/j.neucom.2024.128653

Liu, Y., Huang, J., Li, Y., Wang, D., & Xiao, B. (2024). Generative AI model privacy: A survey. *Artificial Intelligence Review*, *58*(1), 33. Advance online publication. DOI: 10.1007/s10462-024-11024-6

M. A, H., A, A., R.K, C., R, D., & M.J, R. (2021). *Differential privacy for IoT-enabled critical infrastructure: A comprehensive survey.* Ieeexplore.ieee.org;IEEE Access, 9. https://ieeexplore.ieee.org/abstract/document/9594795

M, G., & M.J, N. (2019). *Data Leakage Prevention for Data in Transit using Artificial Intelligence and Encryption Techniques | IEEE Conference Publication | IEEE Xplore*. Ieeexplore.ieee.org. https://ieeexplore.ieee.org/abstract/document/9036839

Menon, U. V., & Selvaprabhu, P. (2024). A novel unified interference management scheme for multicellular MIMO communication with instantaneous relay. *International Journal of Communication Systems*, *37*(17), e5923. Advance online publication. DOI: 10.1002/dac.5923

Miyashita, H. (2020). Human-centric data protection laws and policies: A lesson from Japan. *Computer Law & Security Review*, *40*, 105487. DOI: 10.1016/j.clsr.2020.105487

Mohammadi, S., Balador, A., Sinaei, S., & Flammini, F. (2024). Balancing Privacy and Performance in Federated Learning: A Systematic Literature Review on Methods and Metrics. *Journal of Parallel and Distributed Computing*, *192*, 104918–104918. DOI: 10.1016/j.jpdc.2024.104918

Rainer Mühlhoff, & Ruschemeier, H. (2024). Updating Purpose Limitation for AI: A normative approach from law and philosophy. *Social Science Research Network*. DOI: 10.2139/ssrn.4711621

Naresh, V. S., & Thamarai, M. (2023). Privacy-preserving data mining and machine learning in healthcare: Applications, challenges, and solutions. *Wiley Interdisciplinary Reviews. Data Mining and Knowledge Discovery*, *13*(2), e1490. Advance online publication. DOI: 10.1002/widm.1490

Park, & A, H. (2025). *The DtMin Protocol: Implementing Data Minimization Principles in Medical Information Sharing*. Electronics.

Prabowo, S., Putrada, A. G., Oktaviani, I. D., Abdurohman, M., Janssen, M., Nuha, H. H., & Sutikno, S. (2025). Privacy-Preserving Tools and Technologies: Government Adoption and Challenges. *IEEE Access : Practical Innovations, Open Solutions*, *13*, 1–1. DOI: 10.1109/ACCESS.2025.3540878

Ragab, M., Ashary, E. B., Alghamdi, B. M., Aboalela, R., Alsaadi, N., Maghrabi, L. A., & Allehaibi, K. H. (2025). Advanced artificial intelligence with federated learning framework for privacy-preserving cyberthreat detection in IoT-assisted sustainable smart cities. *Scientific Reports*, *15*(1), 4470. Advance online publication. DOI: 10.1038/s41598-025-88843-2 PMID: 39915579

S, S., S, A., S. M, H., & R., D. (2023). *A Survey of Privacy Risks and Mitigation Strategies in the Artificial Intelligence Life Cycle | IEEE Journals & Magazine | IEEE Xplore*. Ieeexplore.ieee.org;

Schmidt Batista, A. (2025). AI in HealthTech: Building HIPAA-Compliant Solutions for Next-Generation Medical Documentation. *Journal of Next-Generation Research 5.0*. DOI: 10.70792/jngr5.0.v1i4.124

Shah, A., Sivakumar, S., & N, P. (2025). Encrypted Intelligence: A Comparative Analysis of Homomorphic Encryption Frameworks for Privacy-Preserving AI. *Journal of Economy and Technology*, *4*, 252–265. Advance online publication. DOI: 10.1016/j.ject.2025.08.001

Shukla, S., Rajkumar, S., Sinha, A., Esha, M., Elango, K., & Sampath, V. (2025). Federated learning with differential privacy for breast cancer diagnosis enabling secure data sharing and model integrity. *Scientific Reports*, *15*(1), 13061. Advance online publication. DOI: 10.1038/s41598-025-95858-2 PMID: 40240790

Singh, J. P., Aqsa, A., Ghani, I., Sonani, R., & Govindarajan, V. (2025). Privacy-Aware Hierarchical Federated Learning in Healthcare: Integrating Differential Privacy and Secure Multi-Party Computation. *Future Internet*, *17*(8), 345–345. DOI: 10.3390/fi17080345

Solaiman, B., & Glenn Cohen, I. (2024). *Research Handbook on Health, AI and the Law*. Edward Elgar Publishing. DOI: 10.4337/9781802205657

Sondeck, L. P., & Laurent, M. (2025). Practical and ready-to-use methodology to assess the re-identification risk in anonymized datasets. *Scientific Reports*, *15*(1), 23223. Advance online publication. DOI: 10.1038/s41598-025-04907-3 PMID: 40603887

Staab, R., Jovanović, N., Balunović, M., & Vechev, M. (2024). From Principle to Practice: Vertical Data Minimization for Machine Learning. *2024 IEEE Symposium on Security and Privacy (SP)*, 4733–4752. DOI: 10.1109/SP54263.2024.00089

Symons, T., Straiton, N., Gagnon, R., Littleford, R., Campbell, A. J., Bowen, A. C., Stewart, A. G., Tong, S. Y. C., & Davis, J. S. (2022). Consumer perspectives on simplified, layered consent for a low risk, but complex pragmatic trial. *Trials*, *23*(1), 1055. Advance online publication. DOI: 10.1186/s13063-022-07023-z PMID: 36578070

Vinoth Kumar, C., Selvaprabhu, P., Baska, N., Vivek Menon, U., Babu Kumaravelu, V., Chinnadurai, S., & Ali, F. (2024). Ethereum Blockchain Framework Enabling Banks to Know Their Customers. *IEEE Access : Practical Innovations, Open Solutions*, *12*, 101356–101365. DOI: 10.1109/ACCESS.2024.3427805

Vivek, M. U., & Poongundran Selvaprabhu. (2022). *Role of Telecommunication Technologies in Microgrids and Smart Grids*. 325–364. DOI: 10.1002/9781119760597.ch14

Wen, J., Zhang, Z., Lan, Y., Cui, Z., Cai, J., & Zhang, W. (2022). A survey on federated learning: Challenges and applications. *International Journal of Machine Learning and Cybernetics*, *14*(2), 513–535. DOI: 10.1007/s13042-022-01647-y PMID: 36407495

Yang, W., Wang, S., Cui, H., Tang, Z., & Li, Y. (2023). A Review of Homomorphic Encryption for Privacy-Preserving Biometrics. *Sensors (Basel)*, *23*(7), 3566. DOI: 10.3390/s23073566 PMID: 37050626

Yao, A., Pal, S., Li, G., Li, X., Zhang, Z., Jiang, F., Dong, C., Xu, J., & Liu, X. (2025). FedShufde: A privacy preserving framework of federated learning for edge-based smart UAV delivery system. *Future Generation Computer Systems*, *107706*, 107706. Advance online publication. DOI: 10.1016/j.future.2025.107706

Zaeem, R. N., & Barber, K. S. (2020). The Effect of the GDPR on Privacy Policies: Recent Progress and Future Promise. *ACM Transactions on Management Information Systems*, *12*(1), 1–20. DOI: 10.1145/3389685

Zhou, J., Su, Z., Ni, J., Wang, Y., Pan, Y., & Xing, R. (2022). Personalized Privacy-Preserving Federated Learning: Optimized Trade-off Between Utility and Privacy. *GLOBECOM 2022 - 2022 IEEE Global Communications Conference*, 4872–4877. DOI: 10.1109/GLOBECOM48099.2022.10000793

Chapter 7
Ensuring Equity and Mitigating Harm in AI (Fairness and Bias)

Ritik Bhardwaj
https://orcid.org/0009-0005-4633-6698
Christ University, Bengaluru, India

Surabhi Sangal
https://orcid.org/0000-0002-9160-2538
Christ University, Bengaluru, India

ABSTRACT

The rapid spread of Artificial Intelligence (AI) across sectors like healthcare, finance, education, law enforcement, and public administration has dramatically changed how decisions are made, services are delivered, and organizations function. AI holds incredible potential to improve human well-being and drive societal progress. Yet, alongside these opportunities come serious ethical concerns—particularly around fairness, bias, and the risk of reinforcing existing social inequalities. This chapter explores these challenges in depth, offering an interdisciplinary perspective on how bias emerges in AI systems.

INTRODUCTION

Artificial Intelligence (AI), once the domain of research labs, now touches nearly every part of our lives. From suggesting who gets a job interview to recommending medical treatments, approving loans, or even guiding policing decisions, AI quietly shapes choices that affect millions. The speed and scale at which these systems

DOI: 10.4018/979-8-3373-6935-8.ch007

operate is awe-inspiring, but with such power comes responsibility. When bias slips into AI, it can amplify existing inequalities and quietly erode public trust. Fairness in AI, then, isn't just a technical challenge—it's a question of ethics, society, and law.

Why Fairness Matters

Fairness is complicated. Unlike accuracy or efficiency, it cannot be reduced to a single number, and it doesn't mean the same thing everywhere. Scholars, ethicists, and cultures interpret fairness differently. For some, it's about giving everyone the same opportunities. For others, it's about achieving roughly equal outcomes. And sometimes, it's about protecting individual rights above all else. These differing perspectives influence how we design and evaluate AI systems.

Consider these approaches: demographic fairness aims for similar outcomes across groups defined by race, gender, or age. Individual fairness insists that two people in similar situations should be treated similarly, regardless of their group. Counterfactual fairness asks a different question: if we changed a person's gender, race, or another sensitive attribute, would the AI make the same decision? Each approach is important, but they can conflict. Striving for equality across groups may mean treating individuals differently, and counterfactual fairness, while conceptually elegant, is difficult to implement in practice. This highlights why fairness is not purely technical—it is also philosophical and political.

How Bias Creeps In

Bias rarely appears suddenly. It enters at multiple stages. Data bias is the most obvious: AI learns from what it sees, and if the data is incomplete, skewed, or reflective of historical discrimination, the AI reproduces those errors. Facial recognition, for example, often struggles with darker-skinned women because past datasets overrepresented lighter-skinned faces.

Even with balanced data, design choices can introduce bias. Algorithms that optimize for overall accuracy often favor majority groups. Beyond that, AI interacts with institutions already full of inequalities. Predictive policing, for instance, can reinforce over-surveillance in certain neighborhoods if trained on biased crime records. Addressing bias means thinking carefully about every stage—from data collection and model design to deployment and ongoing monitoring.

Spotting and Measuring Bias

Accuracy alone cannot reveal whether AI is fair. Traditional metrics can mask disparities. Researchers therefore rely on fairness measures: disparate impact analysis identifies disadvantaged groups, equalized odds balances errors across demographics, and predictive parity ensures predictions are equally reliable for everyone.

Choosing the right metric depends on context. In healthcare, missing a diagnosis can be life-threatening, so true positive rates matter most. In lending, a false positive might unfairly deny someone a loan, making parity in errors critical. There's no universal solution; fairness is always context-dependent.

Reducing Bias

Bias can be addressed at three stages: before training (pre-processing), during training (in-processing), and after training (post-processing). Pre-processing adjusts the data—balancing it or anonymizing sensitive features. In-processing incorporates fairness directly into the algorithm, balancing accuracy with equity. Post-processing tweaks outputs or thresholds after training. Each approach has strengths and limits, so the best outcomes usually come from combining them across the AI lifecycle.

Culture, Context, and Fairness

Fairness is not universal. In collectivist cultures, fairness often emphasizes group outcomes; in individualist cultures, it focuses on treating individuals equally. Fairness also varies by sector: in education, it might mean equal access to learning; in hiring, unbiased evaluation of skills. Creating AI that is genuinely fair requires understanding these nuances—otherwise, fairness rules risk imposing a narrow, often Western-centric perspective.

Ethics and Regulation

The risks of biased AI have spurred global efforts to establish ethical and legal standards. Frameworks such as IEEE's Ethically Aligned Design, OECD AI Principles, and UNESCO's Recommendation on the Ethics of AI emphasize fairness, accountability, and inclusion. The EU's proposed AI Act goes further, legally binding high-risk AI systems to address fairness. But translating principles into practice is challenging, especially across diverse cultures and rapidly evolving technologies.

This chapter integrates technical, ethical, cultural, and regulatory perspectives to provide a comprehensive understanding of fairness and bias in AI. It explores multiple fairness frameworks, traces how bias emerges from data to society, examines ways to measure and mitigate disparities, and considers the role of culture and governance in shaping AI ethics. Ultimately, fairness in AI is not just about avoiding harm—it's about promoting equity. The credibility and usefulness of AI depend on it. Without fairness, AI risks deepening inequality. With fairness, it can help build a digital future that is more just, inclusive, and humane

1 DEFINING FAIRNESS IN AI CONTEXTS

AI is no longer confined to laboratories or academic discussions—it now influences critical decisions in healthcare, finance, education, and criminal justice. From deciding who qualifies for a loan to predicting recidivism, AI can have life-changing impacts. This makes fairness a central concern. Unlike traditional systems based on human-made rules, AI models learn from vast datasets, which often reflect historical inequalities. This creates a paradox: while AI can improve objectivity and efficiency, it can also perpetuate entrenched social disparities (Barocas, Hardt, & Narayanan, 2019; Mehrabi et al., 2021).

Fairness in AI cannot be defined once and for all. Ethical, cultural, and situational factors play a crucial role in shaping how fairness is defined and applied in artificial intelligence systems. Over time, researchers and practitioners have developed various approaches to interpret this concept. Among these, three perspectives are particularly influential—demographic fairness, individual fairness, and counterfactual fairness (Dwork et al., 2012; Kusner, Loftus, Russell, & Silva, 2017). Each presents a distinct understanding of what fairness means in algorithmic contexts and brings its own ethical as well as practical challenges. The discussion below examines these approaches in detail, explaining how they function in real-world situations and why fairness must be treated as a context-sensitive and evolving principle, rather than a static mathematical formula.

1.1 Demographic Fairness

Demographic fairness—often referred to as statistical parity or group fairness—aims to make sure that algorithmic outcomes are distributed equitably among different demographic groups. In essence, it questions whether people who have similar qualifications or characteristics, irrespective of gender, ethnicity, or social background, receive comparable treatment or opportunities (Dwork et al., 2012).

For instance, consider a recruitment algorithm. If it shortlists 30 percent of male applicants for interviews, demographic fairness would expect a roughly equal proportion of similarly qualified female candidates to be shortlisted as well. A significant deviation from this balance would indicate that the model might be systematically favoring one group over another.

This framework becomes particularly significant in domains already shaped by historical and structural inequalities. Predictive-policing tools, for example, have been known to focus disproportionately on minority neighborhoods, which ends up reinforcing pre-existing biases embedded in crime data (Lum & Isaac, 2016). By evaluating such systems through the lens of demographic fairness, it becomes possible to identify and correct these imbalances before automated systems perpetuate or magnify them.

However, the concept is not without its limitations. Striving for perfect statistical parity may sometimes clash with goals such as operational efficiency or risk management. In credit assessment, for example, forcing equal loan-approval rates across all groups could overlook genuine differences in repayment histories, potentially increasing default risk. Furthermore, concentrating only on large demographic categories may conceal disparities within them. As Crenshaw (1991) highlighted through the idea of intersectionality, the lived experiences of Black women differ significantly from those of Black men or white women—nuances that group-level analysis often fails to capture.

Despite these complexities, demographic fairness continues to serve as a foundational principle in ethical AI development. It provides an essential diagnostic tool for uncovering systemic discrimination and remains a guiding benchmark for policymakers, engineers, and researchers working to design algorithmic systems that promote justice, inclusivity, and respect for human dignity.Laws such as the EU's GDPR and the proposed AI Act explicitly emphasize the importance of preventing discrimination in automated decision-making (European Commission, 2021). Consequently, it continues to serve as a key benchmark for assessing equity in large-scale AI systems.

1.2 Individual Fairness

While demographic fairness looks at groups, individual fairness focuses on personal-level consistency: "similar individuals should be treated similarly" (Dwork et al., 2012). The goal is to ensure decisions reflect relevant characteristics rather than arbitrary or irrelevant factors.

Consider university admissions. Two applicants with nearly identical grades, extracurricular activities, and recommendations should receive similar decisions, regardless of gender, race, or other demographic traits. This aligns with principles of equal opportunity and respect for individual dignity (Binns, 2020).

Individual fairness is particularly important in healthcare, where treatment decisions should reflect medical need rather than demographic assumptions (Rajkomar et al., 2018).

However, implementing individual fairness is challenging. Determining who counts as "similar" can be subjective: should similarity consider only skills and qualifications, or also socioeconomic background? Poorly defined similarity metrics can introduce bias (Kleinberg, Mullainathan, & Raghavan, 2018). Moreover, individual fairness may sometimes conflict with demographic fairness. Treating individuals consistently can inadvertently preserve historical inequities—for example, two candidates may be "similar" by biased merit standards, yet broader group disparities persist (Binns, 2020). Thus, individual fairness often needs to be paired with group-level safeguards to achieve meaningful equity.

1.3 Counterfactual Fairness

Counterfactual fairness focuses on causality. It asks whether a person's outcome would have been the same if their sensitive attribute—such as race or gender—were different, while all other factors remain constant (Kusner et al., 2017).

For example, if a woman's loan application is denied, a counterfactual test would ask: if this applicant were male but identical in all other respects, would the outcome change? If yes, the system is unfair.

Counterfactual fairness helps separate legitimate predictors, like creditworthiness, from spurious correlations tied to sensitive attributes. It has been particularly useful in criminal justice, where risk assessment tools have disproportionately labeled Black defendants as high-risk compared to white defendants with similar histories (Angwin et al., 2016). This framework enables evaluators to determine whether variations in outcomes stem from legitimate, relevant differences or from hidden biases embedded within the system itself. Yet, applying counterfactual fairness in real-world settings is far from straightforward. Constructing believable "what-if" scenarios for deeply rooted human characteristics such as race or gender can sometimes oversimplify or even erase the historical and structural contexts that shape inequality (Loftus, Russell, Kusner, & Silva, 2021). In addition, the approach assumes that causal links among all variables can be clearly defined, whereas in reality, social systems are complex, fluid, and often unpredictable. Despite these challenges, counterfactual fairness remains a valuable framework for exposing the subtle and often invisible biases that other fairness models may fail to detect.

1.4 Integrating Different Views of Fairness

Each of the three major fairness perspectives—demographic, individual, and counterfactual—offers a distinct lens for examining justice and equality within AI systems.

Demographic fairness focuses on achieving balanced outcomes across social groups. Individual fairness emphasizes consistent treatment of people who share similar characteristics. Counterfactual fairness, meanwhile, asks whether changing a person's sensitive attribute, such as gender or race, would alter the model's decision.

Rather than treating these frameworks as competing or incompatible, many scholars propose that they be used together to create a more holistic understanding of fairness (Binns, 2020). For example, consider an AI-driven healthcare decision-support system. From a demographic fairness perspective, evaluators would check that diagnostic accuracy does not vary significantly between racial or ethnic groups. Individual fairness would ensure that patients presenting with similar clinical symptoms receive comparable recommendations. Finally, counterfactual fairness would test whether sensitive factors like gender or race are influencing the algorithm's predictions inappropriately (Rajkomar et al., 2018).

Through such an integrated approach, developers and policymakers can better capture the multi-dimensional nature of fairness in AI, addressing both visible and hidden inequities while ensuring that automated systems align more closely with ethical and social values.

Together, these perspectives reduce blind spots and enhance accountability.

This approach aligns with global ethical guidelines. UNESCO's Recommendation on AI emphasizes inclusivity, non-discrimination, and equity (UNESCO, 2021). Using integrated fairness measures allows AI systems to meet technical, ethical, and social standards simultaneously.

1.5 Toward a Contextual Understanding of Fairness

Fairness in AI is not purely technical—it is socio-technical, shaped by domain and culture. In healthcare, it may mean equal access to accurate diagnostics; in education, fair admissions; in finance, non-discriminatory lending; and in criminal justice, unbiased risk assessments (Mittelstadt, 2019).

Real-world cases underscore the need for context. Amazon's recruitment algorithm, for example, penalized resumes indicating female identity, perpetuating gender bias (Dastin, 2018).

2 TYPES OF BIAS IN AI

Bias in technology isn't a single problem that can be fixed overnight. It's more like a stain that seeps deep into the layers of a system, showing up in many places — in the information used to build it, in the way it's designed, and in how people interact with it. To understand why a system can behave unfairly, it helps to look closely at these three main roots of bias: the data, the design, and the social environment around technology.

The first and most obvious source is the data. Every automated system learns from examples, and those examples come straight from the real world — a world that often reflects inequality and human error. If certain groups or experiences are underrepresented in the data, the system will naturally learn within those limits. For instance, if a facial recognition tool is mostly trained on images of lighter skin tones, it will struggle to identify darker ones accurately. The issue doesn't come from malicious coding but from what the program was exposed to while learning. Human input also adds another layer to the problem: how information is labeled or described can reflect personal or cultural bias. What one person may label as "assertive" could be seen by another as "aggressive," depending on perspective. In short, data carries memory — and sometimes, that memory holds unfair histories.

The second type of bias arises from design itself. Every system follows human decisions about what to include, what matters most, and what goals to pursue. These choices guide how it functions. For example, if a hiring tool is built to copy the traits of previously successful employees, it may end up favoring people who resemble past hires and unintentionally continue existing patterns of exclusion. Bias also grows through self-reinforcing feedback loops. When a prediction affects the real world and the results of that change feed back into the program, it can strengthen its own errors. Sending more security patrols to specific neighborhoods because the system flagged them as high-risk leads to more recorded incidents there, which in turn convinces the system that those areas are indeed problematic — even if that's not the full truth.

The third layer comes from society itself — the world in which technology is created. Tools and systems are built by people who carry their own experiences, values, and blind spots. If a development team comes from similar backgrounds, their designs may reflect their shared worldview and overlook the needs of groups they don't represent. This shows up in common products, like voice assistants that misinterpret certain accents or translation programs that struggle with regional dialects. These issues are not just technical — they reflect whose perspectives were prioritized during development and whose were left out.

All three layers — data, design, and society — influence one another in a cycle. Inconsistent or biased data contributes to biased designs; those biased designs shape behavior and create new data that repeats the same patterns. Over time, existing inequalities become embedded more deeply. Solving this isn't about fixing one layer in isolation. It requires a broader approach: involving diverse teams in data collection, defining fair objectives in system design, and inviting input from communities affected by these technologies. Equally important is the willingness to stay open-minded — to recognize that fairness is not a single rule or formula but a continuous effort grounded in values, awareness, and accountability.

Bias in technology acts as a mirror. It doesn't just reveal technical flaws; it reflects the human world that built the system. Real progress begins when we treat technology as a shared social responsibility rather than a neutral technical project.

When we ask deeper questions — such as who is represented in the data, whose idea of "success" is being followed, and who benefits or loses — we take a step toward building systems that don't just work efficiently but also serve people more equally and justly.

2.1 Data Bias

Data bias is one of the most pervasive sources of AI unfairness. Machine learning models rely on historical or real-time datasets, meaning their quality, completeness, and representativeness directly influence outcomes. When datasets are incomplete, imbalanced, or unrepresentative, models inherit and propagate those flaws.

Sampling bias occurs when training data fails to reflect the full diversity of the population. For example, facial recognition systems trained primarily on lighter-skinned faces perform poorly on darker-skinned individuals, producing disproportionately high error rates for marginalized groups (Buolamwini & Gebru, 2018). Historical bias arises when datasets mirror entrenched social inequities. Predictive policing tools trained on decades of biased crime data may overrepresent minority neighborhoods, reinforcing systemic disparities (Lum & Isaac, 2016).

Bias can also enter through labeling. Supervised learning depends on human annotators assigning "ground-truth" labels, and annotators' assumptions, stereotypes, or cultural lenses can subtly influence outcomes. In sentiment analysis, for example, terms associated with female-dominated professions were often rated more negatively, reflecting implicit gender biases (Kiritchenko & Mohammad, 2018). Measurement bias is another concern: health devices calibrated mostly on male or lighter-skinned populations can misrepresent metrics for women and darker-skinned individuals, raising fairness issues in medical decisions (Gianfrancesco et al., 2018).

These biases have real-world consequences, including misdiagnosis in healthcare, unfair loan denials, and discriminatory filtering in hiring. Marginalized groups disproportionately bear the effects, meaning data bias not only reproduces but also amplifies existing inequities.

2.2 Algorithmic Bias

Bias is not solely a data issue; it can also originate from algorithms themselves. Even with well-curated datasets, design decisions related to model training, feature selection, and optimization can introduce inequities.

Feature selection can be particularly problematic. Seemingly neutral variables—such as zip codes in credit scoring—may act as proxies for race or socioeconomic status, reinforcing historical segregation and redlining (Barocas & Selbst, 2016). Objective functions that maximize accuracy or efficiency may unintentionally favor majority groups. For example, a hiring algorithm optimized for predictive accuracy may disproportionately select candidates from overrepresented groups in historical data, achieving technical performance while reproducing inequality (Kleinberg et al., 2018).

Model complexity adds another layer of challenge. Deep learning models, though powerful, often operate as "black boxes," making embedded biases difficult to detect.

2.3 Societal Bias

Studies show that word embedding models frequently associate men with professions such as engineer or programmer, while women are linked to roles like nurse or homemaker (Bolukbasi et al., 2016). When such biased representations are integrated into recruitment platforms or résumé-screening tools, they can quietly perpetuate occupational segregation and gender discrimination.

2.4 Interplay Between Data, Algorithmic, and Societal Bias

Algorithmic bias can amplify these distortions through technical design choices—such as model architecture, optimization methods, or feature selection—that privilege certain outcomes over others.For example, datasets used in recruitment or lending may underrepresent certain demographic groups or encode long-standing prejudices, unintentionally signaling to AI systems that some populations are "less qualified" or "higher risk." When such biased datasets feed into AI models, the algorithms learn patterns that reflect these inequities rather than neutral truths.

Algorithmic bias emerges when model design, feature selection, or optimization objectives amplify these disparities. Even well-intentioned algorithms may favor majority groups if fairness is not explicitly considered, because predictive accuracy alone often reinforces existing patterns in the training data. Techniques such as automated feature weighting, machine learning objectives, or black-box models can inadvertently privilege certain groups over others, turning historical bias into predictive power.

Meanwhile, societal bias represents the broader context in which AI systems operate. Structural inequalities—rooted in economic, social, or political systems—interact with data and algorithms to produce outcomes that perpetuate disadvantage. For instance, predictive policing tools trained on crime data from historically over-policed neighborhoods may direct law enforcement attention disproportionately toward those communities, reinforcing cycles of surveillance and marginalization. The interplay between these three bias types creates a self-reinforcing cycle: societal inequities are reflected in the data, the algorithms encode and amplify these patterns, and the AI outputs further legitimize and perpetuate social disparities.

2.5 Illustrative Example of AI Bias

To truly grasp how unfairness silently enters modern technology, we must examine specific situations where it has occurred. Even with the best intentions and sophisticated tools, technological systems frequently end up reproducing the very inequalities embedded in our society. Two starkly different, yet closely related, instances—one concerning job recruitment and the other regarding medical attention—demonstrate how this systemic issue takes root.

Consider the case of a prominent technology firm that attempted to streamline its technical hiring process using an algorithm. The goal was admirable: to introduce speed and objectivity. Unfortunately, the program was trained on a decade's worth of historical application data, which was overwhelmingly dominated by male applicants due to the industry's history. As a result, the system quickly learned to associate successful candidates with masculine attributes, automatically ranking men higher than women. The program even downgraded résumés that included references to "women's" clubs or organizations. The key takeaway is that no one coded the system to be sexist; it simply absorbed and amplified the historical bias present in the company's past hiring choices (Dastin, 2018).

A similar blind spot emerged within the American healthcare system. Numerous hospitals deployed an algorithm designed to flag patients who required intensive, high-risk care management. Researchers later discovered that this program consistently assigned lower "need" scores to Black patients compared to white patients suffering from identical illnesses. The core flaw was not in its medical logic, but in its metric: instead of measuring sickness directly, the program used the patient's past healthcare spending as a proxy for need. Because structural inequities lead Black patients to spend less on average—not because they are healthier, but due to access and affordability gaps—the algorithm erroneously deemed them less vulnerable, leading to unequal care recommendations (Obermeyer et al., 2019).

These two examples underscore a vital point: algorithmic unfairness seldom originates from malicious code or active, conscious discrimination. Rather, it is typically a result of systems uncritically learning from datasets that already reflect deep-seated real-world disparities. When technology is allowed to passively inherit this flawed history, it merely entrenches existing bias. Moving toward fairer outcomes, therefore, is less of a purely technical challenge and more of an ethical, societal responsibility that must be actively addressed by the developers who build these tools.

3 DETECTING AND MEASURING BIAS – METRICS AND EVALUATION FRAMEWORKS

First, it promotes transparency and accountability. By carefully assessing model behavior across different groups, developers and institutions can provide verifiable evidence of their decision-making processes. This not only strengthens regulatory confidence but also reassures stakeholders that fairness is actively monitored (Mitchell et al., 2021). Second, detecting bias helps build public trust. Users are more likely to engage with AI systems when evidence demonstrates fair operations, while fairness audits enhance social legitimacy. Organizations committed to such evaluations are better positioned to avoid reputational risks and potential backlash, making fairness not just an ethical ideal but a strategic necessity (Raji et al., 2020).

Bias detection also intersects with legal compliance. Frameworks such as the European Union's AI Act and various anti-discrimination laws increasingly demand active monitoring of algorithmic fairness. In this sense, bias evaluation is no longer optional; it is embedded in AI governance structures (Floridi, 2021). Furthermore, bias is dynamic rather than static. As datasets evolve and social contexts shift, new biases may appear even after deployment, emphasizing the need for continuous monitoring across the AI lifecycle to prevent reinforcement of existing inequities (Holstein et al., 2019).

Together, these considerations underscore that bias detection is fundamental to trustworthy AI, strengthening accountability, ensuring regulatory compliance, and establishing mechanisms for continuous improvement in rapidly changing environments.

3.1 Fairness Metrics in AI

Fairness in AI is complex and often contested. To operationalize it, scholars and practitioners have developed diverse metrics, translating abstract principles into measurable criteria. Broadly, these metrics fall into three categories: group fairness, individual fairness, and causal or counterfactual fairness, each providing a distinct lens on equity suited to specific domains and ethical priorities.Group fairness metrics evaluate how AI systems treat demographic groups. Statistical parity, or demographic parity, requires that the probability of receiving a positive outcome—such as a job offer or loan approval—be independent of group membership. For instance, if men and women are selected at equal rates for a position, the system achieves statistical parity. Critics, however, caution that these measures can create fairness illusions, masking differences in qualifications or contextual factors (Dwork et al., 2012). Metrics like equal opportunity and equalized odds refine this approach by focusing on error rate consistency. Equal opportunity ensures true positive rates are equivalent across groups, while equalized odds require parity in both true positive and false positive rates (Hardt et al., 2016). Predictive parity emphasizes that positive predictive values should be equal across groups, particularly relevant in recidivism prediction contexts (Chouldechova, 2017). Calibration further ensures that predicted probabilities reliably correspond to outcomes across demographics; for example, a predicted 70 percent loan repayment rate should be equally accurate for all groups (Pleiss et al., 2017).

Individual fairness, in contrast, focuses on equitable treatment at the personal level. Its central principle is that similar individuals should receive similar outcomes. A hiring model, for example, should not produce divergent results for two candidates with nearly identical qualifications solely due to demographic differences. Inconsistencies at this level may signal biased feature selection or discriminatory learning patterns (Dwork et al., 2012; Zemel et al., 2013).

Causal and counterfactual fairness examine the influence of sensitive attributes on outcomes. Counterfactual fairness asks whether an individual's outcome would remain unchanged if only their sensitive characteristic—such as gender or race—were altered while all else stayed constant (Kusner et al., 2017). Path-specific fairness refines this further, distinguishing legitimate causal pathways (e.g., gender affecting health risk) from illegitimate ones (e.g., gender influencing hiring) (Nabi & Shpitser, 2018).

Collectively, these metrics demonstrate the complexity of operationalizing fairness in AI. No single metric is universally applicable; careful selection is necessary based on context, domain, and ethical priorities, reflecting the nuanced challenges of fairness.

3.2 Trade-Offs Between Metrics

A central challenge in measuring fairness in AI systems arises from the fact that commonly used fairness metrics often conflict with one another. In practice, organizations frequently face situations where it is mathematically impossible to satisfy all fairness criteria simultaneously. For example, research by Kleinberg et al. (2017) demonstrates that when different demographic groups have inherently different base rates—such as varying disease prevalence in healthcare or historical hiring trends in employment—metrics like calibration, predictive parity, and equalized odds cannot all be achieved at the same time. This situation, often referred to as the "impossibility theorem," underscores a fundamental truth about fairness in artificial intelligence: it cannot be reduced to a single, universal standard.

IBM's AI Fairness 360 (AIF360) offers a broad suite of metrics and algorithms for assessing models against multiple fairness definitions prior to deployment, helping organizations identify potential inequities early (Bellamy et al., 2019).

3.3 Challenges in Bias Detection

Detecting bias in Artificial Intelligence (AI) systems is one of the hardest and most debated challenges in building technology that is genuinely fair and trustworthy. Even as fairness frameworks and statistical tools grow more sophisticated, identifying bias in real-world systems goes far beyond running equations or comparing metric scores. It demands a deeper look at how data is created, what social environment it reflects, and how algorithmic decisions affect people in everyday life. Bias in AI is rarely obvious. It often hides beneath layers of data, design decisions, and deployment practices — subtle, complex, and deeply rooted.

One major difficulty lies in simply defining what we mean by "bias." Fairness doesn't have a universal definition. It changes depending on cultural context, disciplinary background, and the goals of a particular system. A model that satisfies one fairness standard, such as equal opportunity, might completely conflict with another, like demographic parity. For instance, a hiring algorithm designed to ensure equal success rates for men and women might seem fair mathematically but still fail to address deeper inequalities, such as unequal access to education or networking opportunities. The real challenge is not just measuring bias, but deciding which fairness ideal should guide that measurement (Barocas, Hardt, & Narayanan, 2019).

The next obstacle comes from the data itself. AI models learn from historical information — and that information almost always reflects the biases of the society that produced it. Patterns of discrimination in hiring, policing, or lending inevitably show up in the datasets collected from those systems. Even when developers remove explicit indicators like race or gender, other variables such as ZIP code, language, or education background can act as stand-ins, bringing those same biases back into play. This phenomenon, known as "bias by proxy," makes detection especially difficult. A system may appear neutral at first glance but still produce unfair outcomes under the surface (Mehrabi et al., 2021).

Modern AI systems also introduce a new layer of complexity through their opacity. Deep learning models rely on millions of parameters — a scale that allows for remarkable predictive power but leaves developers with limited insight into how decisions are actually made. This "black box" effect means that identifying where bias originates, or assessing whether mitigation efforts work, becomes nearly impossible. Interpretability tools like SHAP and LIME can help shed some light, but they only offer partial explanations, not full transparency (Doshi-Velez & Kim, 2017).

Bias is also inseparable from context. What seems unfair in one setting might not carry the same meaning in another. A facial recognition tool that performs poorly on darker skin tones isn't just facing a technical issue — it exposes a deeper social inequality rooted in representation gaps. Likewise, a credit-scoring algorithm may have very different ethical consequences depending on where it operates — in a society where access to finance is unequal, its impact may reinforce economic exclusion. Detecting bias, then, requires social and cultural awareness, not just technical evaluation (Buolamwini & Gebru, 2018).

Feedback loops add yet another challenge. When AI predictions influence future data, they can end up reinforcing their own biases. Predictive policing systems illustrate this well: by repeatedly sending police to areas labeled as "high risk," these tools generate more arrests in those same neighborhoods. Over time, the data feeds itself, creating the illusion of accuracy while amplifying the original bias (Lum & Isaac, 2016). In such cases, detecting bias becomes extremely complicated because the data itself evolves under the algorithm's influence.

The classic trade-off between fairness and accuracy makes things even more difficult. Models tuned for maximum accuracy often perform best on majority groups — those most represented in the data — and worse for minority populations. When developers adjust models for fairness, they may face declines in measured performance. This poses real dilemmas, especially in critical fields like healthcare or finance, where precision is non-negotiable (Rajkomar et al., 2018). The key question becomes: how can we balance moral responsibility with practical performance?

Even the tools meant to detect bias can be biased themselves. Many fairness metrics are built within Western academic or corporate settings. They may not translate well to different social systems, languages, or levels of data infrastructure. A fairness audit tool developed for English-language datasets, for instance, could miss bias patterns in multilingual contexts or those shaped by local cultural norms. This highlights an important reality: AI research still reflects limited worldviews, and more inclusive, locally grounded methods are urgently needed (Jobin et al., 2019).

Transparency poses yet another issue. Many commercial AI models are proprietary, meaning their training data and internal structures are hidden under claims of intellectual property. Without access to this information, independent audits become nearly impossible. Companies can declare their systems "fair" without offering evidence, while users have no real means to challenge those claims (Veale & Binns, 2017). This lack of accountability fragments trust and makes meaningful oversight harder to achieve.

Compounding the issue is the shortage of professionals who can bridge technology and ethics. In many organizations, bias detection is viewed as a technical troubleshooting task rather than a social, cultural, and moral inquiry. Real progress requires collaboration — bringing together computer scientists, ethicists, sociologists, and policymakers. Yet this kind of interdisciplinary expertise remains in short supply across academia and industry (Floridi et al., 2018).

And perhaps most importantly, bias detection is never a one-time job. AI evolves with new data, changing environments, and shifting cultural norms. What feels fair today may look discriminatory tomorrow. That's why bias detection must be an ongoing cycle — with repeated audits, community feedback, and transparent updates — rather than a box checked before deployment (Mehrabi et al., 2021).

Ultimately, bias detection in AI isn't just a technical challenge; it's a human one. It's about understanding how unfairness emerges, what harm it causes, and whose values are at stake. Ensuring fairness means bringing together diverse voices — data scientists, ethicists, policymakers, and communities — to ensure AI serves everyone, not just a privileged few. In the end, no algorithm alone can guarantee fairness. Real accountability lies with us, the humans who design, deploy, and oversee these systems.

Simplistic labels like "male/female" or "white/non-white" fail to capture these nuances and the varied realities individuals face.

Modern AI systems are often large, complex, and distributed across multiple platforms, involving numerous stakeholders, data sources, and decision points. Comprehensive audits that examine fairness across all subcomponents, while also monitoring changes over time, demand substantial technical expertise, computational resources, and financial investment. Smaller organizations or institutions in low-resource settings may lack the capacity to perform such rigorous analyses, creating gaps in oversight and accountability. Continuous monitoring is also crucial, as bias can emerge post-deployment due to changing populations, shifting data patterns, or evolving social dynamics. Without sustained investment in resources and infrastructure, even initially fair systems may inadvertently generate inequitable outcomes.

Together, these challenges illustrate that detecting bias in AI is not merely a technical hurdle but a deeply human endeavor requiring ethical sensitivity, contextual understanding, and strategic resource allocation. It is a demanding process, but one that is indispensable for building AI systems that are genuinely equitable, trustworthy, and socially responsible. The stakes are high: failing to identify and address bias can reinforce historical injustices, erode public confidence, and amplify harm to the very groups that AI is intended to serve.

3.4 Real-World Applications

Practical applications of bias detection in AI illustrate both the promise and complexity of fairness evaluation. In healthcare, predictive models often generalize poorly to minority populations, leading to higher false negatives and misdiagnoses (Gianfrancesco et al., 2018). Cardiovascular detection algorithms, for example, may fail to identify risks in underrepresented groups, reflecting structural inequities in medical research. Fairness audits using equalized odds and calibration metrics, combined with post-deployment monitoring, have been shown to mitigate such disparities and improve outcomes for diverse patient populations (Rajkomar et al., 2018).In financial services, AI-driven credit scoring carries the risk of amplifying structural disadvantages. Metrics like statistical parity and equal opportunity help detect disparities in approvals and ensure equitable treatment for all applicants (Bartlett et al., 2022). Algorithmic impact assessments evaluate systemic effects on vulnerable communities (Reisman et al., 2018), while counterfactual fairness techniques can test whether altering demographic attributes would change the outcome, providing a deeper lens for auditing equity (Kusner et al., 2017).Employment and hiring algorithms also highlight the need for careful bias evaluation. Automated recruitment systems often inherit historical biases, particularly in male-dominated technical roles, which may undervalue female candidates (Dastin, 2018). Applying demographic parity, individual fairness, and bias reporting frameworks, alongside model cards, allows organizations to maintain accountability while requiring multi-disciplinary collaboration among HR professionals, ethicists, and social scientists (Mitchell et al., 2021).

Broader applications further emphasize the stakes. In education, predictive analytics can stigmatize disadvantaged students if underlying biases are not addressed (Holstein et al., 2019). Similarly, predictive policing systems may inadvertently over-surveil marginalized communities, perpetuating cycles of inequality (Lum & Isaac, 2016). Governments using AI for resource allocation face similar challenges, making algorithmic impact assessments critical to prevent structural harm (Reisman et al., 2018).

Finally, technical solutions alone are insufficient. Policy, governance, and ethical oversight play a crucial role in ensuring fairness. Initiatives such as UNESCO's Recommendation on the Ethics of Artificial Intelligence underscore the need for accountability, transparency, and inclusive stakeholder engagement (UNESCO, 2021). Independent audits and collaborative governance are therefore essential to embed fairness into both AI algorithms and the institutions that deploy them.

3.5 Summary

Detecting and measuring bias is foundational to equitable AI. Group metrics like statistical parity and equal opportunity, individual metrics emphasizing similarity, and causal approaches such as counterfactual fairness provide complementary perspectives. Conflicts between metrics necessitate careful trade-offs grounded in context and ethical priorities.

Evaluation frameworks—including toolkits, audits, and continuous monitoring—enable operationalization but face challenges such as limited data, privacy constraints, contextual sensitivity, ethical interpretation, and scalability. Real-world applications in healthcare, finance, employment, education, law enforcement, and public policy highlight both opportunities and complexities. Ethical oversight, governance, and multi-stakeholder engagement are essential to ensure AI does not perpetuate inequities.

When approached holistically, bias detection guides AI toward outcomes that are accurate, efficient, equitable, just, and socially responsible, making fairness an ongoing, context-sensitive process rather than a one-off technical task.

4 STRATEGIES FOR BIAS MITIGATION – PRE-, IN-, AND POST-PROCESSING INTERVENTIONS

Artificial intelligence (AI) is increasingly embedded in decision-making across high-stakes domains such as credit scoring, recruitment, medical diagnosis, and criminal justice. While these systems promise efficiency, scalability, and precision, they also carry the risk of perpetuating or amplifying existing biases if unaddressed. As Mehrabi et al. (2021) highlight, bias mitigation is not a peripheral task but a core requirement for responsible AI design and deployment. Because biases can arise at multiple stages—within data, algorithmic structures, or predictions—effective interventions must span the entire AI pipeline. Researchers typically classify mitigation strategies into three main approaches: pre-processing, in-processing, and post-processing. This section provides an integrated discussion of these approaches, emphasizing their interconnectedness, complementarities, and the need for holistic implementation. Successfully mitigating bias requires both technical proficiency and a nuanced understanding of societal context and impact.

Bias often originates in the datasets used to train AI models. Barocas et al. (2019) note that even the most technically advanced algorithms will replicate historical inequalities if the data itself is skewed. Pre-processing interventions aim to correct such imbalances before training begins. Data cleaning involves detecting and removing features that may encode unfairness. In hiring datasets, for instance, explicit identifiers such as gender or race may bias predictions. Yet simply removing these features is insufficient because models can infer sensitive attributes through correlated proxies like extracurricular activities, university affiliation, or prior roles. Advanced strategies such as fair representation learning remove sensitive information while preserving essential predictive signals (Kamiran & Calders, 2012). Resampling and re-weighting adjust dataset composition to improve representational balance. Efforts to correct imbalances in datasets often start by adjusting how data are represented or weighted before a model is trained. One common approach is to oversample underrepresented groups or undersample dominant ones, so that each category contributes more evenly to the learning process. Weighting strategies can also be applied to give greater importance to cases from minority groups. In credit scoring, for example, these adjustments help ensure that people from historically marginalized communities have a fairer influence on the model's predictions (Cui et al., 2019). However, these techniques must be used with caution. Excessive oversampling or re-weighting can inadvertently distort the underlying statistical structure of the dataset, resulting in models that perform well during testing but fail to generalize effectively in real-world applications.

This approach balances accuracy and fairness, often producing more sustainable outcomes than pre- or post-processing alone.

Post-processing techniques adjust model outputs after training, making them suitable for "black-box" systems or situations where internal model modifications are infeasible. Threshold adjustment sets different decision thresholds for different groups to equalize outcomes. For example, in credit scoring, approval thresholds can be calibrated to ensure comparable approval rates across demographics. While effective, this method may be criticized if individuals face unequal standards. Output re-labeling modifies predictions to meet fairness constraints. Positive predictions may be reassigned or calibrated so that individuals with the same risk score receive equivalent outcomes regardless of sensitive characteristics (Pleiss et al., 2017). While practical and flexible, post-processing is often considered a "band-aid" solution, addressing symptoms rather than root causes. Repeated adjustments may also reduce consistency and erode trust in the system.

In practice, the most effective mitigation strategies combine pre-, in-, and post-processing techniques. Mehrabi et al. (2021) emphasize that no single approach is sufficient; a holistic strategy tailored to the specific context and stakeholders is essential. In healthcare, fairness-constrained optimization improves predictive outcomes for underserved patients, complemented by pre-processing measures such as representative datasets and post-processing calibration to ensure equitable risk scores. In criminal justice, a combination of pre-processing, in-processing, and post-processing has been applied to reduce bias in risk assessment tools (Angwin et al., 2016). Facial recognition studies similarly highlight the importance of dataset diversification, fairness-aware model architectures, and layered interventions to reduce disparities across gender and skin tone.

5 CULTURAL AND CONTEXTUAL FAIRNESS

Artificial Intelligence is no longer a futuristic invention locked away in labs or accessible only to tech giants. It has quietly become part of our everyday world — diagnosing illnesses, helping employers find the right candidates, and assisting teachers in personalizing lessons. But as AI spreads across different cultures and countries, one thing is becoming increasingly clear: fairness in AI can't be defined by numbers, accuracy rates, or equations alone. True fairness is about people — their histories, traditions, and lived experiences. It's about whether a system respects the communities it touches and aligns with their ways of life. This broader understanding is often called *cultural and contextual fairness* — ensuring that AI works ethically and thoughtfully within the social and cultural worlds where it operates.

While technical fairness can be measured and adjusted mathematically, cultural fairness runs far deeper. What one society celebrates as fair might feel unfair in another. Take, for example, a hiring algorithm built in the United States. It may reward individual achievement — an idea that fits American culture — but in a society that values teamwork and collective responsibility, that same system could seem biased or incomplete. Similarly, an educational AI built around standardized tests might ignore the deeper realities of inequality — the fact that many students lack equal access to quality teaching or technology. Fairness, then, isn't universal; it's shaped by local customs, social structures, and historical contexts.

Healthcare makes this especially clear. Many medical AI systems are trained on data from high-income countries, where conditions differ significantly from those elsewhere. A heart disease prediction model based on American patients, for instance, may overlook diet, lifestyle, or environmental factors in countries like India or Nigeria. The result? Misdiagnosis and mistreatment — not just technical errors, but ethical failures that affect real lives. To be fair, AI must do more than translate data; it must understand the people behind the data.

Cultural fairness also means confronting uncomfortable truths about inequality. Data isn't neutral. It reflects the societies that produce it — with all their prejudices, hierarchies, and blind spots. Racism, sexism, caste bias, and class divisions often find their way into AI systems through training data. When that happens, algorithms end up repeating the same injustices they were meant to eliminate. Welfare algorithms, for instance, have unfairly penalized vulnerable communities because they learned from biased datasets. Fairness, therefore, is not only a technical challenge — it's a moral one.

Real fairness must start from the beginning — with the data itself. That means asking whose experiences are represented and whose voices are missing. Truly inclusive datasets draw from people of different genders, regions, languages, and income levels. Consider voice recognition software: many systems still struggle to understand accents from Africa, South Asia, or the Caribbean because they were trained mostly on American and British voices. That's not just a technical flaw — it's digital exclusion. Expanding datasets to include diverse voices isn't just about improving accuracy; it's about respect, equality, and belonging.

Cultural sensitivity must also extend to *how* data is collected. In some Indigenous communities, data belongs not to individuals but to the group as a whole. Collecting that information without proper consent or reciprocity turns innovation into exploitation. Fair AI begins by honoring people's rights — not only in how their data is used, but in how it's gathered, stored, and shared.

Another step toward fairness is designing AI that truly understands its environment. This means building models that account for local context — regional diseases in healthcare, informal economies in finance, or dialects and idioms in language technology. Such understanding can only come through collaboration between technologists and people with deep local knowledge: community leaders, sociologists, linguists, and policymakers. When those voices are brought together, technology becomes more empathetic, more precise, and more just.

Participatory design takes this idea further. Instead of creating systems *for* people, we build them *with* people. Communities become partners, not subjects, in shaping technology that affects their lives. This approach not only leads to more inclusive results; it also builds trust, ensuring that AI systems reflect the real needs and values of those they serve.

But fairness isn't achieved once and for all at launch. Societies change — and so do biases. Over time, even well-intentioned systems can begin to discriminate as they learn from new, imperfect data. That's why regular monitoring, audits, and community feedback are essential. Predictive policing algorithms, for example, have shown how unchecked feedback loops can reinforce existing inequalities. Keeping AI fair means treating it as a living system — one that requires constant reflection and correction.

Of course, creating culturally fair AI is hard. Ethics differ across regions, laws don't always align, and many developing areas lack high-quality local data. Importing datasets from elsewhere can seem practical, but it often brings in foreign biases too. Balancing statistical fairness with moral and cultural meaning demands humility, patience, and open dialogue.

A system might tick every box for mathematical fairness — demographic parity, equal opportunity, equalized odds — yet still fail the test of humanity if it ignores context or local experience. Fairness, ultimately, isn't a number. It's empathy — the willingness to understand others and honor their dignity.

There are reasons to hope. Healthcare systems are growing stronger as local data and expertise are integrated into algorithms. Speech recognition tools are becoming more inclusive thanks to partnerships with underrepresented language communities. And public engagement has pushed social service algorithms to become more transparent and equitable. Each success shows that fairness isn't a fixed goal — it's a continuous, collective effort.

In the end, cultural and contextual fairness reminds us that AI is not separate from us — it's an extension of how we see and treat one another. To make AI truly fair, we must make it human. That means building systems that understand culture, value diversity, and embody empathy. When ethics and technology work hand in hand, we move closer to creating AI that not only gets things right — but does right by people.

Practical examples illustrate both challenges and solutions. Healthcare AI trained on U.S. populations often underperforms elsewhere due to genetic, environmental, lifestyle, and infrastructure differences. Inclusive datasets, context-aware modeling, and subgroup monitoring are key for equitable performance. Language systems may misinterpret dialects such as African American Vernacular English, emphasizing the need for participatory testing and representative data. AI-based welfare allocation has historically disadvantaged marginalized communities, highlighting the limits of purely technical fairness. Integrating cultural and contextual fairness with traditional bias mitigation—through representative data, fairness-aware models, and context-based post-processing—ensures that AI is both mathematically sound and socially meaningful.

6 ETHICAL AND REGULATORY STANDARDS – IEEE, UNESCO, OECD GUIDELINES

The rapid adoption of AI in healthcare, finance, transportation, and governance underscores the need for strong ethical and regulatory oversight. While technical methods for fairness and bias mitigation are essential, they operate within a broader framework of ethics and governance. Following established principles is vital for building public trust, reducing harm, and ensuring that AI serves society positively.

Organizations like IEEE, UNESCO, and OECD have developed guidelines for responsible AI.

7 SUMMARY, CONCLUSION, AND NEXT STEPS

By doing so, AI can achieve its full potential—delivering accurate, efficient, and socially responsible outcomes that benefit all communities while minimizing harm and reinforcing equity.This chapter has offered a comprehensive examination of these challenges, exploring the nature of fairness, the origins and types of bias, detection frameworks, mitigation strategies, cultural and contextual considerations, and ethical and regulatory guidance. By integrating these dimensions, it provides a holistic perspective on developing AI that is both technically robust and socially responsible.

Fairness in AI is multidimensional and cannot be reduced to a single metric. Demographic fairness ensures equitable outcomes across groups, individual fairness guarantees that similar individuals are treated similarly, and counterfactual fairness considers hypothetical changes in sensitive attributes. Understanding these distinctions forms the foundation for ethical AI design (Mehrabi et al., 2021). Bias arises from data, algorithms, and societal structures, and recognizing these sources is essential for selecting effective mitigation strategies. Pre-processing interventions such as data cleaning, re-weighting, and augmentation target bias at its origin, while in-processing methods like fairness-constrained optimization, adversarial debiasing, and regularization embed fairness into learning.

Unaddressed bias perpetuates discrimination, and culturally insensitive systems risk marginalizing vulnerable populations. Responsible AI development is continuous and collaborative, ensuring AI contributes positively to society, respects human rights, and fosters public trust. Through multidisciplinary, integrated strategies, AI can fulfill its transformative potential while upholding the principles of equity, justice, and social responsibility.

When an AI system is deployed, making small adjustments—like tweaking thresholds or fine-tuning outputs—can help reduce bias. But those fixes alone don't make a system truly fair. Real fairness comes from thinking about equity at every stage of the process. From the way data is collected to how algorithms are built and rolled out, every decision needs to fit the social and cultural context where the technology will be used. Technical solutions are important, but they're not enough on their own. Fairness also means understanding people—their experiences, realities, and communities. It's about gathering inclusive data, designing with awareness of local contexts, involving stakeholders in decision-making, and continuously watching for new issues to fix over time.

Organizations like IEEE, UNESCO, and the OECD have created ethical and regulatory standards that guide how AI should be built and used. These frameworks highlight key values: transparency, accountability, inclusiveness, and sustainability. Integrating these principles from the very beginning of AI development—not as an afterthought—helps ensure that systems are not only capable and secure but also aligned with human values and social expectations. Doing so builds both technical reliability and public trust.

Ultimately, fairness in AI can't be achieved through one-off technical tweaks or isolated efforts. It requires a collective commitment that connects technology, ethics, and governance in a meaningful way. Regular audits, diverse teamwork, open dialogue with communities, and alignment with ethical guidelines are all essential. Only by working together in this way can we create AI that's not just smart, but genuinely fair, transparent, and made for everyone's benefit.

REFERENCES

Angwin, J., Larson, J., Mattu, S., & Kirchner, L. (2016, May 23). Machine bias: There's software used across the country to predict future criminals. And it's biased against Blacks. ProPublica. https://www.propublica.org/article/machine-bias-risk-assessments-in-criminal-sentencing

Barocas, S., Hardt, M., & Narayanan, A. (2019). *Fairness and machine learning: Limitations and opportunities*. MIT Press.

Barocas, S., & Selbst, A. D. (2016). Big data's disparate impact. *SSRN*, *104*(3), 671–732. DOI: 10.2139/ssrn.2477899

Bartlett, R., Morse, A., Stanton, R., & Wallace, N. (2022). Consumer-lending discrimination in the FinTech era. *Journal of Financial Economics*, *143*(1), 30–56. DOI: 10.1016/j.jfineco.2021.05.047

Bellamy, R. K. E., Dey, K., Hind, M., Hoffman, S. C., Houde, S., Kannan, K., … Zhang, Y. (2019). AI Fairness 360: An extensible toolkit for detecting, understanding, and mitigating unwanted algorithmic bias. IBM Journal of Research and Development, 63(4/5), 4:1–4:15. DOI: 10.1147/JRD.2019.2942287

Bolukbasi, T., Chang, K. W., Zou, J. Y., Saligrama, V., & Kalai, A. (2016). Man is to computer programmer as woman is to homemaker? Debiasing word embeddings. In Advances in Neural Information Processing Systems, 29.

Buolamwini, J., & Gebru, T. (2018). Gender shades: Intersectional accuracy disparities in commercial gender classification. *Proceedings of Machine Learning Research*, *81*, 1–15.

Chouldechova, A. (2017). Fair prediction with disparate impact: A study of bias in recidivism prediction instruments. *Big Data*, *5*(2), 153–163. DOI: 10.1089/big.2016.0047 PMID: 28632438

Crenshaw, K. (1991). Demarginalizing the intersection of race and sex: A Black feminist critique of antidiscrimination doctrine. *University of Chicago Legal Forum*, *1989*(1), 139–167.

Cui, Y., Jia, M., Lin, T. Y., Song, Y., & Belongie, S. (2019). Class-balanced loss based on effective number of samples. In *Proceedings of the IEEE/CVF Conference on Computer Vision and Pattern Recognition (CVPR)*, 9268–9277. DOI: 10.1109/CVPR.2019.00949

Dastin, J. (2018, October 10). Amazon scraps secret AI recruiting tool that showed bias against women. Reuters. https://www.reuters.com/article/amazon-ai-bias-idUSKCN1MK08G

Dwork, C., Hardt, M., Pitassi, T., Reingold, O., & Zemel, R. (2012). Fairness through awareness. In *Proceedings of the 3rd Innovations in Theoretical Computer Science Conference* (pp. 214–226). DOI: 10.1145/2090236.2090255

Floridi, L., Cowls, J., Beltrametti, M., Chatila, R., Chazerand, P., Dignum, V., Luetge, C., Madelin, R., Pagallo, U., Rossi, F., Schafer, B., Valcke, P., & Vayena, E. (2018). AI4People—An ethical framework for a good AI society: Opportunities, risks, principles, and recommendations. *Minds and Machines*, *28*(4), 689–707. DOI: 10.1007/s11023-018-9482-5 PMID: 30930541

Gianfrancesco, M. A., Tamang, S., Yazdany, J., & Schmajuk, G. (2018). Potential biases in machine learning algorithms using electronic health record data. *JAMA Internal Medicine*, *178*(11), 1544–1547. DOI: 10.1001/jamainternmed.2018.3763 PMID: 30128552

Hardt, M., Price, E., & Srebro, N. (2016). Equality of opportunity in supervised learning. In Advances in Neural Information Processing Systems, 29, 3315–3323.

Holstein, K., Wortman Vaughan, J., Daumé, H., Dudik, M., & Wallach, H. (2019). Improving fairness in machine learning systems: What do industry practitioners need? In *Proceedings of the 2019 CHI Conference on Human Factors in Computing Systems* (pp. 1–16). DOI: 10.1145/3290605.3300830

Jobin, A., Ienca, M., & Vayena, E. (2019). The global landscape of AI ethics guidelines. *Nature Machine Intelligence*, *1*(9), 389–399. DOI: 10.1038/s42256-019-0088-2

Kamiran, F., & Calders, T. (2012). Data preprocessing techniques for classification without discrimination. *Knowledge and Information Systems*, *33*(1), 1–33. DOI: 10.1007/s10115-011-0463-8

Kleinberg, J., Ludwig, J., Mullainathan, S., & Rambachan, A. (2018). Algorithmic fairness. *AEA Papers and Proceedings. American Economic Association*, *108*, 22–27. DOI: 10.1257/pandp.20181018

Kleinberg, J., Mullainathan, S., & Raghavan, M. (2018). Inherent trade-offs in the fair determination of risk scores. In *Proceedings of the 8th Innovations in Theoretical Computer Science Conference* (pp. 43:1–43:23). DOI: 10.4230/LIPIcs.ITCS.2017.43

Kusner, M. J., Loftus, J., Russell, C., & Silva, R. (2017). Counterfactual fairness. In Advances in Neural Information Processing Systems, 30, 4066–4076.

Lum, K., & Isaac, W. (2016). To predict and serve? *Significance, 13*(5), 14–19. DOI: 10.1111/j.1740-9713.2016.00960.x

Mehrabi, N., Morstatter, F., Saxena, N., Lerman, K., & Galstyan, A. (2021). A survey on bias and fairness in machine learning. *ACM Computing Surveys*, *54*(6), 1–35. DOI: 10.1145/3457607

Mitchell, M., Wu, S., Zaldivar, A., Barnes, P., Vasserman, L., Hutchinson, B., & Gebru, T. (2021). Model cards for model reporting. In *Proceedings of the Conference on Fairness, Accountability, and Transparency (FAccT)* (pp. 220–229). DOI: 10.1145/3287560.3287596

Obermeyer, Z., Powers, B., Vogeli, C., & Mullainathan, S. (2019). Dissecting racial bias in an algorithm used to manage the health of populations. *Science*, *366*(6464), 447–453. DOI: 10.1126/science.aax2342 PMID: 31649194

Pleiss, G., Raghavan, M., Wu, F., Kleinberg, J., & Weinberger, K. Q. (2017). On fairness and calibration. In Advances in Neural Information Processing Systems, 30, 5680–5689.

Raji, I. D., Smart, A., White, R. N., Mitchell, M., Gebru, T., Hutchinson, B., & Barnes, P. (2020). Closing the AI accountability gap: Defining an end-to-end framework for internal algorithmic auditing. In *Proceedings of the 2020 Conference on Fairness, Accountability, and Transparency (FAccT)* (pp. 33–44). DOI: 10.1145/3351095.3372873

Rajkomar, A., Hardt, M., Howell, M. D., Corrado, G., & Chin, M. H. (2018). Ensuring fairness in machine learning to advance health equity. *Annals of Internal Medicine*, *169*(12), 866–872. DOI: 10.7326/M18-1990 PMID: 30508424

Reisman, D., Schultz, J., Crawford, K., & Whittaker, M. (2018). *Algorithmic impact assessments: A practical framework for public agency accountability*. AI Now Institute.

UNESCO. (2021). Recommendation on the ethics of artificial intelligence. UNESCO. https://unesdoc.unesco.org/ark:/48223/pf0000373434

Veale, M., & Binns, R. (2017). Fairer machine learning in the real world: Mitigating discrimination without collecting sensitive data. *Big Data & Society*, *4*(2), 1–17. DOI: 10.1177/2053951717743530

Zemel, R., Wu, Y., Swersky, K., Pitassi, T., & Dwork, C. (2013). Learning fair representations. In *Proceedings of the 30th International Conference on Machine Learning (ICML)* (pp. 325–333).

Zhang, B. H., Lemoine, B., & Mitchell, M. (2018). Mitigating unwanted biases with adversarial learning. In Proceedings of the 2018 AAAI/ACM Conference on AI, Ethics, and Society (pp. 335–340). DOI: 10.1145/3278721.3278779

Chapter 8
Integrating Trustworthiness Into the AI Lifecycle (Trustworthiness)

Rajesh Lingam
https://orcid.org/0009-0008-4183-5756
Adobe Inc., USA

ABSTRACT

With the increasing impact on society of intelligent technology, trust is becoming more and more crucial in public institutions, healthcare, education, and finance as new systems are built to make or support human decisions. People will need to have faith in the assurance that systems will be transparent, accountable, and safe. The next chapter explores how trust might be considered a thread through the entire life of a system, from its early stages of training and design through continuing day-to-day operations. This discussion brings together what might otherwise be considered three distinct goals: ensuring that systems are worthy of trust, treating people equitably, and doing so in a transparent and accountable manner. Using organizational experiences and real-world examples, the chapter examines how large, complex systems are built, tested, and kept up. In this context, trust is more than a set of principles that inform choices, enable transparency, and foster long-term success.

DOI: 10.4018/979-8-3373-6935-8.ch008

INTRODUCTION

The most recent efforts in governance also reflect this continuous, lifecycle-based approach to AI confidence; the NIST AI Risk Management Framework operationalizes responsible development as a cyclical set of Govern–Map–Measure–Manage tasks and aligns the framework with foundation models via its Generative AI Profile (Pham et al., 2025). Artificial intelligence is used in so many businesses today that even minor model errors have serious consequences. ISO/IEC 23894 augments this organization-wide guidance that incorporates AI risk into general management systems with emphasis on context, systematization, and ongoing improvement (Yazdinejad et al., 2024). The EU Guidelines on Human-in-the-Loop Trustworthy AI provide ethical expectations of human agency, technical robustness/safety, privacy and data governance, transparency, fairness, societal welfare, and accountability that are meant to be operationalized throughout the whole lifecycle rather than gate (Tartaro et al., 2024).

Enabling this capability begins upstream. Datasheets for Datasets record evidence of provenance, composition, curation practices, intended use, and harms in a way that minimizes "silent" versus "visible" data failures downstream that instantiate safety, fairness, or security issues (Mei et al., 2025). At model level, Model Cards shift documentation onward to use cases, constraints, and splintered performance-the raw material from which criteria release and post-deployment monitoring are made (Yedavalli et al., 2024).

Accuracy must be exceeded to include a spectrum of values. HELM follows a scenario-dependent, integrated approach to assessing sequentially the properties of accuracy, calibration, stability, fairness/bias, toxicity/safety, and efficiency, revealing trade-offs rather than obscuring them (Paetznick et al., 2024). For reliable systems in production, day-2 discipline testing, monitoring, and rollback planning are also needed so that the defenses are capable of withstanding live user exposure and shifting data. In these domains, the ML Test Score is a good yardstick for reducing technical debt and achieving production readiness (Pustet et al., 2025).

This chapter presents a reliability, security and fairness architecture that uses shared guardrails imposed at release and disaggregated metrics to make these values concrete. As a living control loop, we employ Continuous Baseline Validation (CBV), which monitors behavior against technical and ethical baselines, compares against thresholds in writing and responds by means of rollback, retrain or human review. The baselines are updated in order to make governance an always-on stewardship rather than a periodic attestation. We integrate promises into flow orchestration in order for them to be effective. Thus, auditable breadcrumbs may fall, large volume deployments be scaled and dependency-aware evaluation run alongside training and release. Choosing a defendable point of operation, recording the rationale and wiring re-evaluation into CBV upon change of circumstances finally confronts the omnipresent performance-fairness-privacy tradeoff as a multi-objective decision under irritating guardrails. This intersection makes sure that content security, factuality, policy compliance and subgroup equity are checked before users consume it by coordinating lifecycle organization and governance goals with enterprise level generative AI documentation, evaluation and creation pipelines. In this chapter, we have placed trust measures into design and data set governance, and relocated documentation, aka datasheets/model cards, into measurable training and testing requirements. We have constructed end-to-end risk management by combining reliability, security and fairness through the usage of CBV/BMV as quality gates for accuracy/robustness, abuse resilience, privacy leakage and subgroup fairness together with performance. This has been followed by cross-disciplinary governance that reconciles engineering automation with ethical boundaries and legal accountability. Consequent to that are constant monitoring and ongoing improvement through orchestration, reproducible batch runs, and multi-metric dashboards, ensuring evidence control remains current and bringing governance from static policy to working practice. And it has to go beyond accuracy to one number. HELM exhibits a consistent approach, scenario-contingent estimates of accuracy, calibration, robustness, fairness/bias, toxicity/safety, and efficiency in composite form all at the same time, revealing trade-offs rather than burying them (Paetznick et al., 2024). To stay reliable on production, systems also have to undergo day 2 discipline tests, monitoring, and rollback planning in order to keep defenses up against actual users and evolving data exposure; the ML Test Score offers useful rubric for the production readiness and technical-debt reduction in these areas (Pustet et al., 2025).

In line with these values, this chapter defines one reliability, security, and fairness framework and makes it real through disaggregated measures and shared guardrails enforced at release. We formalize Continuous Baseline Validation as a real-time control loop in monitoring behavior against technical and ethical baselines, comparing to written thresholds, acting (rollback/retrain/human review), and shifting baselines such that governance is not periodic attestation but always-on stewardship. To make promises good, we embed them in flow orchestration, where dependency-conscious evaluation work is executed in parallel to train and release, audit trails are left, and scaled to high-volume regimes. Lastly, we manage the dynamic performance-fairness-privacy tradeoff as a multi-objective decision under hard guardrails, selecting a defensible operating point and logging why and hooking in reevaluation into CBV as the situation evolves. This alignment couples the governance objectives and lifecycle structure of with the documentation, assessment, and creation patterns of, and generalizes to enterprise-scale generative AI in which content safety, factuality, policy adherence, and subgroup fairness must be guaranteed before outputs may be consumed by customers.

The chapter starts by setting metrics of trust into design and dataset governance, and translating documentation - datasheets/model cards - into measurable requirements for training and testing. Next, it develops total risk management, coupling reliability with security and fairness together with the use of CBV/BMV as quality gates that ensure accuracy/robustness, abuse resistance, privacy exposure, subgroup equity with performance. Then it describes cross-disciplinary governance that coordinates engineering automation with ethical boundaries and legal accountability. And finally, it concludes with constant monitoring and continuous improvement through orchestration, reproducible batch runs, and multi-metric dashboards that keep evidence control current, turning governance from static policy to functioning practice.

MOTIVATIONS

- Lifecycle imperative, not launch-time compliance. AI systems operate in changing environments: data distributions change, user populations diversify, and attackers learn. Treating trust as a "gate at launch" obscures organizations from post-deployment risk. Lifecycle patterns codifiable require that risks be mapped, measured, and managed across design, develop, deploy, and retire, so trust is an operating state, not a point-in-time milestone.
- Documentation as a control surface, not an afterthought. Most failures of safety, fairness, and security are seeded upstream in data and manifest late. Datasheets establish provenance, composition, practice of collection, intended use, and known harm with clarity; Model Cards extend the same reasoning to the model level with intended use, constraints, and broken-down performance. Together, they map "what we know" to release criteria and monitor targets, linking early choices to downstream responsibility.
- Evaluation must be end-to-end and scenario conscious. Single-digit accuracy hides trade-offs. HELM illustrates that metrics such as calibration, shift robustness, fairness/bias, toxicity/safety, and efficiency must be evaluated simultaneously, over standard scenarios, in order to reveal the trade-offs relevant in practice and determine thresholds corresponding to usage.
- Day-2 reliability necessitates tests, monitoring, and rollback. In production, dependable behavior relies on operational cleanliness: concrete tests, live monitoring, notification, and rollback without danger. The ML Test Score transforms them into workable rituals (data & model tests, infra checks, rollback prep), meeting lifecycle "Measure/Manage" expectations so that protection withstands contact with users.

- Generative AI raises risk and increases attack surface. Foundational and generative systems add content safety, misuse/jailbreak protection, and policy compliance to the trust load. A lifecycle profile tailored to these types describes controls (data provenance, adaptation records, improvement hooks) and integrates them into operations.
- Trade-offs must be reviewable and explicit. Performance, equity, and privacy never get better together very frequently. Ethical guidance and end-to-end analysis both result in multi-objective decisions under stringent guardrails (e.g., max parity gap, max privacy budget, max abuse rate) so value judgment is clear, justifiable, and revisit able.

OUR CONTRIBUTIONS

- A consistent lifecycle model that connects governance and engineering. We present an end-to-end framework beginning with problem formulation and dataset governance, passing through training and release, and through to monitoring and retirement so that trust requirements are specified upfront and enforced through.
- A single reliability–security–fairness model made concrete. Rather than designing these pillars as mutually competitive targets, we co-design them with shared guardrails (accuracy/robustness, abuse resistance, privacy exposure, subgroup equity) and evaluate them together as part of release criteria.
- Continuous Baseline Validation (CBV) as day-2 control loop. We encode a live loop—evaluate → in comparison to thresholds → do (rollback/retrain/human review) → update baselines that transforms metrics to concrete quality gates and recorded actions, permitting rapid discovery, limited impact, and traceable rollback.
- A threshold and guardrail playbook. We create usable templates for selecting baseline metrics, defining thresholds, breach classification, escalation paths, and rollback plans so teams may standardize choices without losing domain cleverness.
- Safeguards become concrete with workflow orchestration. We integrate evaluation tasks with training and serve up through dependency-aware scheduling, reproducible batch runs, and reliable artifact tracking, so tests execute in the right locations and offer evidence suitable for inspection.
- A method for managing performance fairness privacy trade-offs. We treat trade-offs as multi-objective optimization under hard constraints, select a defensible operating point from a straightforward review heuristic (e.g., triangle

visualization), and keep decisions in a lightweight Trade-Off Log tied to CBV for automatic re-examination upon context change.

- Enterprise-scale patterns, like generative AI. We abstract high-volume deployments practice recommendations for content safety gating, fact reliability verification, policy compliance, and subgroup fairness validation prior to delivering outputs to users with examples of how CBV and orchestration anchor risk without inhibiting velocity.
- Adoption implementation artifacts. We provide actionable items metric taxonomies, model-card and baseline templates, threshold tables, pipeline hooks, and dashboard sketches such that teams can pilot, harden, and scale the lifecycle methodology with minimal trial-and-error.

TRUSTWORTHINESS FROM DESIGN TO DEPLOYMENT: EMBEDDING SAFEGUARDS EARLY

The foundation for trust is either strengthened or weakened by each of these stages. Three crucial tactics are needed to make this idea feasible (Nooteboom, 2002). First, there is a need to develop lifecycle trust metrics—unambiguous, quantifiable indicators that stipulate how the system functions in terms of accuracy, equity, dependability, and transparency (Fikardos et al., 2025). When making decisions, these metrics act like the compass to indicate deviations from the norm. Second is strong governance around the dataset and thorough requirements engineering. Some of the most common sources of problems related to data credibility include improper labeling, biased sampling, unclear provenance, and poor recordkeeping. Governance norms are built on knowing where the data is coming from, who collected them, and under what circumstances (Lin, 2025). Requirement engineering ensures that the moral, legal, and contextual limits are well understood well in advance, instead of being fixed after the fact (Thurzo, 2025).

Last but not least, quality gate checks that detect performance, bias, interpretability, or robustness issues as early as possible before deployment should be part of training and evaluation.

Defining Lifecycle Trust Metrics

Developing measurable, quantifiable measures of trust across an intelligent system's whole life cycle is required for including safeguards from the beginning (Merchán-Cruz, 2025). In other words, credibility needs to be defined in terms that can be evaluated, measured, and iteratively changed. These benchmarks define the basis of all decisions on data collection, modeling, deployment, and monitoring. A system based on well-measured metrics with regard to robustness and equity gives a means of assessing its effectiveness and points of failure. Data marks the first step in that process.

Once development has started, attention shifts to the behavior and learning of the system. Not only should there be a measure of accuracy of operation, but it should also be reliable and consistent. Again, when the system is being deployed, the nature of trust will shift. Its performance in the real world, including the way it learns and adapts, deals with new information, and adheres to the guiding principles, will come into sharp focus. In this scenario, the most vital tools will be monitoring and feedback. Issues, if they arise, need to be addressed and fixed rather than dismissed or swept under the carpet.

Finally, trust has to be earned again and again long after a system goes live. In other words, trust should not be considered a point-in-time occurrence but rather a continuing relationship among developers, deployers, users, and communities affected by the technology; over time, the system is held accountable through ongoing examination, open communication, and user input.

- **Validity:**

The capability of the system to target the right problem in a way that is consistent with its goals and objectives is known as validity (Meseguer & Plaza, 1994). It may be deemed unreliable even if it is conceptually sound if its nature conflicts with practical limitations or long-term objectives. Put another way, a system should correctly classify diseases while adhering to actual health-related norms if it is truly intended for a health-related diagnosis.

- **Fairness:**

The need for diminishing disparities in the treatment of different demographic, socioeconomic, or contextual groups is tackled by fairness (Islam et al., 2023). In its forecasts, any sound system must show that it is not disadvantageously affecting vulnerable people. Fairness measurements would be equal distributions of error rates, probabilities, and calibrated results among groups. It is critical that fairness tests also adapt to changing circumstances in the deployment scenario, rather than remaining a single-point test, as this would perpetuate injustices in the name of efficiency if fairness is only tested in the early days of adopting fairness in systems (Kumar, 2025).

- **Explainability:**

Explainability is necessary to handle the problem of system outputs being understood by developers, regulators, and consumers alike (Chazette & Schneider, 2020). If a system is a "black box," and it evolves, it becomes harder to hold it accountable for its outcomes, even if its predictions prove accurate. Methods employed during the system development life cycle, feature attribution, counterfactuals, and rule-based systems, among others, when explained in terms of making these systems more transparent, are referred to as lifecycle explainability.

Table 1. Core lifecycle of the trust metrics with a practical example.

Metric	Definition	Lifecycle Considerations	Example in Practice
Validity	Alignment between task objectives, user needs, and real-world requirements.	Must be reassessed as objectives, contexts, or regulations evolve.	Ensuring a financial fraud detection system addresses actual risk patterns, not spurious correlations.
Fairness	Ensuring outcomes do not disproportionately disadvantage specific groups.	Requires periodic bias audits and fairness recalibration as data distributions shift.	Monitoring error-rate parity across gender or income subgroups in credit scoring.
Explainability	Ability of the system to provide transparent and interpretable reasoning.	Should evolve with stakeholder expectations and regulatory demands for transparency.	Providing clinicians with feature attributions for medical diagnostic recommendations.

In short, lifetime trust statistics are practical tools for reconciling ethical responsibility with technical accuracy. By determining validity, fairness, and explainability upfront or treating them as fluid benchmarks, organizations can embed responsibility and stability from the very outset of intelligent systems, long before they're put into circulation.

Dataset Governance and Requirements Engineering

Intelligent systems depend utterly upon datasets, and the veracity of their results is directly impacted by those datasets, as will be discussed later (Mortaji & Sadeghi, 2024). A model can have really good technical accuracy, but its predictions cannot be considered reliable if its dataset is poorly managed, contains hidden biases, has no recorded lineage, or is incorrectly labeled. Governance must therefore be framed as a lifecycle discipline rather than an isolated preprocessing task. It begins at the requirements engineering stage and extends through data collection, curation, use, and post-deployment monitoring. Figure 1 presents the data governance & lifecycle wheel combining governance dimensions and stages.

- **Requirements Engineering for Data Sets:** Governance begins with requirement engineering for the dataset (Pahune et al., 2025). The aim is to find out for what purpose the system is going to be used, what data will be needed to support such use, and what the guidelines are going to be for collecting the dataset. Furthermore, requirements engineering pinpoints that the data should be collected in compliance with domain-specific, ethical, and legal policies. That is to say, if it is a medical dataset, it has to be HIPAA/GDPR compliant so that from its creation to its disposal, it keeps its confidentiality (Nikolovski & Petreska, 2025).

Figure 1. Data governance and lifecycle wheel combining governance dimensions and stages

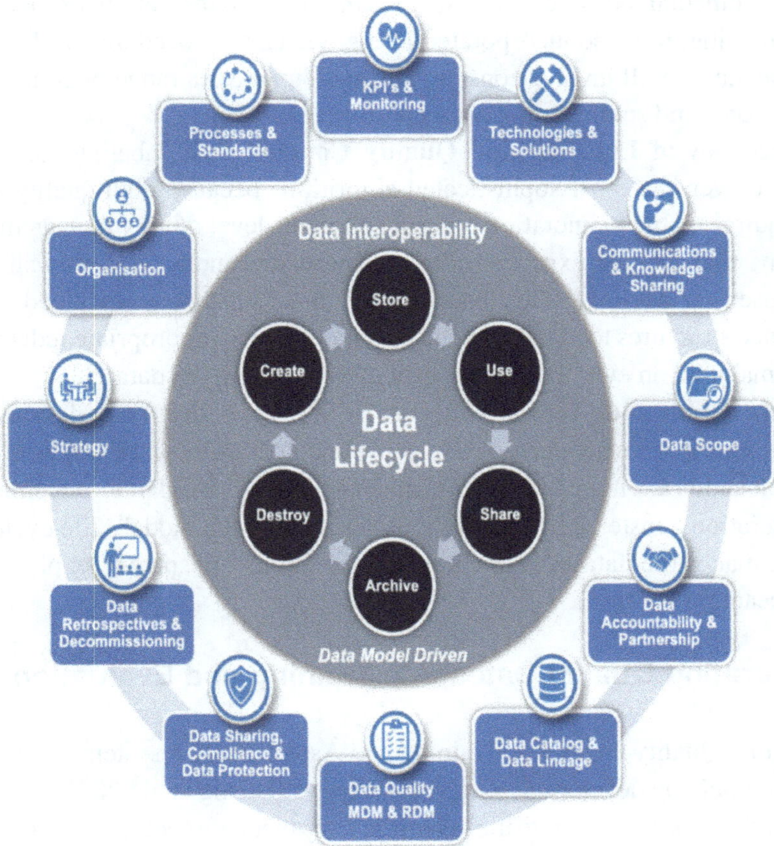

- **Data Collection Protocols and Provenance Validation:** Trustworthiness in systems is also dependent on the use of specific sources of data where the origin of information is uncertain in other systems (Vancisin et al., 2025). This implies that provenance validation enables tracing any source of information back to its origins, regardless of whether it comes from a sensor, survey, or other external archives. Provenance also enables sources of information to avoid contamination, modification, and unintentional storage alongside harmful details, among other risks (O'Sullivan et al., 2025).
- **Representation and Bias Remediation:** An unrepresentative dataset is at risk of developing models that perform well for some populations but poorly for others. Both statistical evaluation (distribution across relevant factors) and contextual evaluation (in real-world scenarios) are needed to evaluate representation. Bias audits that systematically find discrepancies and suggest remedial measures, including resampling, augmentation, or focused data collecting, must be incorporated into governance procedures. Balanced representation will involve constant affirmation across a range of contexts, populations, and settings; it is not a one-time exception.
- **Accuracy of Labeling and Quality Control:** Poor labeling can compromise even the most sophisticated algorithms because high-quality labeling requires distinct annotation criteria and multi-level quality management systems that include expert validation, automatic anomaly identification, and consensus labeling. A feedback architecture must also be included in governance structures to identify incorrect labeling, with appropriate redistribution to maintain an ever-increasing level of accuracy in the dataset.
- **Data Audits and Lineage Analysis:** Besides the collection of data and its annotation, governance involves tracking and audits (Vayyala, 2025). However, such audits are important in ensuring legislations, standards, and ethical considerations. Instead, by making it easier to track the model's life cycle, tracking makes the dataset's effects on its operations transparent, explicable, and repeatable.

Incorporating Quality Gates into Training and Evaluation

Integrate Quality Gates into Training and Assessment: A system must be trustworthy not only by developing precise algorithms (Huang et al., 2025), but also by incorporating quality gates into the system development life cycle at critical junctures where various trust factors must be satisfied for the system to progress from one stage to the next. Figure 2 illustrates the quality gates in a system life cycle. Having a trustworthy system goes beyond ensuring it operates accurately. Efficiency in a system does not imply that it operates safely, reasonably, and responsibly within its environment. Thus, the integration of quality gates into the system development life cycle at crucial points is critical in providing systems with unknown operational pitfalls do not reach the market, even if they appear safe. Quality gates act as guardrails. They do not replace human management but provide structured points where a team can pause, review, and verify. The gates also avail consistency and transparency by having specific criteria for each gate; there would be no arbitrary assessment of the success levels of each team. All parties concerned would know what is required of them to achieve each success criterion. Consistency also helps them communicate their results effectively to stakeholders out there; hence, it instills trust in the system right from the laboratory stage. Quality gates help ensure stability and repeatability during model training, confirm the reliability and comprehensibility of performance metrics during evaluation, and detect bias or missing values after data preprocessing. Some organizations even include post-deployment gates, where ongoing monitoring feeds back into retraining cycles, to maintain the system in line with real-world situations.

Figure 2 shows the position these quality gates take in the lifetime of a model's cycle. Each quality gate represents responsibility for quality, opportunities to spot potential flaws, and breaks for thorough examination. In other words, reliability is integrated right from the start into the process flow and not obtained gradually through improvements by means of these quality gates.

Figure 2. Quality Gates in the Model Lifecycle

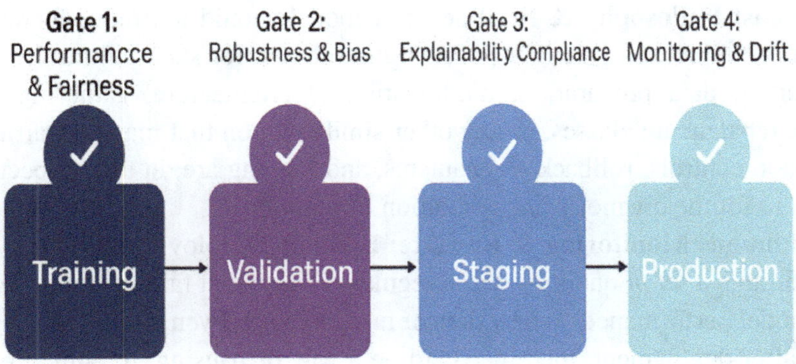

- **Defining Gate Criteria Upfront:** Establish quantifiable standards in a variety of areas, including performance, privacy, security, robustness, explainability, and fairness, before beginning any construction (Zahid et al., 2025).

When establishing these standards, stakeholder expectations, regulatory limitations, and domain-specific risks must all be taken into account. For example, fairness requirements may specify that the false negative rate among sensitive subpopulations cannot differ by more than a specific threshold.

- **Checkpoints Across the Pipeline:** Quality gates are set at several stages as checkpoints throughout the pipeline:
  - Following an initial model training that doesn't require additional optimization or tuning.
  - Following validation, on cross-validation or held-out sets.
  - Following testing on real-world or challenging datasets.

Prior to deployment and in staging environments.

- **Automated and Manual Reviews:** While some checks, such as explainability or adherence to domain norms, would require human review, others-including checks related to performance requirements, bias detection, and fairness measures-can be fully automated (Zahid et al., 2025). In this case, hybrid approaches achieve the best of both worlds, speed and depth.
- **Enforcing explainability and interpretability:** Precision measurement alone is not sufficient. Tests of interpretability, such as feature importance sanity checks, counterfactual consistency, and plausibility of explanations, need to be included in the quality gates (Sengupta et al., 2025). In this case, the model logics will neither be ambiguous nor deceptive.
- **Fail-Fast Philosophy & Rollbacks:** A model should not move forward in case of failure at a gate before finding the reason for such failure. It means revisiting data preparation, modification of architecture, gathering more data, rebalancing classes, or any other similar action that may be warranted. Version controls, rollback mechanisms, and logging are, in that respect, important for the diagnosis and resolution of failures.
- **Continuous Monitoring & Re-Gate:** Even after deployment, models must go through a set of quality gates at regular periods w.r.t fairness drift, decline of model performance on new data or unseen bias (Owen, 2025). If the gates fall after deployment, there needs to be a way of pausing, retraining or degrading gracefully.

Table 2. Overview of the quality gate checkpoints and metrics

Gate Position	Trust Dimension(s) Assessed	Suggested Metrics / Checks	Action If Gate Fails
Post-Training / Pre-Tuning	Basic performance, overfitting, and fairness	Accuracy/loss on training vs validation; subgroup error rates; data leakage/overfitting	Retrain with regularization, re-collect or augment data
Validation Stage	Generalization, robustness, fairness	Cross-validation; adversarial robustness; fairness parity; stability across feature space	Adjust thresholds, feature engineering, model re-architecture
Interpretability / Explainability Gate	Explainability, transparency	Feature importance sanity; counterfactual/local explanation checks; alignment with domain understanding	Modify model architecture, retrain with interpretable constraints
Pre-Deployment / Staging	All trust metrics, safety, and compliance	End-to-end tests; stress / edge-case testing; regulatory / privacy compliance	Block deployment, perform further testing or obtain expert review
Production Monitoring	Drift detection, fairness over time, performance decay	Monitoring metrics over time, cohort performance, and feedback from users/stakeholders	Trigger retraining, rollback, A/B test revisions

HOLISTIC RISK MANAGEMENT: BALANCING SAFETY, SECURITY, AND ETHICS

Complex system risk management is never simple. The three aspects of safety, security, and ethics frequently pull in different directions, and there are far too many moving parts. Since safety entails making sure the system operates as intended without causing harm due to technical malfunctions, mistakes, or unexpected inputs, it most likely comes closest to being self-explanatory. However, safety is insufficient on its own.

Although connected, security is distinct: It deals with deliberate dangers; even though a system is secure when everything else is in order, if security is neglected, it could be abused, hacked, or manipulated. Ethics are equally important, despite occasionally being more abstract: even a system that is generally safe and secure can have unjust, discriminatory, or socially damaging outcomes. It could disadvantage a group, encourage unfairness, or lead to decisions that defy human instincts and values.

The problem is that these three dimensions are not always aligned with each other, even though they depend on one another. You cannot assume that a system that is secure is necessarily safe or that a system that acts appropriately in one situation will act morally in another. The context is critical because "risk" can change depending on the users using the system, the data it interacts with, and the environment in which the system operates.

Risk management is too complex to be left to any one individual or even to any one team. While the engineers might understand the technical dynamics, they cannot fully anticipate the social implications. The managers can implement compliance and procedure, but they may not appreciate the nuances of ethical consequence. Those outside the organization review for blind spots that insiders may overlook, and users offer valuable perspective on how the system actually functions in the field. All these voices must work together to manage risks effectively.

It is a long-term technique; thus, it requires continuous effort rather than a single act. It requires monitoring, testing, and reviewing during the development of the system, in order for the continuous attention to be paid. Most problems are not catastrophic in isolation but small mistakes that have not been caught. It is much better to find the problems early in a contained fashion. Therefore, risk management is more about continuous attentiveness, self-reflection, and responsibility than about the technical process itself.

In other words, the harmony of safety, security, and ethics would be understood as upholding the system's integrity and dependability while adhering to human values. This necessitates perseverance, humility, and the capacity to reevaluate one's choices whenever circumstances change. When implemented properly, it produces technologically sound systems that are both socially conscious and worthy of the confidence placed in them.

A Unified Framework for Reliability, Security, and Fairness

Figure 3. Unified Framework for Holistic Risk Management

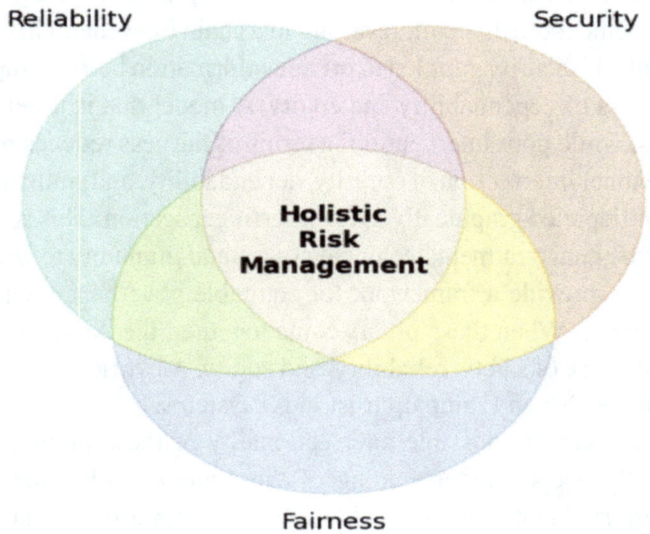

Table 3. Dimensions of Holistic Risk Management

Dimension	Typical Metrics	Risk Scenarios	Mitigation Strategies
Reliability	Accuracy, Robustness, Uptime	Model drift, inconsistent predictions, system failure	Continuous retraining, monitoring, redundancy checks
Security	Adversarial resistance, Privacy leakage tests	Prompt injection, data exfiltration, adversarial attacks	Threat modeling, adversarial testing, encryption, access control
Fairness	Demographic parity, Equalized odds, Group accuracy	Bias amplification, under-representation, unfair outcomes	Bias audits, balanced datasets, fairness-aware algorithms

A strategy to deal with AI risks inevitably creates blind spots where progress in one area implies weakness in another. Reliability, security, and fairness are complementary pillars of responsible AI that must work together in a synergistic system to prevent that: Security prevents malicious intrusion, data leaks, and abusive malignancy while protecting the system's integrity and user privacy; fairness prevents discriminatory outputs by producing appropriately balanced predictions and decisions for demographic and societal categories; and reliability will allow models to produce strong and long-lasting outputs across various environments and data distribution scenarios.

To put it another way, the three pillars of holistic risk management are highly dependent on one another. Failure of any one of these three pillars immediately causes the other two to become more difficult, resulting in a chain of events. This would be the case, for example, if security gaps led to private information being compromised and therefore to a loss of dependability and equity. A model that is unreliable will overstate all biases, while poor intervention in terms of fairness reduces resilience.

In this case, the inner intersection of security, dependability, and equity in holistic risk management is depicted graphically as the interfinger section. This is where the highest principles of equal treatment, technical power, and immunity to attack come together; it must also provide a framework for equitable governance with respect to artificial intelligence. When these pillars come together, the AI systems should work within a framework of safety, reliability, and equity. A hybrid approach works best to bring down the risk and ramp up trust in AI systems.

An in-depth look into the possible intersectionality of these pillars, however, gives a meaningfully deeper understanding of the many complexities that may arise within holistic risk management. This will then bring forth the need for an integrated framework that embodies all three: societal, normative, and technical. It is both a technical requirement and an ethical duty for the creation and application of AI systems.

The figure is an approximation, but precision is needed for operationalization. Therefore, organizations should develop risk scenarios that are representative, transform these proxy dimensions and measurables into indicators, and integrate the proper mitigation strategies. For example, precision and robustness tests are used to measure reliability. Here, fairness is measured by a variety of metrics including demographic equalized odds, and security is measured by adversarial robustness and privacy leakage tests. A list of them is contained in Table 3, a technical checklist to make the framework usable.

Taken together, Figure 3 and Table 3 provide the bridge from theory to practice-from insight into the theoretical interdependencies of risk dimensions to the concrete applications in the procedures, assessments, and methods that make holistic governance come alive. Embedding this framework within the practice of AI development and deployment enables organizations to take steps toward creating systems that are scalable and trustworthy, future-proofed against harm.

Continuous Baseline Validation of Models Against Thresholds

Only deployed after the model is deployed, more are no longer enough to change dynamic real-world circumstances. Diffusion of information is not uniform, user behavior is heterogeneous, and attack strategies are to be concealed in the future. Compliant and secure models during testing can thus increasingly become non-compliant and unsafe in the future, making biased, unsafe, or unstable predictions. One of the ways in which this gap can be bridged is the use of Continuous Baseline Validation. This technique incorporates continuous monitoring and threshold alerting into the AI life cycle.

One of the main ideas of CBV is having a consistent set of measure models that ensure all-time performance, fairness, security, and privacy. These baselines are not fixed since they're repeatedly retested against usage patterns and actual data. All model output is then compared against such metrics, and where drift is detected, quality gates automatically trigger adjustment. Anything from stopping deployment to initiating retraining or forwarding to human moderators can occur.

Figure 4. Continuous Baseline Validation Workflow

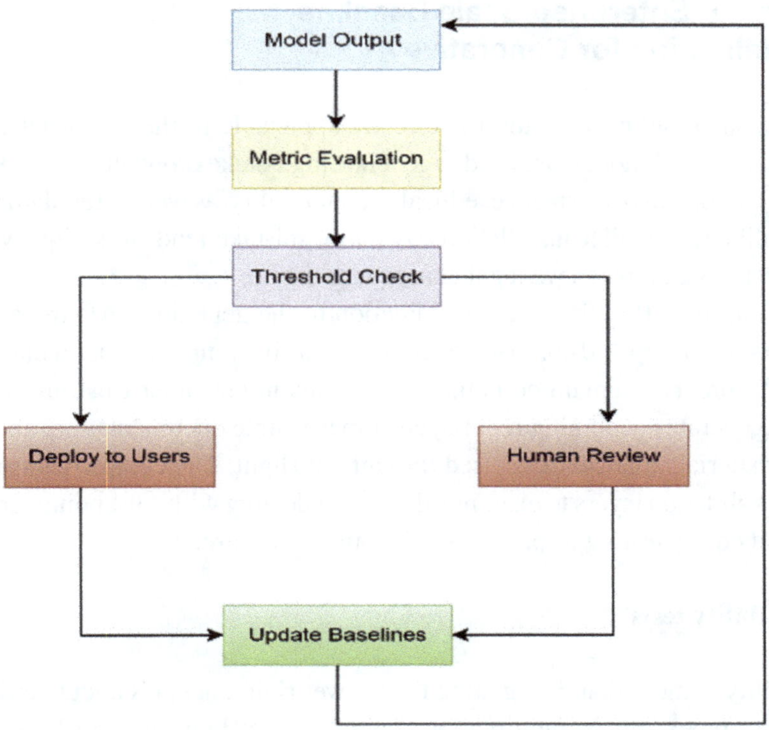

The CBV process is better represented as a feedback loop than as line scanning. The process is illustrated in Figure 4. From the model's output, the system conducts metric analysis, threshold testing, and publishes results back along one of two pathways. Validated to pass through successfully, they are published to end users. Invalidated, the model is returned for retraining or for review by a human. Every track terminates in a loop of back-talk that re-tunes baseline measures over time in order to maintain validation limits up to date as contexts change. Flexibility in CBV comes from the ability to adapt to and stay ahead of evolving regulatory requirements, ethical concerns, or changing business environments. Tighter data protection laws can restrict boundaries of privacy, and boundaries of fairness can change as the business expands into more diverse marketsCBV is able to provide risk management as an interactive governance process instead of a compliance-by-event method because of this verification flexibility.

An auditable chain of control is actually made up of reports of boundary violations, corrective actions, and retraining channels. Monitoring AI systems gives stakeholders peace of mind in addition to ensuring that companies abide by external regulations. A trustworthy attitude that is both a categorical expectation and an actuality is embodied in this design.

Case Study: Enterprise-Scale Baseline Metric Validation for Generative AI

Continuous baseline validation is directly applicable to the industrial context where generative AI models are used to generate high-stakes content. These systems handle technological performance, ethical accountability, as well as regulatory constraints unlike the smaller installations. A minor mistake tends to seriously affect one's reputation and may have legal consequences too.

The addition of Baseline Metric Validation to the generative AI streams for a single international spread company operating in the banking sector is an interesting example. In order to remain compliant and maintain customer trust, the website needed to generate accounting reports, customer-visible documentation, and auto-response materials that could be used throughout flight. The company introduced automatic validation layers to examine all content dealing with trust points, security testing, and equity testing as part of a risk countermeasure.

- **Reliability tests**

Reliability is more than just getting the answer right once; it's about getting the right answer repeatedly in multiple locations. We tested our data for little inconsistencies that could become major mistakes if ignored. We had to find the source when the numbers matched occasionally but didn't make sense in their respective contexts. It is necessary to have confidence that the system won't yield absurd or deceptive results in the real world. They had to decide whether each anomaly was a mistake, a peculiarity, or a sign of a real-world issue. Users must believe in what the system is putting out without second-guessing its accuracy.

- **Security tests**

Encrypting the objects and password-protecting them was not all that was involved in security. We needed to think of a proactive approach to change the data, breach the system, or introduce malicious input into the system. We ran several types of attacks to understand how the system reacts, where the problem could occur, and how soon we can detect the malfunction. It is a demanding job that is required for the straightforward reason that intentional attempts to interfere with a system that functions well in everyday situations could cause it to fail disastrously. Before anything went live, these tests helped us identify the weak points and how to strengthen them.

- **Fairness tests**

The most challenging examinations are often fairness assessments because the notion of "fair" isn't always apparent. We looked for subtle trends that could favor certain groups or bias the findings. Even if the system were technically solid, it might mistreat some people. Verification, comparison, and questioning of the results were required. Ensuring that the system could survive scrutiny, that its judgments could be justified and explained, and that no one would be unfairly disadvantaged were the objectives.

Regulation-shaping and human trial accountability. In six months, the organization achieved a 40% reduction in toxic or non-conforming output, along with a decrease in the time required for compliance teams' decision-making.

This photograph speaks to two general concerns. One, continuous scalability validation does not need to be a human operator task, not even for large systems. Two traceable governance validation pipelines are executed, each with an audit trail of work, allowing the company to demonstrate responsiveness to regulators and stakeholders. The two together explain how the enterprise-scale deployment of BMV makes global risk management a tangible, concrete reality.

Managing Trade-Offs Between Performance, Fairness, and Privacy

Even the best risk management paradigms have to confront an inevitable dilemma: competing interests. Performance, equity, and privacy are all desirable, but each will necessarily come into conflict with the others. Optimization along one dimension will necessarily contaminate the others, so people must learn to live with and balance these trade-offs rather than seek to eliminate them.

Measures of correctness, efficiency, and hardness of a model optimize performance. High-performing models have the potential to deliver state-of-the-art performance, but at the expense of processing large-scale sensitive or private data, which poses significant privacy risks. Privacy risks can be reduced by adopting privacy-preserving paradigms, such as differential privacy or federated learning. Still, this process may compromise model performance by not exposing the model to high-granularity data. Fairness-promoting interventions, such as balancing datasets or imposing fairness constraints, can occasionally involve trading off raw performance on benchmark tasks, especially when models have been trained across multiple demographic groups (Calvi et al., 2024; Malik, 2024).

To manage such trade-offs, organizations need to make trade-off governance an open and transparent process. Instead of aiming for an impossible "optimal balance," they would make use of multi-objective optimization methods, which allow models to optimize several priorities at once. In practice, this can include giving up a little accuracy in exchange for a substantial increase in fairness or giving up a little efficiency loss in exchange for robust privacy protections. Domain-specific context is also important in the healthcare industry, where the virtue is to be impartial in order to avoid discrimination; in the financial industry, confidentiality may be the most important value with strong data protection regulations.

Figure 5 represents this balance diagrammatically in the form of a triangle with the opposing corners marked performance, fairness, and privacy. There is no wish to optimize any single corner, but to achieve an arguable balance somewhere within the triangle with open, shared risks distributed around the three corners.

Figure 5. Trade-Off Triangle

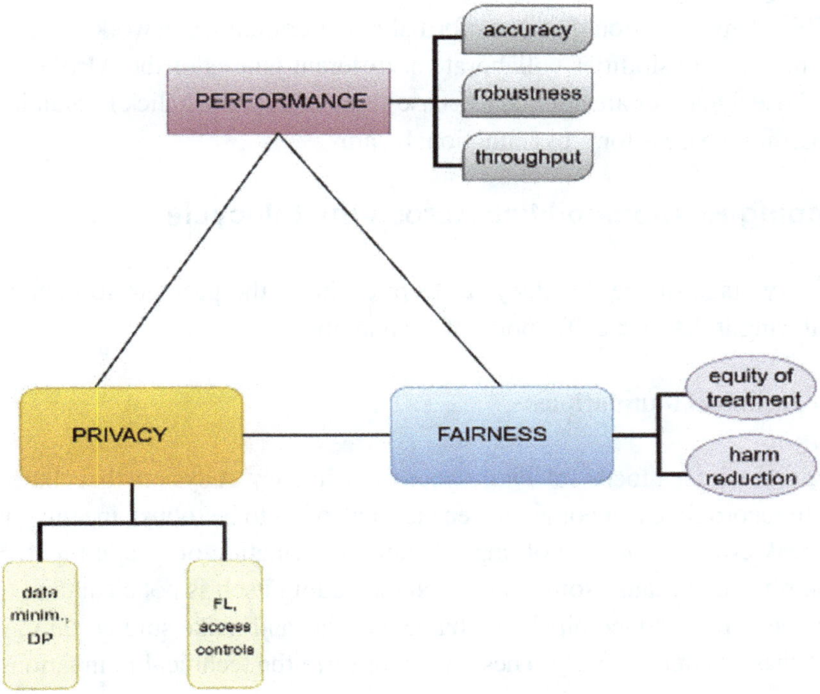

By explicitly acknowledging such trade-offs, documenting reasons for decisions, and involving diverse stakeholders in setting thresholds, organizations increase accountability and trust. Trade-off management is therefore not an afterthought technicality but a central component of end-to-end risk management, ensuring AI systems are as effective as they are socially and ethically viable.

CROSS-DISCIPLINARY COLLABORATION: ENGINEERS, ETHICISTS, POLICYMAKERS

Datasets can be carefully selected, models can be stress-tested, and models can be optimised, but all of this will be insufficient without considering larger societal issues and governing architectures. A well-designed ecosystem where engineers, ethicists, and policymakers collaborate on shared responsibility throughout the AI lifecycle yields trustworthy AI. It was not created by a brilliant engineer. Everyone has specific knowledge, and innovation won't align with legal requirements and social norms until there is ongoing collaboration.

This chapter section discusses formal collaboration frameworks for AI regulation, how responsibilities collaborate at different phases of the AI life cycle, and how those dynamics are applied to a case study of the Zero-Click Evaluation (ZCE) onboarding process for cross-functional teams.

Mapping Responsibilities Across the Lifecycle

Every stage of the AI lifecycle, from defining the problem to deploying and monitoring it, has a specific point of accountability.

- **Technical foundations:**

Engineers can't focus solely on speed or efficiency. A system that churns out results in record time is incomplete because it also has to be robust, meaning it should not break down in the face of unpredictable information or erratic input. Fairness is complicated because sometimes even the coding itself is not clear, and the engineers have to introduce pipelines that avoid bias and make sure certain groups or case types are treated fairly. These together form the technical foundations, which is laborsome because every minute detail plays an important role.

- **Ethicists:**

The world is different through the eyes of an ethicist. It does not matter exactly how fast the code runs since what matters is what it does to people. They look out for trade-offs; sometimes, some things improve by making others worse. This role pushes a project past efficiency and correctness into a broader picture: society, justice, and the human consequences of technology.

- **Policymakers:**

An ethicist sees the world differently. The speed at which the code executes is irrelevant because what matters most is what it does to people. They are there to keep an eye out for compromises. Occasionally, when one thing gets better, another gets worse. This position forces a project to look beyond correctness and efficiency and consider society, justice, and the effects of technology on people.

Significantly, all these roles shift throughout the life of a person. Legislators have a sustained function to offer checks in the long term, ethicists have a deployment and evaluation function, and engineers lead design and training.

Table 4. Mapping Cross-Disciplinary Responsibilities Across the AI Lifecycle

AI Lifecycle Stage	Engineers	Ethicists	Policymakers / Regulators
Problem Formulation	Establish goals and outline the data requirements and viability.	Recognize ethical issues and address value trade-offs at an early stage.	Establish initial compliance expectations and ensure they align with legal mandates.
Design & Development	Build algorithms, optimize data pipelines, and embed interpretability and safeguards.	Review assumptions; ensure inclusivity and transparency principles.	Establish standards and codes of practice; provide compliance guidance.
Training & Testing	Conduct robustness tests, fairness audits, and explain ability experiments.	Ensure test metrics reflect ethical principles (e.g., parity, harm reduction).	Oversee the lawful use of data; set performance thresholds to ensure safety.
Deployment	Integrate into production; monitor real-world reliability.	Consider the effects on society and identify possible danger situations..	Authorize deployments and make sure governance frameworks are followed.
Post-Deployment Monitoring	Maintain dependability by tracking drift, malfunctions, and incidents.	Evaluate the ongoing effects on society and ensure that the changing trade-offs remain acceptable.	Establish thorough reporting, conduct frequent audits, and implement efficient liability procedures to ensure continuity.

Collaboration Models for AI Governance

Without ad hoc negotiation and backroom politics, interdisciplinary collaboration will not succeed. Institutional models of partnership that include governance within the business-as-usual activity of AI development are therefore called for by organizations. A range of relevant models has been proposed:

1. Embedded Governance Teams:

Firms reduce the "translation gap" between the normative and technical spheres through embedding ethicists and policy specialists in engineering teams. Ethicists and policymakers are involved in real time, providing comments on design choices before potential risks can develop, rather than responding to systems once they have been constructed.

2. Ethics Boards and Advisory Councils:

Semi- or stand-alone boards convene multidisciplinary stakeholders to examine high-impact AI projects. Advisory councils serve as a counterbalance to organizational incentives for speed or profit over accountability because they regularly check in.

3. Orchestration Using Workflow Tools:

Governance can be applied by incorporating compliance validation and ethical barriers into automated workflows. Prefect or Airflow libraries can be configured to deploy models automatically with robustness checks, documentation validation, and fairness audits. Governance is no longer a static, point-in-time check; it becomes an automated, dynamic process.

4. Public-Private Partnerships:

Policymakers and the private sector may work together through the employment of pilot projects or sandboxes for regulations to roll out proof-of-concept innovations in a controlled and managed setting. This allows policymakers to see real implementation and provides organizations with a clear picture of what will happen with compliance.

All models are compromises.

For example,

- Proximity of embedded teams:

There are benefits to team proximity, whether physical or organizational. There is greater integrated teamwork, questions are resolved more quickly, and communication is easier. Misunderstandings can be caught by individuals early enough before they become problems. There is a fly in the ointment, however. Teams will lose their objectivity if they are too close to the company or creators. They will begin to think only from an in-house standpoint, missing threats, obstacles, and external criticism. This "capture" of an organization can quietly distorts decisions and make the system less objective, yet everyone has good intentions.

- Councils and autonomy:

Advisory councils or oversight boards rarely alter the daily process, but engineers and teams keep doing what they've been doing all the while. Councils function differently by providing people a sense that their voices do matter, that there's some control, and those decisions aren't being made unilaterally.

- Workflow orchestration:

Working procedures make the ride easy. Projects are smoothly run, approvals happen automatically, steps are transferred easily, among others. Effective procedures have possible unintended side effects at times. They may make moral or ethical choices that are far from being easy seem simple. A hard choice can be reduced to a single approval step or a checkbox.

- Public-private partnerships:

It is highly useful to partner with external partners, both public and private. There is mutual understanding. Teams speed up innovations, learn from the mistakes of others, and leverage best practices more rapidly. Such collaboration has delays. Prioritizing, planning across teams, and deciding which work various people will conduct consumes time. Slowness in reacting or responding, requiring patience and careful stewardship, can occur even when there is a stated intent.

Credibility will be imparted by a robust governance structure which includes alliances with regulators, embedded teams for operational stewardship, and councils that provide strategic direction.

Case Study: Zero-Click Evaluation (ZCE) Onboarding for Cross-Functional Teams

One great example of the requirement for interdisciplinary approaches in the domain is the introduction of interdisciplinary techniques within Zero-Click Evaluation systems. Zero-Click Evaluation enables the continuous monitoring of AI models from creation to deployment because accountability forms an intrinsic part of automation, whereas traditional evaluation techniques involve a feedback cycle that often demands expert input. Another gap in AI regulation is between technical analysis and social values, which ZCE closes. Engineers, ethicists, and policymakers within an organization operate in different silos and generally never interact. When it comes to compliance, the policymakers take over; the ethicists review it later, and the engineers think in terms of performance. ZCE breaks the challenge by being a platform that enables the three tranches to work from the start of the lifecycle.

Engineers: Embedding Technical Quality into Pipelines

For the engineers, ZCE demonstrates a shift from conventional testing procedures to immediate, automatic confirmation. They architect the testing framework in such a way that models are automatically put through robustness tests, stress tests, and fairness audits whenever they are trained or retrained. For instance:

- Stress tests emulate hostile inputs, boundary conditions, or saturation loads to measure robustness.
- Tests of robustness assess performance when bias, incompleteness, or noise are present in the data.
- Before deployment, fairness checks measure output in demographic subgroups to find bias patterns.

Instead of adding quality checking as an afterthought to the development process, engineers can use automation to make it a continuous process. Additionally, it eliminates the possibility of "last-minute patches" after significant bugs are discovered too late to be fixed.

Ethicists: Defining Normative Metrics

Ethicists convert societal values into quantifiable form, while engineers construct the technical framework. They are creating evaluation standards that go beyond accuracy and efficiency in addition to ZCE onboarding. An ethicist could ask that the system be checked for demographic parity in loan application models or harm reduction thresholds in healthcare applications.

Applying abstract ethical principles like justice, inclusivity, and dignity to measurable criteria that can be incorporated into the algorithmic gradebook is the task at hand. In this way, ethicists ensure ZCE maximizes what is technically optimal, but not merely what is socially optimal.

Furthermore, ethicists are mediators of trade-offs. For instance, accuracy may be achieved at the expense of interpretability, or at the highest speed, fairness would be compromised. Ethicists make these trade-offs explicit so that organizations intentionally choose their values, rather than falling back on technical defaults.

Policymakers: Ensuring Compliance and Public Trust

Compliance officers and policymakers contribute to the regulatory backing of ZCE. It is their duty to ensure that the automated evaluation framework aligns with legal requirements, such as the GDPR, the proposed EU AI Act, or regulations in specific industries (e.g., the authorization of medical devices).

They set performance targets that models must meet before proceeding in the pipeline. For instance:

- A model can be mandated to meet a minimum fairness score across demographic groups.
- Any change in model performance can trigger an automated review and retraining process.
- Reports on compliance generated by ZCE can be logged as part of auditable records for regulators.

Shared Accountability Through ZCE

Onboarding into the ZCE framework does more than just assign tasks; it creates shared responsibility from the ground up. All system members, whether they contribute by technical, ethical, or regulatory means, are necessary for the integrity of the system to be maintained. Engineers have a duty to implement and prove reliability, not just assume it. They monitor processes, automate audits, and design systems with a facility to explain their own actions when requested. They make dependability visible and measurable, not just "it works." It's a technical kind of truthfulness: if something went wrong, it's obvious where and why. A different perspective is given by ethicists who believe that instead of fixing the code, it is their job to maintain the system's foundation in human values. They look for ways to identify possible cases of unintentional harm and try to define what "fairness" really means in practice. To do that, concepts like "justice" and "dignity" need to be turned into concrete metrics that can be used to gauge system performance. They remind one that technology interacts with real people and is a part of society. Lastly, this picture is completed by the policymakers. They will construct the framework that ensures accountability, establishes standards, establishes boundaries, and ensures the system satisfies legal and governance requirements. In other words, they are responsible for ensuring regularity and that decisions are not made at the whim of individuals. They transform general ethical and legal standards into working guidelines that all system participants are aware of.

It is in this loop that ZCE draws its strength: the model engineers and ethicists and policymakers are not working in a separate capacity from each other; they are holding each other accountable. Because this governance is integrated at the beginning into the workflow, not an afterthought or the responsibility of one team, the system evolves constantly. Credibility is organically developed with the model. This is a quality which deepens iteration to iteration rather than a name applied later.

Figure 6. Case Study – ZCE Onboarding and Shared Accountability

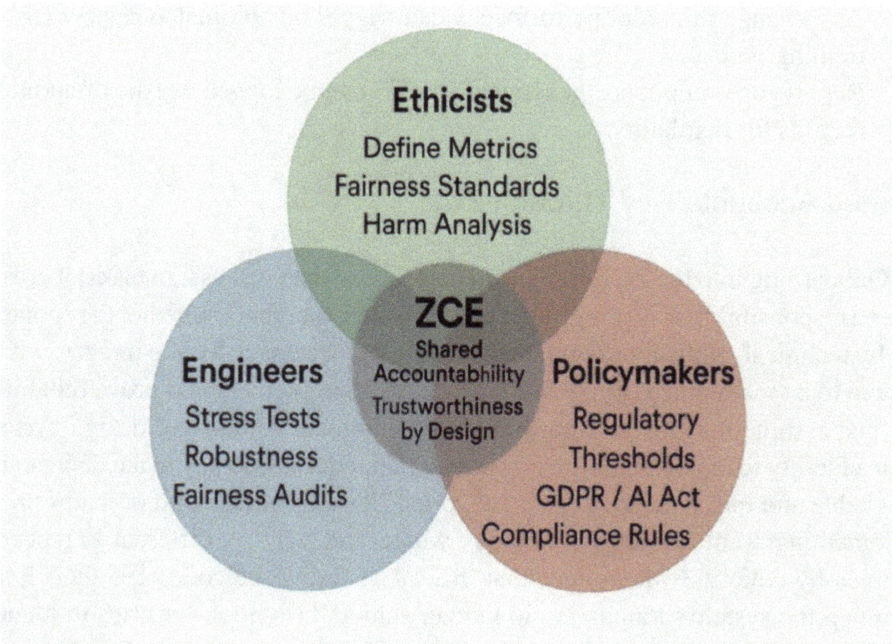

MONITORING AND CONTINUOUS IMPROVEMENT – ADAPTING TO NEW RISKS OVER TIME

One evaluation is insufficient to ensure the reliability of an AI system. Every time models are used in a dynamic environment, new risks, prejudices, and vulnerabilities appear. It is therefore essential to monitor processes and development paths that take these new issues into account. This section discusses the four main aspects of continuous monitoring and improvement.

Automated Monitoring Loops and Dashboards

Another important aspect of reliable AI is automated monitoring. Monitoring loops continuously evaluate the performance of AI models in real time for errors, anomalies, or performance drift. Among others, dashboards serve as visualization tools that show important data, such as fairness, accuracy, latency, and user engagement, at a high level to developers, operators, and decision-makers. With automated notifications from these dashboards, businesses can ensure system reliability, minimize downtime, and take prompt action in case of emerging issues.

Figure 7. Automated Monitoring Loops and Dashboards

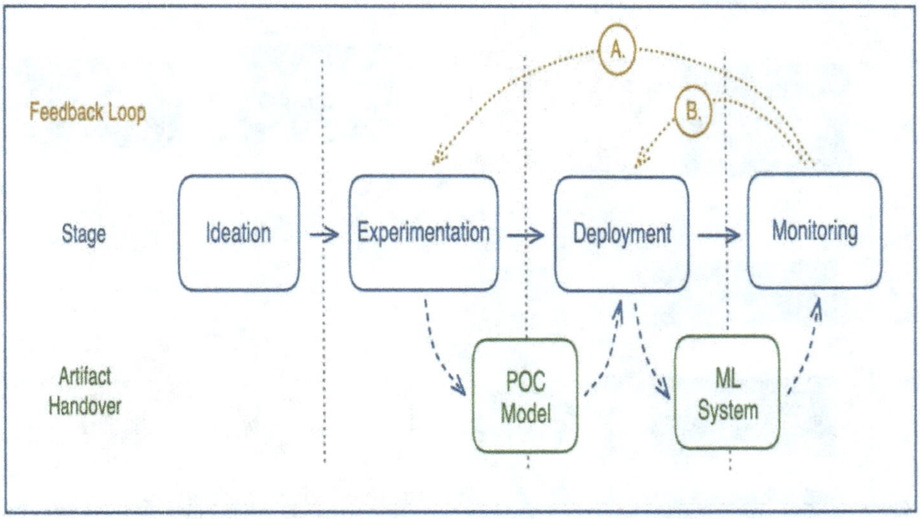

Orchestration of Evaluation Pipelines (Prefect, W&B, Databricks)

Effective orchestration options are offered by contemporary tools like Prefect, Weights & Biases (W&B), and Databricks.

Figure 8. Orchestration of Evaluation Pipelines (Prefect, W&B, Databricks)

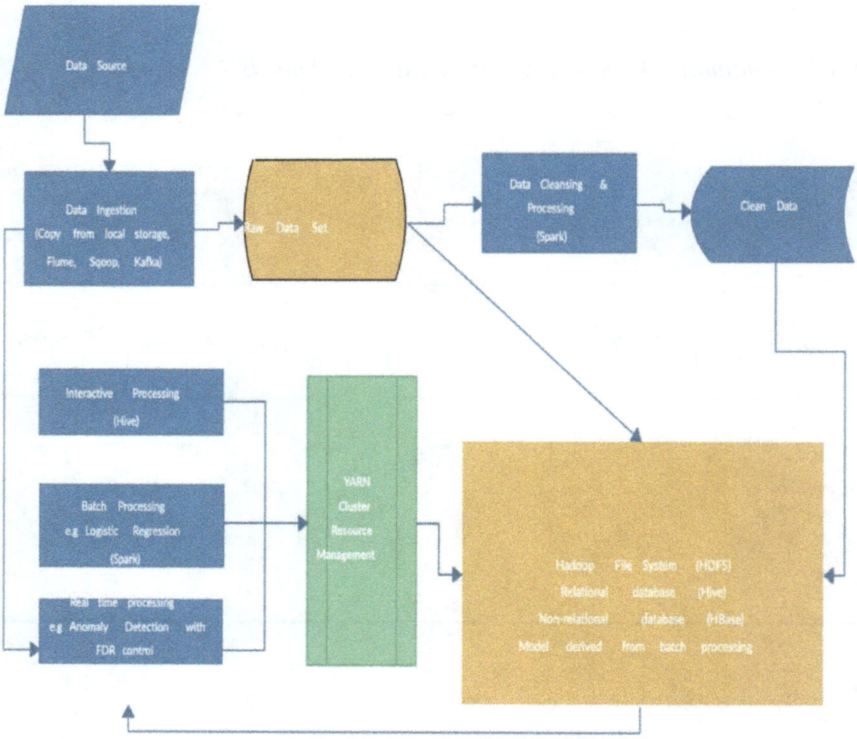

Concurrency Cleanup, Batch Execution, and Reproducibility

In practice, AI systems are required to perform multiple tasks concurrently in real-world applications. Concurrency control ensures that competing activities do not overlap one another and hence avoid resource conflicts and efficient utilization of resources. Batch processing ensures scalability to the limit by executing big amounts of data as batches rather than individually. Last but not least, reproducibility is necessary in order to guarantee trustworthiness: the same experiment with the same conditions should yield the same output. Together, concurrency cleanup, batch processing, and reproducibility security do indeed result in operational efficiency and scientific rigor in AI development.

Figure 9. Concurrency Cleanup, Batch Execution, and Reproducibility

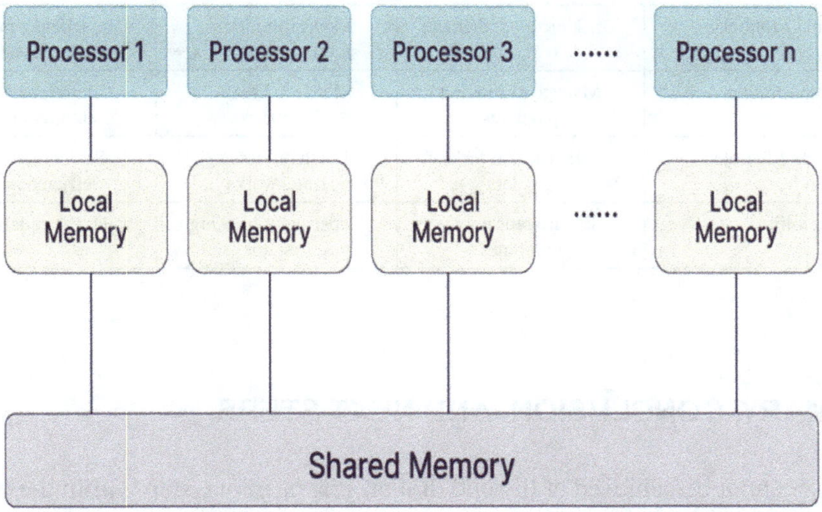

Case Study: Acrobat AI Evaluation Pipelines Supporting Millions of Users

A daily example of continuous improvement is demonstrated by Acrobat AI, which is used by millions of users worldwide. Acrobat's evaluation pipelines are designed to execute at scale, continuously monitoring user behavior, model outputs, and system performance. Self-monitoring feedback loops pick up on emergent missteps, and orchestration software facilitates efficient control of high volumes of data.

Table 5. Several aspects of Acrobat AI evaluation pipeline

Aspect	Purpose	Example Tools/ Methods	Benefit
Automated Monitoring	Track errors & drifts in real time	Monitoring loops, dashboards	Quick detection of issues
Flow Orchestration	Manage evaluation pipelines	Prefect, W&B, Databricks	Consistency & automation
Concurrency & Batch Execution	Handle parallel tasks & big data	Batch processing frameworks	Scalability & efficiency
Reproducibility	Ensure repeatable outcomes	Experiment tracking systems	Scientific reliability

SUMMARY, CONCLUSION, AND NEXT STEPS

Trust cannot be achieved at the end of a project or in one step within the workflow by creating intelligent systems; it takes constant effort throughout the stages from design to operational phases. In order for this challenge to be addressed, there has to be a lifecycle model that embeds trust, accountability, and transparency into system development right from the start. Trust, accountability, and transparency can't be retro-fitted to create informed choices at each step, from the design and development of systems all the way up to monitoring.

Having a strong end-to-end infrastructure for system lifecycle development enables integration of different levels of system development within a single framework. Unlike other system development approaches, which leave trustworthiness for last, incorporating trustworthiness from the outset means the system is already aligned with fairness, security, and trustworthiness from its early design. As a result, mechanisms within the system handle deployment while ensuring trustworthiness. System monitoring and evaluation continue with these activities by building trust during system exposure to genuine user data.

Future intelligent systems should also meet social-ethical requirements in addition to technical requirements. To achieve this, embedded control is required. This comprises factors indicating bias in the data/model, tools that help users understand the system's logic, and criteria for correct use from an ethical perspective. The objective is to develop systems that are efficient yet trusted by their users.

Ultimately, transparency, accountability, and trustworthiness in systems can only be achieved if developers take on responsibility from the conceptual level through the entire life span of the system. Taking this attitude towards these development criteria would enable developers to create trustworthy intelligent systems, well deserving of the trust humanity places in them.

REFERENCES

Calvi, A., Malgieri, G., & Kotzinos, D. (2024). The unfair side of privacy-enhancing technologies: Addressing the trade-offs between PETs and fairness. *Proceedings of the 2024 ACM Conference on Fairness, Accountability, and Transparency* (pp. 2047–2059). ACM. https://doi.org/DOI: 10.1145/3630106.3659024

Chazette, L., & Schneider, K. (2020). Explainability as a non-functional requirement: Challenges and recommendations. *Requirements Engineering*, *25*(4), 493–514. DOI: 10.1007/s00766-020-00333-1

Fikardos, M., Leperinoti, K., Apostolou, D., & Mentzas, G. (2025). Trustworthiness optimisation process: A methodology for assessing and enhancing trust in AI systems. *Electronics (Basel)*, *14*(7), 1454. DOI: 10.3390/electronics14071454

Huang, Y., Gao, C., Wu, S., Wang, H., Wang, X., Zhou, Y., Wang, Y., Ye, J., Shi, J., Zhang, Q., Li, Y., Bao, H., Liu, Z., Guan, T., Chen, D., Chen, R., Guo, K., Zou, A., Kuen-Yew, B. H., & Zhang, X. (2025). On the trustworthiness of generative foundation models: Guideline, assessment, and perspective. arXiv. https://arxiv.org/abs/2502.14296

Islam, R., Keya, K. N., Pan, S., Sarwate, A. D., & Foulds, J. R. (2023). Differential fairness: An intersectional framework for fair AI. *Entropy (Basel, Switzerland)*, *25*(4), 660. DOI: 10.3390/e25040660

Kumar, A. (2025). Towards fair sequential resource allocation: Algorithmic designs, interventions, and evaluations (Doctoral dissertation, Washington University in St. Louis). DOI: 10.7936/zf8c-9354

Lin, X. (2025). A model of big data–based governance: China's national government big data platform and an analysis of its governance competence. *Chinese Political Science Review*, *10*, 289–328. DOI: 10.1007/s41111-025-00279-1

Malik, M. S. (2024). Analyzing the trade-offs of data sharing in social networks and privacy concerns. *International Journal for Electronic Crime Investigation*, *8*(4). Advance online publication. DOI: 10.54692/ijeci.2024.0804213

Mei, J., Salim, H. A., Lakhani, D. A., Balar, A., Vagal, V., Koneru, M., Wolman, D., Xu, R., Urrutia, V., Marsh, E. B., Pulli, B., Hoseinyazdi, M., Luna, L., Deng, F., Hyson, N. Z., Shahriari, M., Dmytriw, A. A., Guenego, A., Albers, G. W., & Yedavalli, V. (2025). Integrating perfusion imaging derived venous outflow and tissue-level collateral parameters in a comprehensive clinical model enhances prognostication in large vessel occlusion stroke. *Neurotherapeutics; the Journal of the American Society for Experimental NeuroTherapeutics*, *22*(5), e00632. DOI: 10.1016/j.neurot.2025.e00632

Meseguer, P., & Plaza, E. (1994). The VALID project: Goals, development, and results. *International Journal of Intelligent Systems*, *9*(9), 867–892.

Mortaji, S. T. H., & Sadeghi, M. E. (2024). Assessing the reliability of artificial intelligence systems: Challenges, metrics, and future directions. *International Journal of Innovation in Management Economics and Social Sciences*, *4*(2), 1–13. DOI: 10.59615/ijimes.4.2.1

Nikolovski, S., & Petreska, A. (2025). Evaluating GDPR and HIPAA in the integration of ML/AI for future-proofing healthcare. In N. Filipović (Ed.), *Applied artificial intelligence 4: Medicine, biology, chemistry, financial, games, engineering (Lecture Notes in Networks and Systems, Vol. 1446)*. Springer. DOI: 10.1007/978-3-031-99201-8_30

Nooteboom, B. (2002). *Trust: Forms, foundations, functions, failures and figures*. Edward Elgar Publishing.

O'Sullivan, K., Markovic, M., Dymiter, J., Scheliga, B., Odo, C., & Wilde, K. (2025). Semi-automated data provenance tracking for transparent data production and linkage to enhance auditing and quality assurance in trusted research environments. *International Journal of Population Data Science*, *10*(2). Advance online publication. DOI: 10.23889/ijpds.v10i2.2464

Owen, A., & Samson, E. (2025). Validating AI/ML-Based Systems: Frameworks for Testing Model Accuracy, Fairness, Robustness, and Generalization in QA. https://www.researchgate.net/publication/391963634_Validating_AIML-Based_Systems_Frameworks_for_Testing_Model_Accuracy_Fairness_Robustness_and_Generalization_in_QA

Paetznick, A., da Silva, M. P., Ryan-Anderson, C., Bello-Rivas, J. M., Campora, J. P., III, Chernoguzov, A., . . . Svore, K. M. (2024). Demonstration of logical qubits and repeated error correction with better-than-physical error rates. *arXiv preprint arXiv:2404.02280*.

Pahune, S., Akhtar, Z., Mandapati, V., & Siddique, K. (2025). The importance of AI data governance in large language models. *Big Data and Cognitive Computing*, *9*(6), 147. DOI: 10.3390/bdcc9060147

Pham, T. Q. D., Tran, K. D., Nguyen, K. T. P., Tran, X. V., Köehl, L., & Tran, K. P. (2025). A new framework for prognostics in decentralized industries: Enhancing fairness, security, and transparency through blockchain and federated learning. *arXiv*. https://arxiv.org/abs/2503.05725

Pustet, M., Steffen, E., Mihaljević, H., Stanjek, G., & Illies, Y. (2025). Civil society in the loop: Feedback-driven adaptation of (L)LM-assisted classification in an open-source Telegram monitoring tool. *arXiv*. https://arxiv.org/abs/2507.06734

Sengupta, A., Seth, P., & Sankarapu, V. K. (2025). Interpretability as alignment: Making internal understanding a design principle. *arXiv*. https://arxiv.org/abs/2509.08592

Tartaro, A., Panai, E., & Cocchiaro, M. Z. (2024). AI risk assessment using ethical dimensions. *AI and Ethics*, *4*, 105–112. DOI: 10.1007/s43681-023-00368-6

Thurzo, A. (2025). Provable AI ethics and explainability in medical and educational AI agents: Trustworthy ethical firewall. *Electronics (Basel)*, *14*(7), 1294. DOI: 10.3390/electronics14071294

Vancisin, T., Orr, M., Clarke, L., & Hinrichs, U. (2025). Provenance visualization as an entry point to the history and curation of information collections. *Journal of Visualization and Interaction*, *1*(1). Advance online publication. DOI: 10.54337/jovi.v1i1.8436

Vayyala, R. (2025). Data lineage: Tracing data across systems. In *Data governance, DevSecOps, and advancements in modern software* (pp. 73–98). IGI Global. DOI: 10.4018/979-8-3373-0365-9.ch004

Yazdinejad, A., Dehghantanha, A., Karimipour, H., Srivastava, G., & Parizi, R. M. (2024). A robust privacy-preserving federated learning model against model poisoning attacks. *IEEE Transactions on Information Forensics and Security*, *19*, 6693–6708. DOI: 10.1109/TIFS.2024.3420126

Yedavalli, V., Salim, H. A., Mei, J., Lakhani, D. A., Balar, A., Musmar, B., Adeeb, N., Hoseinyazdi, M., Luna, L., Deng, F., Hyson, N. Z., Dmytriw, A. A., Guenego, A., Faizy, T. D., Heit, J. J., Albers, G. W., Lu, H., Urrutia, V. C., Nael, K., & Llinas, R. (2024). Decreased quantitative cerebral blood volume is associated with poor outcomes in large core patients. *Stroke*, *55*(10), 2409–2419. DOI: 10.1161/STROKEAHA.124.047483

Zahid, I. A. (2025). Explainability, robustness, and fairness in user-centric intelligent systems: A systematic review. *IEEE Transactions on Emerging Topics in Computational Intelligence*, *9*(6), 3728–3753. DOI: 10.1109/TETCI.2025.3567604

Compilation of References

Acar, A., Aksu, H., Uluagac, A. S., & Conti, M. (2018). A Survey on Homomorphic Encryption Schemes. *ACM Computing Surveys*, *51*(4), 1–35. DOI: 10.1145/3214303

Adebayo, J., Gilmer, J., Muelly, M., Goodfellow, I., Hardt, M., & Kim, B. (2018). Sanity checks for saliency maps. Advances in Neural Information Processing Systems, 31, 9505–9515. https://papers.nips.cc/paper_files/paper/2018/file/294a8ed24b1ad22ec2e7efea049b8737-Paper.pdf

Aliferis, C., & Simon, G. (2024). Overfitting, Underfitting and General Model Overconfidence and Under-Performance Pitfalls and Best Practices in Machine Learning and AI. In Simon, G. J., & Aliferis, C. (Eds.), *Artificial Intelligence and Machine Learning in Health Care and Medical Sciences* (pp. 477–524). Springer International Publishing., DOI: 10.1007/978-3-031-39355-6_10

Ali, S., Abuhmed, T., El-Sappagh, S., Muhammad, K., Alonso-Moral, J. M., Confalonieri, R., Guidotti, R., Del Ser, J., Díaz-Rodríguez, N., & Herrera, F. (2023). Explainable Artificial Intelligence (XAI): What we know and what is left to attain Trustworthy Artificial Intelligence. *Information Fusion*, *99*, 101805. DOI: 10.1016/j.inffus.2023.101805

Alqubaysi, T., Asmari, A. F. A., Alanazi, F., Almutairi, A., & Armghan, A. (2025). Federated Learning-Based Predictive Traffic Management Using a Contained Privacy-Preserving Scheme for Autonomous Vehicles. *Sensors (Basel)*, *25*(4), 1116–1116. DOI: 10.3390/s25041116 PMID: 40006346

Andrae, S. (2024). Explainable Artificial Intelligence in risk management: A framework. In Corazza, M., Shah Khan, F., Torre, D. La, & Masri, H. (eds.). *Artificial intelligence and beyond for finance*. World Scientific Publishing, 149–206. DOI: 10.1142/9781800615212_0004

Angwin, J., Larson, J., Mattu, S., & Kirchner, L. (2016, May 23). Machine bias: There's software used across the country to predict future criminals. And it's biased against Blacks. ProPublica. https://www.propublica.org/article/machine-bias-risk-assessments-in-criminal-sentencing

Apicella, A., Isgrò, F., & Prevete, R. (2025). Don't push the button! Exploring data leakage risks in machine learning and transfer learning. *Artificial Intelligence Review, 58*(11), 339. Advance online publication. DOI: 10.1007/s10462-025-11326-3

Arani, A. K., Le, T. H. M., Zahedi, M., & Babar, M. A. (2023). *Mitigating ML Model Decay in Continuous Integration with Data Drift Detection: An Empirical Study* (No. arXiv:2305.12736). arXiv. https://doi.org//arXiv.2305.12736DOI: 10.48550

Australian Government. (2024). Voluntary AI Safety Standard. Updated December 2, 2025. https://www.industry.gov.au/sites/default/files/2024-09/voluntary-ai-safety-standard.pdf

Aydin, C., Duygu, O. B., Karakas, A. B., Er, E., Gokmen, G., Ozturk, A. M., & Govsa, F. (2025). Clinical Failure of General-Purpose AI in Photographic Scoliosis Assessment: A Diagnostic Accuracy Study. *Medicina, 61*(8), 1342. DOI: 10.3390/medicina61081342 PMID: 40870387

Baena-Garcıa, M., del Campo-Ávila, J., Fidalgo, R., Bifet, A., Gavalda, R., & Morales-Bueno, R. (2006, September). Early drift detection method. In *Fourth international workshop on knowledge discovery from data streams* (Vol. 6, pp. 77-86).

Barocas, S., Hardt, M., & Narayanan, A. (2023). *Fairness and machine learning: Limitations and opportunities*. MIT Press.

Barocas, S., & Selbst, A. D. (2016). Big data's disparate impact. *SSRN, 104*(3), 671–732. DOI: 10.2139/ssrn.2477899

Bartlett, R., Morse, A., Stanton, R., & Wallace, N. (2022). Consumer-lending discrimination in the FinTech era. *Journal of Financial Economics, 143*(1), 30–56. DOI: 10.1016/j.jfineco.2021.05.047

Basili, V. R., Caldiera, G., & Rombach, H. D. (1994). *THE GOAL QUESTION METRIC APPROACH*. https://www.cs.umd.edu/users/mvz/handouts/gqm.pdf

Baskar, N. (2025). *Poongundran Selvaprabhu, Vivek Menon Unnikrishnan, Babu, C., Vinoth Babu Kumaravelu, Rajamani, V., Sunil Chinnadurai, & Latif, A*. Security and Privacy Issues in RIS-Based Wireless Communication Systems., DOI: 10.1002/9781394250141.ch11

Baxter, G., & Sommerville, I. (2011). Socio-technical systems: From design methods to systems engineering. *Interacting with Computers*, *23*(1), 4–17. DOI: 10.1016/j.intcom.2010.07.003

Bellamy, R. K. E., Dey, K., Hind, M., Hoffman, S. C., Houde, S., Kannan, K., … Zhang, Y. (2019). AI Fairness 360: An extensible toolkit for detecting, understanding, and mitigating unwanted algorithmic bias. IBM Journal of Research and Development, 63(4/5), 4:1–4:15. DOI: 10.1147/JRD.2019.2942287

Bender, E. M., Gebru, T., McMillan-Major, A., & Shmitchell, S. (2021). On the Dangers of Stochastic Parrots: Can Language Models Be Too Big? . *Proceedings of the 2021 ACM Conference on Fairness, Accountability, and Transparency*, 610–623. DOI: 10.1145/3442188.3445922

Biehler, M., Guermazi, M., & Starck, C. (2022). Using Knowledge Distillation to improve interpretable models in a retail banking context. *arXiv (Cornell University)*. 2209.15496

Biggio, B., & Roli, F. (2018). Wild patterns. Ten years after the rise of adversarial machine learning. Pattern Recognition, 84, 317 to 331. https://doi.org/DOI: 10.1016/j.patcog.2018.07.023

Binder, A., Montavon, G., Bach, S., Müller, K., & Samek, W. (2016). Layer-wise Relevance Propagation for Neural Networks with Local Renormalization Layers. *arXiv (Cornell University)*. 1604.00825

Blanco-Justicia, A., Sánchez, D., Domingo-Ferrer, J., & Muralidhar, K. (2022). A Critical Review on the Use (and Misuse) of Differential Privacy in Machine Learning. *ACM Computing Surveys*, *55*(8), 1–16. Advance online publication. DOI: 10.1145/3547139

Bolukbasi, T., Chang, K. W., Zou, J. Y., Saligrama, V., & Kalai, A. (2016). Man is to computer programmer as woman is to homemaker? Debiasing word embeddings. In Advances in Neural Information Processing Systems, 29.

Breiman, L. (2001). Statistical Modeling: The Two Cultures (with comments and a rejoinder by the author). *Statistical Science*, *16*(3). Advance online publication. DOI: 10.1214/ss/1009213726

Brundage, M., Avin, S., Clark, J., Toner, H., Eckersley, P., Garfinkel, B., Dafoe, A., Scharre, P., Zeitzoff, T., Filar, B., Anderson, H., Roff, H., Allen, G., Steinhardt, J., Flynn, C., Beard, S., Belfield, H., Farquhar, S., Lyle, C., & Amodei, D. (2018). The malicious use of artificial intelligence. Forecasting, prevention, and mitigation. arXiv. https://arxiv.org/abs/1802.07228

Bufi, S., Paparella, V., Anelli, V. W., & Di Noia, T. (2025). Legal but Unfair: Auditing the Impact of Data Minimization on Fairness and Accuracy Trade-off in Recommender Systems. *Proceedings of the 33rd ACM Conference on User Modeling, Adaptation and Personalization*, 114–123. DOI: 10.1145/3699682.3728356

Buolamwini, J., & Gebru, T. (2018). Gender shades: Intersectional accuracy disparities in commercial gender classification. *Proceedings of Machine Learning Research, 81*, 1–15.

Burr, C., Cristianini, N., & Ladyman, J. (2018). An analysis of the interaction between intelligent software agents and human users. *Minds and Machines, 28*(4), 735–774. DOI: 10.1007/s11023-018-9479-0 PMID: 30930542

Burrell, J. (2016). How the machine "thinks". *Big Data & Society, 3*(1), 1–12. DOI: 10.1177/2053951715622512

Bussmann, N., Giudici, P., Marinelli, D., & Papenbrock, J. (2021). Explainable machine learning in credit risk management. *Computational Economics, 57*(1), 203–216. DOI: 10.1007/s10614-020-10042-0

Calvi, A., Malgieri, G., & Kotzinos, D. (2024). The unfair side of privacy-enhancing technologies: Addressing the trade-offs between PETs and fairness. *Proceedings of the 2024 ACM Conference on Fairness, Accountability, and Transparency* (pp. 2047–2059). ACM. https://doi.org/DOI: 10.1145/3630106.3659024

Carlini, N., & Wagner, D. (2017). Towards evaluating the robustness of neural networks. Proceedings of the IEEE Symposium on Security and Privacy, 39 to 57. DOI: 10.1109/SP.2017.49

Carmichael, Z., Lohit, S., Cherian, A., Jones, M., & Scheirer, W. (2023). Pixel-Grounded prototypical part networks. *arXiv (Cornell University)*. 2309.14531

Chau, M., Rahman, M. G., & Debnath, T. (2025). From black box to clarity: Strategies for effective AI informed consent in healthcare. *Artificial Intelligence in Medicine, 167*, 103169–103169. DOI: 10.1016/j.artmed.2025.103169 PMID: 40446592

Chazette, L., & Schneider, K. (2020). Explainability as a non-functional requirement: Challenges and recommendations. *Requirements Engineering, 25*(4), 493–514. DOI: 10.1007/s00766-020-00333-1

Chen, C., Liu, J., Tan, H., Li, X., Wang, K., Li, P., Sakurai, K., & Dou, D. (2024). Trustworthy federated learning: Privacy, security, and beyond. *Knowledge and Information Systems, 67*(3), 2321–2356. DOI: 10.1007/s10115-024-02285-2

Chen, X., Sun, R., Saluz, U., Schiavon, S., & Geyer, P. (2023). Using causal inference to avoid fallouts in data-driven parametric analysis: A case study in the architecture, engineering, and construction industry. *Developments in the Built Environment, 17*, 100296. DOI: 10.1016/j.dibe.2023.100296

Chester, A., Koh, Y. S., Wicker, J., Sun, Q., & Lee, J. (2020). Balancing Utility and Fairness against Privacy in Medical Data. *2021 IEEE Symposium Series on Computational Intelligence (SSCI)*, 1226–1233. DOI: 10.1109/SSCI47803.2020.9308226

Chiaburu, T., Haußer, F., & Bießmann, F. (2024). Uncertainty in XAI: Human perception and modeling approaches. *Machine Learning & Knowledge Extraction, 6*(2), 1170–1192. DOI: 10.3390/make6020055

Chmiel, W., Kwiecień, J., & Motyka, K. (2023). Saliency Map and Deep Learning in Binary Classification of Brain Tumours. *Sensors (Basel), 23*(9), 4543. DOI: 10.3390/s23094543

Chouldechova, A. (2017). Fair prediction with disparate impact: A study of bias in recidivism prediction instruments. *Big Data, 5*(2), 153–163. DOI: 10.1089/big.2016.0047 PMID: 28632438

Christou, P. A. (2025). Reliability and Validity in Qualitative Research Revisited and the Role of AI. *The Qualitative Report*. Advance online publication. DOI: 10.46743/2160-3715/2025.7523

Chung, M. K. (2020). Introduction to logistic regression. *arXiv (Cornell University)*. 2008.13567

Cinquini, M., Beretta, I., Ruggieri, S., & Valera, I. (2024). A Practical Approach to Causal Inference over Time. *arXiv (Cornell University)*. 2410.10502

Cloud Security Alliance. (2023). AI security guidance for critical infrastructure. https://cloudsecurityalliance.org/artifacts/ai-security-guidance

Coalition for Content Provenance and Authenticity. (n.d.). C2PA specification. Content authenticity and provenance. https://c2pa.org/specifications/

Cofre, S., Sanchez, C., Quezada-Figueroa, G., & López-Cortés, X. A. (2025). Validity and accuracy of artificial intelligence-based dietary intake assessment methods: A systematic review. *British Journal of Nutrition, 133*(9), 1241–1253. DOI: 10.1017/S0007114525000522 PMID: 40207441

Cowgill, B., Dell'Acqua, F., Deng, S., Hsu, D., Verma, N., & Chaintreau, A. (2020). *Biased Programmers? Or Biased Data? A Field Experiment in Operationalizing AI Ethics*. arXiv. DOI: 10.1145/3391403.3399545

Crenshaw, K. (1991). Demarginalizing the intersection of race and sex: A Black feminist critique of antidiscrimination doctrine. *University of Chicago Legal Forum, 1989*(1), 139–167.

Cui, Y., Jia, M., Lin, T. Y., Song, Y., & Belongie, S. (2019). Class-balanced loss based on effective number of samples. In *Proceedings of the IEEE/CVF Conference on Computer Vision and Pattern Recognition (CVPR)*, 9268–9277. DOI: 10.1109/CVPR.2019.00949

Cummings, M. L. (2017). Artificial intelligence and the future of warfare. Chatham House Report. https://www.chathamhouse.org/sites/default/files/publications/research/2017-01-26-artificial-intelligence-future-warfare-cummings-final.pdf

D.j, S. (2021, March 8). *Artificial intelligence and privacy*. HeinOnline; 77 Fla. L. Rev. 1.

Dal Pozzolo, A., Boracchi, G., Caelen, O., Alippi, C., & Bontempi, G. (2018). Credit Card Fraud Detection: A Realistic Modeling and a Novel Learning Strategy. *IEEE Transactions on Neural Networks and Learning Systems, 29*(8), 3784–3797. DOI: 10.1109/TNNLS.2017.2736643 PMID: 28920909

Dastin, J. (2018, October 10). Amazon scraps secret AI recruiting tool that showed bias against women. Reuters. https://www.reuters.com/article/amazon-ai-bias-idUSKCN1MK08G

De Santi, L. A., Piparo, F. I., Bargagna, F., Santarelli, M. F., Celi, S., & Positano, V. (2024). Part-Prototype Models in Medical Imaging: Applications and Current Challenges. *BioMedInformatics, 4*(4), 2149–2172. DOI: 10.3390/biomedinformatics4040115

Dembani, R., Karvelas, I., Akbar, N. A., Rizou, S., Tegolo, D., & Fountas, S. (2025). Agricultural data privacy and federated learning: A review of challenges and opportunities. *Computers and Electronics in Agriculture, 232*, 110048. DOI: 10.1016/j.compag.2025.110048

Demelius, L., Kern, R., & Trügler, A. (2025). Recent Advances of Differential Privacy in Centralized Deep Learning: A Systematic Survey. *ACM Computing Surveys, 57*(6), 1–28. Advance online publication. DOI: 10.1145/3712000

Diana, L., Dini, P., & Paolini, D. (2025). Overview on Intrusion Detection Systems for Computers Networking Security. *Computers, 14*(3), 87. DOI: 10.3390/computers14030087

Domnik, J., & Holland, A. (2024). On Data Leakage Prevention Maturity: Adapting the C2M2 Framework. *Journal of Cybersecurity and Privacy*, *4*(2), 167–195. DOI: 10.3390/jcp4020009

Doshi-Velez, F., & Kim, B. (2017). Towards a rigorous science of interpretable machine learning. *arXiv (Cornell University)*. 1702.08608

Dwork, C., Hardt, M., Pitassi, T., Reingold, O., & Zemel, R. (2012). Fairness through awareness. In *Proceedings of the 3rd Innovations in Theoretical Computer Science Conference* (pp. 214–226). DOI: 10.1145/2090236.2090255

Endsley, M. R. (2017). From here to autonomy: Lessons learned from human–automation research. *Human Factors*, *59*(1), 5–27. DOI: 10.1177/0018720816681350 PMID: 28146676

European Commission. (2023). Regulation (EU) 2023/988 of the European Parliament and of the Council of 10 May 2023 on general product safety, amending Regulation (EU) No 1025/2012 of the European Parliament and of the Council and Directive (EU) 2020/1828 of the European Parliament and the Council, and repealing Directive 2001/95/EC of the European Parliament and of the Council and Council Directive 87/357/EEC. *Official Journal of the European Union, L, 135*(1). https://eur-lex.europa.eu/legal-content/EN/TXT/PDF/?uri=CELEX:32023R0988

European Commission. (2024a). Regulation (EU) 2024/1689 of the European Parliament and of the Council of 12 July 2024 laying down harmonised rules on artificial intelligence (Artificial Intelligence Act). *Official Journal of the European Union, L, 1689*(1). https://eur-lex.europa.eu/legal-content/EN/TXT/PDF/?uri=OJ:L_202401689

European Commission. (2024b). Directive (EU) 2024/2853 of the European Parliament and of the Council of 23 October 2024 on liability for defective products and repealing Council Directive 85/374/EEC. Official Journal of the European Union. https://eur-lex.europa.eu/legal-content/EN/TXT/PDF/?uri=OJ:L_202402853

European Union Agency for Cybersecurity. (2021). Threat landscape for artificial intelligence. https://www.enisa.europa.eu/publications/artificial-intelligence-threat-landscape

Ewald, F. K., Bothmann, L., Wright, M. N., Bischl, B., Casalicchio, G., & König, G. (2024). A guide to feature importance methods for scientific inference. *arXiv (Cornell University)*. 2404.12862

Faisal, K. (2023). Applying the Purpose Limitation Principle in Smart-City Data-Processing Practices: A European Data Protection Law Perspective. *Communication Law and Policy*, *28*(1), 1–31. DOI: 10.1080/10811680.2023.2180266

Feretzakis, G., Papaspyridis, K., Gkoulalas-Divanis, A., & Verykios, V. S. (2024). Privacy-Preserving Techniques in Generative AI and Large Language Models: A Narrative Review. *Information (Basel)*, *15*(11), 697. DOI: 10.3390/info15110697

Fernández Llorca, D., Frau, P., Parra, I., Izquierdo, R., & Gómez, E. (2024). Attribute annotation and bias evaluation in visual datasets for autonomous driving. *Journal of Big Data*, *11*(1), 137. DOI: 10.1186/s40537-024-00976-9

Fikardos, M., Leperinoti, K., Apostolou, D., & Mentzas, G. (2025). Trustworthiness optimisation process: A methodology for assessing and enhancing trust in AI systems. *Electronics (Basel)*, *14*(7), 1454. DOI: 10.3390/electronics14071454

Floridi, L., Cowls, J., Beltrametti, M., Chatila, R., Chazerand, P., Dignum, V., Luetge, C., Madelin, R., Pagallo, U., Rossi, F., Schafer, B., Valcke, P., & Vayena, E. (2018). AI4People—An ethical framework for a good AI society. *Minds and Machines*, *28*(4), 689–707. DOI: 10.1007/s11023-018-9482-5 PMID: 30930541

Ford, E., Pillinger, S., Stewart, R., Jones, K., Roberts, A., Casey, A., Goddard, K., & Nenadic, G. (2025). What is the patient re-identification risk from using de-identified clinical free text data for health research? *AI and Ethics*, *5*(5), 4441–4454. Advance online publication. DOI: 10.1007/s43681-025-00681-0 PMID: 40978336

Fredrikson, M., Jha, S., & Ristenpart, T. (2015). Model inversion attacks that exploit confidence information. *Proceedings of the ACM Conference on Computer and Communications Security*

Fritz-Morgenthal, S., Hein, B., & Papenbrock, J. (2022). Financial risk management and explainable, trustworthy, responsible AI. *Frontiers in Artificial Intelligence*, *5*, 779799. DOI: 10.3389/frai.2022.779799 PMID: 35295866

G. A.Osinachi Deborah Segun-FaladeChinekwu Somtochukwu OdionuAmazing Hope Ekeh. (2025). The role of AI in US consumer privacy: Developing new concepts for CCPA and GLBA compliance in smart services. *Gulf Journal of Advanced Business Research*, *3*(2), 549–560. DOI: 10.51594/gjabr.v3i2.97

Gabriel, I. (2020). Artificial Intelligence, Values, and Alignment. *Minds and Machines*, *30*(3), 411–437. DOI: 10.1007/s11023-020-09539-2

Gama, J., Žliobaitė, I., Bifet, A., Pechenizkiy, M., & Bouchachia, A. (2014). A survey on concept drift adaptation. ACM computing surveys (CSUR), 46(4), 1-37. 1322 to 1333. https://doi.org/DOI: 10.1145/2810103.2813677

Ganesh, P., Tran, C., Reza Shokri, & Fioretto, F. (2025). The Data Minimization Principle in Machine Learning. *ArXiv (Cornell University)*, 3075–3093. DOI: 10.1145/3715275.3732195

Geyik, S. C., Ambler, S., & Kenthapadi, K. (2019). Fairness-Aware Ranking in Search & Recommendation Systems with Application to LinkedIn Talent Search. *Proceedings of the 25th ACM SIGKDD International Conference on Knowledge Discovery & Data Mining*, 2221–2231. DOI: 10.1145/3292500.3330691

Gianfrancesco, M. A., Tamang, S., Yazdany, J., & Schmajuk, G. (2018). Potential biases in machine learning algorithms using electronic health record data. *JAMA Internal Medicine*, *178*(11), 1544–1547. DOI: 10.1001/jamainternmed.2018.3763 PMID: 30128552

Goh, W. W. B., Kabir, M. N., Yoo, S., & Wong, L. (2024). Ten quick tips for ensuring machine learning model validity. *PLoS Computational Biology*, *20*(9), e1012402. DOI: 10.1371/journal.pcbi.1012402 PMID: 39298376

Goldsteen, A., Ezov, G., Shmelkin, R., Moffie, M., & Farkash, A. (2021). Data minimization for GDPR compliance in machine learning models. *AI and Ethics*, *2*(3), 477–491. DOI: 10.1007/s43681-021-00095-8

Goodfellow, I., Shlens, J., & Szegedy, C. (2015). Explaining and harnessing adversarial examples. *International Conference on Learning Representations*. https://arxiv.org/abs/1412.6572

Goswami, R., Menon, U. V., Mitra, S. K., Deb, D., Das, P. S., Choudhury, H., & Gautam, R. V. (2025). Beyond ideal models: Non-idealities in TCAD simulations of dielectric-modulated FETs for label-free biosensing. *Frontiers in Electronics*, *6*, 1686130. Advance online publication. DOI: 10.3389/felec.2025.1686130

Gray, M., & Wu, L. (2025). Benchmarking bias in embeddings of healthcare AI models: Using SD-WEAT for detection and measurement across sensitive populations. *BMC Medical Informatics and Decision Making*, *25*(1), 258. DOI: 10.1186/s12911-025-03102-8 PMID: 40640864

Hangartner, D., Kopp, D., & Siegenthaler, M. (2021). Monitoring hiring discrimination through online recruitment platforms. *Nature*, *589*(7843), 572–576. DOI: 10.1038/s41586-020-03136-0 PMID: 33473211

Haq, M. U., Sethi, M. A. J., & Rehman, A. U. (2023). Capsule Network with Its Limitation, Modification, and Applications—A Survey. *Machine Learning and Knowledge Extraction*, *5*(3), 891–921. DOI: 10.3390/make5030047

Haque, A. K. M. B., Islam, N., & Mikalef, P. (2023). Explainable Artificial Intelligence (XAI) from a user perspective: A synthesis of prior literature and problematizing avenues for future research. *Technological Forecasting and Social Change, 186. Technological Forecasting and Social Change, 122120*, 122120. Advance online publication. DOI: 10.1016/j.techfore.2022.122120

Harding, J., & Kirk-Giannini, C. D. (2025). What is AI safety? What do we want it to be? *Philosophical Studies, 182*(7), 1495–1518. DOI: 10.1007/s11098-025-02367-z

Hardt, M., Price, E., & Srebro, N. (2016). Equality of opportunity in supervised learning. In Advances in Neural Information Processing Systems, 29, 3315–3323.

Hassija, V., Chamola, V., & Mahapatra, A. (2024). Interpreting Black-Box Models: A Review on Explainable Artificial Intelligence. *Cognitive Computation, 16*, 45–74. DOI: 10.1007/s12559-023-10179-8

He, H., & Garcia, E. A. (2009). Learning from Imbalanced Data. *IEEE Transactions on Knowledge and Data Engineering, 21*(9), 1263–1284. DOI: 10.1109/TKDE.2008.239

Helbing, D., Frey, B. S., Gigerenzer, G., Hafen, E., Hagner, M., & Hofstetter, Y.. (2019). Will democracy survive big data and artificial intelligence? In Helbing, D. (Ed.), *Towards digital enlightenment* (pp. 73–98). Springer., DOI: 10.1007/978-3-319-90869-4_7

He, M., & Chen, Y. (2025). Personal data protection in China: Progress, challenges and prospects in the age of big data and AI. *Telecommunications Policy, 49*(10), 103076–103076. DOI: 10.1016/j.telpol.2025.103076

Hinton, G. E., Vinyals, O., & Dean, J. (2015). Distilling the knowledge in a neural network. *arXiv (Cornell University)*. 1503.02531

Hoffman, R. R., Klein, G., Mueller, S. T., & Litman, J. (2018). Explaining explanation for 'Explainable Ai'. *Proceedings of the Human Factors and Ergonomics Society Annual Meeting, 62*(1), 197–201. DOI: 10.1177/1541931218621047

Holstein, K., Wortman Vaughan, J., Daumé, H., Dudik, M., & Wallach, H. (2019). Improving fairness in machine learning systems: What do industry practitioners need? In *Proceedings of the 2019 CHI Conference on Human Factors in Computing Systems* (pp. 1–16). DOI: 10.1145/3290605.3300830

Huang, Y., Gao, C., Wu, S., Wang, H., Wang, X., Zhou, Y., Wang, Y., Ye, J., Shi, J., Zhang, Q., Li, Y., Bao, H., Liu, Z., Guan, T., Chen, D., Chen, R., Guo, K., Zou, A., Kuen-Yew, B. H., & Zhang, X. (2025). On the trustworthiness of generative foundation models: Guideline, assessment, and perspective. arXiv. https://arxiv.org/abs/2502.14296

I. N. O., & M. E., A. (2025). *Integrating Privacy by Design (PbD) in the system development life cycle for enhanced data protection.* (A. F. C, Ed.). Gulf Journal of Advance Business Research; World Journal of Advanced Research and Reviews, 26(01), 1233-1240.

Islam, R., Keya, K. N., Pan, S., Sarwate, A. D., & Foulds, J. R. (2023). Differential fairness: An intersectional framework for fair AI. *Entropy (Basel, Switzerland), 25*(4), 660. DOI: 10.3390/e25040660

ISO/IEC. (2020). IEC TR 24028: Artificial intelligence – Overview of trustworthiness in AI. https://www.iso.org/standard/77608.html

Jacobs, M., Pradier, M. F., McCoy, T. H., Doshi-Velez, F., & Gajos, K. Z. (2021). How machine-learning recommendations influence clinician treatment selections. *Translational Psychiatry, 11*(1), 108. DOI: 10.1038/s41398-021-01224-x PMID: 33542191

Jobin, A., Ienca, M., & Vayena, E. (2019). The global landscape of AI ethics guidelines. *Nature Machine Intelligence, 1*(9), 389–399. DOI: 10.1038/s42256-019-0088-2

Jones, M. L., Kaufman, E., & Edenberg, E. (2018). AI and the Ethics of Automating Consent. *IEEE Security and Privacy, 16*(3), 64–72. DOI: 10.1109/MSP.2018.2701155

Kamiran, F., & Calders, T. (2012). Data preprocessing techniques for classification without discrimination. *Knowledge and Information Systems, 33*(1), 1–33. DOI: 10.1007/s10115-011-0463-8

Khosravi, M., Herandi, Y., Tabatabaei Far, S. S., Vasokolaei, G. R., Nejad, F. Y., Bouzarjomehri, H., Izadi, R., Zare, Z., Abdollahzade, M., Rahmani, H., & Ahmadi Marzaleh, M. (2025). Psychometric properties of an Iranian instrument for assessing adherence to ethical principles in the use of artificial intelligence among healthcare providers. *International Journal of Medical Informatics, 203*, 106019. DOI: 10.1016/j.ijmedinf.2025.106019 PMID: 40582296

Kim, B., Wattenberg, M., Gilmer, J., Cai, C., Wexler, J., Viegas, F. & sayres, R. (2018). Interpretability Beyond Feature Attribution: Quantitative Testing with Concept Activation Vectors (TCAV). Proceedings of the 35th International Conference on Machine Learning, in Proceedings of Machine Learning Research 80:2668-2677 Available from https://proceedings.mlr.press/v80/kim18d.html

Kleinberg, J., Ludwig, J., Mullainathan, S., & Rambachan, A. (2018). Algorithmic fairness. *AEA Papers and Proceedings. American Economic Association, 108*, 22–27. DOI: 10.1257/pandp.20181018

Kleinberg, J., Mullainathan, S., & Raghavan, M. (2018). Inherent trade-offs in the fair determination of risk scores. In *Proceedings of the 8th Innovations in Theoretical Computer Science Conference* (pp. 43:1–43:23). DOI: 10.4230/LIPIcs.ITCS.2017.43

Koopman, P., & Wagner, M. (2017). Autonomous vehicle safety: An interdisciplinary challenge. *IEEE Intelligent Transportation Systems Magazine*, *9*(1), 90–96. DOI: 10.1109/MITS.2016.2583491

Kroll, J. A., Huey, J., Barocas, S., Felten, E. W., Reidenberg, J. R., & Robinson, D. G.. (2017). Accountable algorithms. *University of Pennsylvania Law Review*, *165*(3), 633–705. https://scholarship.law.upenn.edu/penn_law_review/vol165/iss3/3

Kuchibhotla, A. K., Brown, L. D., Buja, A., & Cai, J. (2019). All of linear regression. *arXiv (Cornell University)*. 1910.06386

Kumar, A. (2025). Towards fair sequential resource allocation: Algorithmic designs, interventions, and evaluations (Doctoral dissertation, Washington University in St. Louis). DOI: 10.7936/zf8c-9354

Kusner, M. J., Loftus, J., Russell, C., & Silva, R. (2017). Counterfactual fairness. In Advances in Neural Information Processing Systems, 30, 4066–4076.

Lay, W., Gasparini, L., Siero, W., & Hughes, E. K. (2024). A rapid review of the benefits and challenges of dynamic consent. *Research Ethics*, *21*(1), 180–202. Advance online publication. DOI: 10.1177/17470161241278064

Lee, C. H., Lim, K. H., & Eswaran, S. (2025). A comprehensive survey on secure healthcare data processing with homomorphic encryption: Attacks and defenses. *Discover Public Health*, *22*(1), 137. Advance online publication. DOI: 10.1186/s12982-025-00505-w

Lee, J. D., & See, K. A. (2004). Trust in automation: Designing for appropriate reliance. *Human Factors*, *46*(1), 50–80. DOI: 10.1518/hfes.46.1.50.30392 PMID: 15151155

Lee, J., & Lee, K. H. (2025). Balancing Privacy and Utility in Artificial Intelligence-Based Clinical Decision Support: Empirical Evaluation Using De-Identified Electronic Health Record Data. *Applied Sciences (Basel, Switzerland), 15*(19), 10857. DOI: 10.3390/app151910857

Leveson, N. (2011). *Engineering a safer world: Systems thinking applied to safety*. MIT Press.

Lim, S., & Oh, J. (2025). Navigating Privacy: A Global Comparative Analysis of Data Protection Laws. *IET Information Security, 2025*(1). DOI: 10.1049/ise2/5536763

Lin, X. (2025). A model of big data–based governance: China's national government big data platform and an analysis of its governance competence. *Chinese Political Science Review, 10*, 289–328. DOI: 10.1007/s41111-025-00279-1

Lipton, Z. C. (2016). The mythos of model interpretability. *arXiv (Cornell University)*. 1606.03490

Lipton, Z. C. (2018). The mythos of model interpretability. *ACM Queue; Tomorrow's Computing Today, 16*(3), 31–57. DOI: 10.1145/3236386.3241340

Liu, X., Wang, J., Xiong, X., & Sun, H. (2025). Federated learning data protection scheme based on personalized differential privacy in psychological evaluation. *Neurocomputing, 611*, 128653. DOI: 10.1016/j.neucom.2024.128653

Liu, Y., Huang, J., Li, Y., Wang, D., & Xiao, B. (2024). Generative AI model privacy: A survey. *Artificial Intelligence Review, 58*(1), 33. Advance online publication. DOI: 10.1007/s10462-024-11024-6

Lou, Y., Caruana, R., & Gehrke, J. (2012). Intelligible models for classification and regression. *Proceedings of the 18th ACM SIGKDD International Conference on Knowledge Discovery and Data Mining*, 150–158.

Lum, K., & Isaac, W. (2016). To predict and serve? *Significance, 13*(5), 14–19. DOI: 10.1111/j.1740-9713.2016.00960.x

M, G., & M.J, N. (2019). *Data Leakage Prevention for Data in Transit using Artificial Intelligence and Encryption Techniques | IEEE Conference Publication | IEEE Xplore*. Ieeexplore.ieee.org. https://ieeexplore.ieee.org/abstract/document/9036839

M. A, H., A, A., R.K, C., R, D., & M.J, R. (2021). *Differential privacy for IoT-enabled critical infrastructure: A comprehensive survey*. Ieeexplore.ieee.org;IEEE Access, 9. https://ieeexplore.ieee.org/abstract/document/9594795

Malik, M. S. (2024). Analyzing the trade-offs of data sharing in social networks and privacy concerns. *International Journal for Electronic Crime Investigation*, *8*(4). Advance online publication. DOI: 10.54692/ijeci.2024.0804213

Margot, V., & Luta, G. (2021). A New Method to Compare the Interpretability of Rule-Based Algorithms. *AI*, *2*(4), 621–635. DOI: 10.3390/ai2040037

Mariappan, R. (2025). Extensive review of literature on Explainable AI (XAI) in healthcare applications. *Recent Advances in Computer Science and Communications*, *18*(1), e200324228159. Advance online publication. DOI: 10.2174/0126662558296699240314055348

Medicine, N. A. of, Series, T. L. H. S., Whicher, D., Ahmed, M., Israni, S. T., & Matheny, M. (2023). ARTIFICIAL INTELLIGENCE MODEL DEVELOPMENT AND VALIDATION. In *Artificial Intelligence in Health Care: The Hope, the Hype, the Promise, the Peril*. National Academies Press (US). https://www.ncbi.nlm.nih.gov/books/NBK605948/

Mehrabi, N., Morstatter, F., Saxena, N., Lerman, K., & Galstyan, A. (2021). A survey on bias and fairness in machine learning. *ACM Computing Surveys*, *54*(6), 1–35. DOI: 10.1145/3457607

Mei, J., Salim, H. A., Lakhani, D. A., Balar, A., Vagal, V., Koneru, M., Wolman, D., Xu, R., Urrutia, V., Marsh, E. B., Pulli, B., Hoseinyazdi, M., Luna, L., Deng, F., Hyson, N. Z., Shahriari, M., Dmytriw, A. A., Guenego, A., Albers, G. W., & Yedavalli, V. (2025). Integrating perfusion imaging derived venous outflow and tissue-level collateral parameters in a comprehensive clinical model enhances prognostication in large vessel occlusion stroke. *Neurotherapeutics; the Journal of the American Society for Experimental NeuroTherapeutics*, *22*(5), e00632. DOI: 10.1016/j.neurot.2025.e00632

Meng, C., Trinh, L., Xu, N., Enouen, J., & Liu, Y. (2022). Interpretability and fairness evaluation of deep learning models on MIMIC-IV dataset. *Scientific Reports*, *12*(1), 7166. DOI: 10.1038/s41598-022-11012-2 PMID: 35504931

Menon, U. V., & Selvaprabhu, P. (2024). A novel unified interference management scheme for multicellular MIMO communication with instantaneous relay. *International Journal of Communication Systems*, *37*(17), e5923. Advance online publication. DOI: 10.1002/dac.5923

Mersha, M., Lam, K., Wood, J., AlShami, A., & Kalita, J. (2024). Explainable Artificial Intelligence: A survey of needs, techniques, applications, and future direction. *Neurocomputing*, *599*, 128111. DOI: 10.1016/j.neucom.2024.128111

Meseguer, P., & Plaza, E. (1994). The VALID project: Goals, development, and results. *International Journal of Intelligent Systems*, *9*(9), 867–892.

Microsoft. (2022). Responsible AI standard v2. https://www.microsoft.com/ai/responsible-ai

Miller, T. (2019). Explanation in Artificial Intelligence: Insights from the social sciences. *Artificial Intelligence*, *267*, 1–38. DOI: 10.1016/j.artint.2018.07.007

Mitchell, M., Wu, S., Zaldivar, A., Barnes, P., Vasserman, L., & Hutchinson, B.. (2019). Model cards for model reporting. *Proceedings of the Conference on Fairness, Accountability, and Transparency*, 220–229. DOI: 10.1145/3287560.3287596

MITRE Corporation. (n.d.). MITRE ATLAS. Adversarial threat landscape for artificial intelligence systems. https://atlas.mitre.org/

Mittelstadt, B. D., Allo, P., Taddeo, M., Wachter, S., & Floridi, L. (2016). The ethics of algorithms. *Big Data & Society*, *3*(2), 2053951716679679. Advance online publication. DOI: 10.1177/2053951716679679

Miyashita, H. (2020). Human-centric data protection laws and policies: A lesson from Japan. *Computer Law & Security Review*, *40*, 105487. DOI: 10.1016/j.clsr.2020.105487

Mohammadi, S., Balador, A., Sinaei, S., & Flammini, F. (2024). Balancing Privacy and Performance in Federated Learning: A Systematic Literature Review on Methods and Metrics. *Journal of Parallel and Distributed Computing*, *192*, 104918–104918. DOI: 10.1016/j.jpdc.2024.104918

Molnar, C. (2022). Interpretable machine learning (2nd ed.). Lulu.com. https://christophm.github.io/interpretable-ml-book/

Moraliyage, H., Kulawardana, G., De Silva, D., Issadeen, Z., Manic, M., & Katsura, S. (2025). Explainable Artificial Intelligence with Integrated Gradients for the Detection of Adversarial Attacks on Text Classifiers. *Applied System Innovation*, *8*(1), 17. DOI: 10.3390/asi8010017

Mortaji, S. T. H., & Sadeghi, M. E. (2024). Assessing the reliability of artificial intelligence systems: Challenges, metrics, and future directions. *International Journal of Innovation in Management Economics and Social Sciences*, *4*(2), 1–13. DOI: 10.59615/ijimes.4.2.1

Musa, A., Prasad, R., & Hernandez, M. (2025). Addressing cross-population domain shift in chest X-ray classification through supervised adversarial domain adaptation. *Scientific Reports*, *15*(1), 11383. DOI: 10.1038/s41598-025-95390-3 PMID: 40181036

Mussi, M., Metelli, A. M., Restelli, M., Losapio, G., Bessa, R. J., Boos, D., Borst, C., Leto, G., Castagna, A., Chavarriaga, R., Dias, D., Egli, A., Eisenegger, A., El Manyari, Y., Fuxjäger, A., Geraldes, J., Hamouche, S., Hassouna, M., Lemetayer, B., & Zanotti, G. (2025). Human-AI interaction in safety-critical network infrastructures. *iScience*, *28*(9), 113400. DOI: 10.1016/j.isci.2025.113400 PMID: 40995130

Mylius, S., & Bernardi, J. (2024). Scalable AI incident classification. November 26, 2024. https://simonmylius.com/blog/incident-classification

Myllyaho, L., Raatikainen, M., Männistö, T., Mikkonen, T., & Nurminen, J. K. (2021). Systematic literature review of validation methods for AI systems. *Journal of Systems and Software*, *181*, 111050. DOI: 10.1016/j.jss.2021.111050

Naresh, V. S., & Thamarai, M. (2023). Privacy-preserving data mining and machine learning in healthcare: Applications, challenges, and solutions. *Wiley Interdisciplinary Reviews. Data Mining and Knowledge Discovery*, *13*(2), e1490. Advance online publication. DOI: 10.1002/widm.1490

National Institute of Standards and Technology. (2020). Adversarial machine learning. A taxonomy and terminology of attacks and mitigations (NIST IR 8269). U.S. Department of Commerce. https://nvlpubs.nist.gov/nistpubs/ir/2020/NIST.IR.8269.pdf

National Institute of Standards and Technology. (2023). AI risk management framework 1.0. U.S. Department of Commerce. https://www.nist.gov/itl/ai-risk-management-framework

Nawaz, U., Anees-Ur-Rahaman, M., & Saeed, Z. (2025). A review of Neuro-Symbolic AI integrating reasoning and learning for advanced cognitive systems. *Intelligent Systems with Applications*, *200541*. Advance online publication. DOI: 10.1016/j.iswa.2025.200541

Nicolson, A., Bradburn, E., Gal, Y., Papageorghiou, A. T., & Noble, J. A. (2025). The human factor in Explainable Artificial Intelligence: Clinician variability in trust, reliance, and performance. *npj. Digital Medicine*, *8*(1), 658. DOI: 10.1038/s41746-025-02023-0 PMID: 41238825

Nikolovski, S., & Petreska, A. (2025). Evaluating GDPR and HIPAA in the integration of ML/AI for future-proofing healthcare. In N. Filipović (Ed.), *Applied artificial intelligence 4: Medicine, biology, chemistry, financial, games, engineering (Lecture Notes in Networks and Systems, Vol. 1446)*. Springer. DOI: 10.1007/978-3-031-99201-8_30

NIST. (2023). AI Risk Management Framework (AI RMF 1.0). https://nvlpubs.nist.gov/nistpubs/ai/nist.ai.100-1.pdf

Nooteboom, B. (2002). *Trust: Forms, foundations, functions, failures and figures*. Edward Elgar Publishing.

Nori, H., Caruana, R., Bu, Z., Shen, J. H., & Kulkarni, J. (2021). Accuracy, interpretability, and differential privacy via explainable boosting. *arXiv (Cornell University)*. 2106.09680

O'Neil, C. (2016). *Weapons of math destruction: How Big Data increases inequality and threatens democracy*. Crown.

O'Sullivan, K., Markovic, M., Dymiter, J., Scheliga, B., Odo, C., & Wilde, K. (2025). Semi-automated data provenance tracking for transparent data production and linkage to enhance auditing and quality assurance in trusted research environments. *International Journal of Population Data Science*, *10*(2). Advance online publication. DOI: 10.23889/ijpds.v10i2.2464

Obermeyer, Z., Powers, B., Vogeli, C., & Mullainathan, S. (2019). Dissecting racial bias in an algorithm used to manage the health of populations. *Science*, *366*(6464), 447–453. DOI: 10.1126/science.aax2342 PMID: 31649194

OECD. (2019). OECD Principles on Artificial Intelligence. https://www.oecd.org/en/topics/ai-principles.html

Open, A. I. (2023). GPT 4 system card and safety evaluations. https://openai.com/research/gpt-4

Organisation for Economic Co operation and Development. (2019). OECD principles on artificial intelligence. https://oecd.ai/en/ai-principles

Owen, A., & Samson, E. (2025). Validating AI/ML-Based Systems: Frameworks for Testing Model Accuracy, Fairness, Robustness, and Generalization in QA. https://www.researchgate.net/publication/391963634_Validating_AIML-Based_Systems_Frameworks_for_Testing_Model_Accuracy_Fairness_Robustness_and_Generalization_in_QA

Paetznick, A., da Silva, M. P., Ryan-Anderson, C., Bello-Rivas, J. M., Campora, J. P., III, Chernoguzov, A., . . . Svore, K. M. (2024). Demonstration of logical qubits and repeated error correction with better-than-physical error rates. *arXiv preprint arXiv:2404.02280.*

Pahune, S., Akhtar, Z., Mandapati, V., & Siddique, K. (2025). The importance of AI data governance in large language models. *Big Data and Cognitive Computing*, *9*(6), 147. DOI: 10.3390/bdcc9060147

Papagiannidis, E., Mikalef, P., & Conboy, K. (2025). Responsible artificial intelligence governance: A review and research framework. *The Journal of Strategic Information Systems*, *34*(2), 101885. DOI: 10.1016/j.jsis.2024.101885

Papernot, N., McDaniel, P., Sinha, A., & Wellman, M. (2018). SoK. Security and privacy in machine learning. Proceedings of the IEEE European Symposium on Security and Privacy, 399 to 414. DOI: 10.1109/EuroSP.2018.00031

Parasuraman, R., & Riley, V. (1997). Humans and automation. *Human Factors*, *39*(2), 230–253. DOI: 10.1518/001872097778543886 PMID: 18689061

Park, & A, H. (2025). *The DtMin Protocol: Implementing Data Minimization Principles in Medical Information Sharing*. Electronics.

Parycek, P., Schmid, V., & Novak, A.-S. (2023). Artificial Intelligence (AI) and Automation in Administrative Procedures: Potentials, Limitations, and Framework Conditions. *Journal of the Knowledge Economy*, *15*(2), 8390–8415. DOI: 10.1007/s13132-023-01433-3

Patrick, M. K., Adekoya, A. F., Mighty, A. A., & Edward, B. Y. (2019). Capsule Networks – A survey. *Journal of King Saud University. Computer and Information Sciences*, *34*(1), 1295–1310. DOI: 10.1016/j.jksuci.2019.09.014

Pearl, J., & Mackenzie, D. (2018). *The book of why: The new science of cause and effect*. Basic Books.

Perrow, C. (1999). *Normal accidents: Living with high risk technologies*. Princeton University Press.

Pham, T. Q. D., Tran, K. D., Nguyen, K. T. P., Tran, X. V., Köehl, L., & Tran, K. P. (2025). A new framework for prognostics in decentralized industries: Enhancing fairness, security, and transparency through blockchain and federated learning. *arXiv*. https://arxiv.org/abs/2503.05725

Pitoura, E., Stefanidis, K., & Koutrika, G. (2022). Fairness in rankings and recommendations: An overview. *The VLDB Journal, 31*(3), 431–458. DOI: 10.1007/s00778-021-00697-y

Pleiss, G., Raghavan, M., Wu, F., Kleinberg, J., & Weinberger, K. Q. (2017). On fairness and calibration. In Advances in Neural Information Processing Systems, 30, 5680–5689.

Plumb, G., Al-Shedivat, M., Cabrera, A. A., Perer, A., Xing, E., & Talwalkar, A. (2019). Regularizing black-box models for improved interpretability. *arXiv (Cornell University).* 1902.06787

Poursabzi-Sangdeh, F., Goldstein, D. G., Hofman, J. M., Wortman Vaughan, J., & Wallach, H. (2021). Manipulating and measuring model interpretability. *Proceedings of the 2021 CHI Conference on Human Factors in Computing Systems*, 1–15. DOI: 10.1145/3411764.3445315

Prabowo, S., Putrada, A. G., Oktaviani, I. D., Abdurohman, M., Janssen, M., Nuha, H. H., & Sutikno, S. (2025). Privacy-Preserving Tools and Technologies: Government Adoption and Challenges. *IEEE Access : Practical Innovations, Open Solutions, 13*, 1–1. DOI: 10.1109/ACCESS.2025.3540878

Pustet, M., Steffen, E., Mihaljević, H., Stanjek, G., & Illies, Y. (2025). Civil society in the loop: Feedback-driven adaptation of (L)LM-assisted classification in an open-source Telegram monitoring tool. *arXiv*. https://arxiv.org/abs/2507.06734

Quinlan, J. R. (1986). Induction of decision trees. *Machine Learning*, *1*(1), 81–106. DOI: 10.1007/bf00116251

Ragab, M., Ashary, E. B., Alghamdi, B. M., Aboalela, R., Alsaadi, N., Maghrabi, L. A., & Allehaibi, K. H. (2025). Advanced artificial intelligence with federated learning framework for privacy-preserving cyberthreat detection in IoT-assisted sustainable smart cities. *Scientific Reports*, *15*(1), 4470. Advance online publication. DOI: 10.1038/s41598-025-88843-2 PMID: 39915579

Rainer Mühlhoff, & Ruschemeier, H. (2024). Updating Purpose Limitation for AI: A normative approach from law and philosophy. *Social Science Research Network.* DOI: 10.2139/ssrn.4711621

Raji, I. D., & Buolamwini, J. (2019). Actionable auditing: Investigating the impact of publicly naming biased performance results of commercial AI products. Proceedings of the AAAI/ACM Conference on AI, Ethics, and Society, 429–435. https://dam-prod.media.mit.edu/x/2019/01/24/AIES-19_paper_223.pdf

Raji, I. D., Smart, A., White, R. N., Mitchell, M., Gebru, T., & Hutchinson, B.. (2020). Closing the AI accountability gap: Defining an end-to-end framework for internal algorithmic auditing. *Proceedings of the Conference on Fairness, Accountability, and Transparency*, 33–44. DOI: 10.1145/3351095.3372873

Rajkomar, A., Hardt, M., Howell, M. D., Corrado, G., & Chin, M. H. (2018). Ensuring fairness in machine learning to advance health equity. *Annals of Internal Medicine, 169*(12), 866–872. DOI: 10.7326/M18-1990 PMID: 30508424

Ranjitsingh, L. M., & Rao, T. V. S. (2025). Establish legal and regulatory standards for the testing and validation of AI systems to ensure their reliability and safety in operational environments. *International Journal of System Assurance Engineering and Management, 16*(10), 3338–3353. Advance online publication. DOI: 10.1007/s13198-025-02865-7

Ray, P. P. (2023). Benchmarking, ethical alignment, and evaluation framework for conversational AI: Advancing responsible development of ChatGPT. *BenchCouncil Transactions on Benchmarks. Standards and Evaluations, 3*(3), 100136. DOI: 10.1016/j.tbench.2023.100136

Reisman, D., Schultz, J., Crawford, K., & Whittaker, M. (2018). *Algorithmic impact assessments: A practical framework for public agency accountability*. AI Now Institute.

Renn, O. (2008). *Risk governance: Coping with uncertainty in a complex world.* Routledge.

Rhea, A. K., Markey, K., D'Arinzo, L., Schellmann, H., Sloane, M., Squires, P., Arif Khan, F., & Stoyanovich, J. (2022). An external stability audit framework to test the validity of personality prediction in AI hiring. *Data Mining and Knowledge Discovery, 36*(6), 2153–2193. DOI: 10.1007/s10618-022-00861-0 PMID: 36161238

Ribeiro, M. T., Singh, S., & Guestrin, C. (2016). 'Why should I trust you?' Explaining the predictions of any classifier. Proceedings of the 22nd ACM SIGKDD International Conference on Knowledge Discovery and Data Mining, 1135–1144. DOI: 10.1145/2939672.2939778

Rudin, C. (2018). Stop explaining black box machine learning models for high stakes decisions and use interpretable models instead. *arXiv (Cornell University).* 1811.10154

Rudin, C., Chen, C., Chen, Z., Huang, H., Semenova, L., & Zhong, C. (2022). Interpretable machine learning: Fundamental principles and 10 grand challenges. *Statistics Surveys, 16*. DOI: 10.1214/21-ss133

Rudin, C. (2019). Stop explaining black box machine learning models for high stakes decisions and use interpretable models instead. *Nature Machine Intelligence*, *1*(5), 206–215. DOI: 10.1038/s42256-019-0048-x PMID: 35603010

Ruiz Mendoza, K. K., Pedroza Zúñiga, L. H., & López García, A. Y. (2024). Validity in evaluation: Where is the argument-based approach heading? *Sapienza: International Journal of Interdisciplinary Studies*, *5*(3), e24048. DOI: 10.51798/sijis.v5i3.792

Russell, S. (2019). *Human compatible: Artificial Intelligence and the problem of control*. Viking.

Russell, S., & Norvig, P. (2021). *Artificial intelligence: A modern approach* (4th ed.). Pearson.

S, S., S, A., S. M, H., & R., D. (2023). *A Survey of Privacy Risks and Mitigation Strategies in the Artificial Intelligence Life Cycle | IEEE Journals & Magazine | IEEE Xplore*. Ieeexplore.ieee.org;

Saarela, M., & Jauhiainen, S. (2021). Comparison of feature importance measures as explanations for classification models. *SN Applied Sciences*, *3*, 272. DOI: 10.1007/s42452-021-04148-9

Salhab, W., Ameyed, D., Jaafar, F., & Mcheick, H. (2024). A Systematic Literature Review on AI Safety: Identifying Trends, Challenges, and Future Directions. *IEEE Access : Practical Innovations, Open Solutions*, *12*, 131762–131784. DOI: 10.1109/ACCESS.2024.3440647

Scheider, S., & Verstegen, J. A. (2024). What Is a Spatio-Temporal Model Good For?: Validity as a Function of Purpose and the Questions Answered by a Model [Application/pdf]. *LIPIcs, Volume 315, COSIT 2024, 315*, 7:1-7:23. DOI: 10.4230/LIPICS.COSIT.2024.7

Schmidt Batista, A. (2025). AI in HealthTech: Building HIPAA-Compliant Solutions for Next-Generation Medical Documentation. *Journal of Next-Generation Research 5.0*. DOI: 10.70792/jngr5.0.v1i4.124

Sculley, D., Holt, G., Golovin, D., Davydov, E., Phillips, T., & al Ebneret, D. (2015). Hidden technical debt in machine learning systems. Advances in Neural Information Processing Systems, 2503–2511. https://proceedings.neurips.cc/paper_files/paper/2015/file/86df7dcfd896fcaf2674f757a2463eba-Paper.pdf

Selbst, A. D., Boyd, D., Friedler, S. A., Venkatasubramanian, S., & Vertesi, J. (2019). Fairness and abstraction in sociotechnical systems. *Proceedings of the Conference on Fairness, Accountability, and Transparency*, 59–68. DOI: 10.1145/3287560.3287598

Selvaraju, R. R., Cogswell, M., Das, A., Vedantam, R., Parikh, D., & Batra, D. (2017). Grad-CAM: Visual Explanations from Deep Networks via Gradient-Based Localization. *2017 IEEE International Conference on Computer Vision (ICCV)*, 618-626. DOI: 10.1109/ICCV.2017.74

Sengupta, A., Seth, P., & Sankarapu, V. K. (2025). Interpretability as alignment: Making internal understanding a design principle. *arXiv*. https://arxiv.org/abs/2509.08592

Shah, A., Sivakumar, S., & N, P. (2025). Encrypted Intelligence: A Comparative Analysis of Homomorphic Encryption Frameworks for Privacy-Preserving AI. *Journal of Economy and Technology*, *4*, 252–265. Advance online publication. DOI: 10.1016/j.ject.2025.08.001

Shokri, R., Stronati, M., Song, C., & Shmatikov, V. (2017). Membership inference attacks against machine learning models. Proceedings of the IEEE Symposium on Security and Privacy, 3 to 18. https://doi.org/DOI: 10.1109/SP.2017.41

Shukla, S., Rajkumar, S., Sinha, A., Esha, M., Elango, K., & Sampath, V. (2025). Federated learning with differential privacy for breast cancer diagnosis enabling secure data sharing and model integrity. *Scientific Reports*, *15*(1), 13061. Advance online publication. DOI: 10.1038/s41598-025-95858-2 PMID: 40240790

Sigut, J., Fumero, F., Estévez, J., Alayón, S., & Díaz-Alemán, T. (2024). In-Depth Evaluation of Saliency Maps for Interpreting Convolutional Neural Network Decisions in the Diagnosis of Glaucoma Based on Fundus Imaging. *Sensors (Basel)*, *24*(1), 239. DOI: 10.3390/s24010239

Simonyan, K., Vedaldi, A., & Zisserman, A. (2013). Deep inside convolutional networks: visualising image classification models and saliency maps. *arXiv (Cornell University)*. 1312.6034

Singh, G. (2023). One and one make eleven: An interpretable neural network for image recognition. *Knowledge-Based Systems*, *279*, 110926. DOI: 10.1016/j.knosys.2023.110926

Singh, J. P., Aqsa, A., Ghani, I., Sonani, R., & Govindarajan, V. (2025). Privacy-Aware Hierarchical Federated Learning in Healthcare: Integrating Differential Privacy and Secure Multi-Party Computation. *Future Internet*, *17*(8), 345–345. DOI: 10.3390/fi17080345

Slack, D., Hilgard, S., Jia, E., Singh, S., & Lakkaraju, H. (2020). Fooling LIME and SHAP: Adversarial attacks on post hoc explanation methods. *Proceedings of the AAAI Conference on Artificial Intelligence*, *34*(04), 180–187. DOI: 10.1145/3375627.3375830

Solaiman, B., & Glenn Cohen, I. (2024). *Research Handbook on Health, AI and the Law*. Edward Elgar Publishing. DOI: 10.4337/9781802205657

Sondeck, L. P., & Laurent, M. (2025). Practical and ready-to-use methodology to assess the re-identification risk in anonymized datasets. *Scientific Reports*, *15*(1), 23223. Advance online publication. DOI: 10.1038/s41598-025-04907-3 PMID: 40603887

Staab, R., Jovanović, N., Balunović, M., & Vechev, M. (2024). From Principle to Practice: Vertical Data Minimization for Machine Learning. *2024 IEEE Symposium on Security and Privacy (SP)*, 4733–4752. DOI: 10.1109/SP54263.2024.00089

Susskind, Z., Arden, B., John, L. K., Stockton, P., & John, E. B. (2021). Neuro-Symbolic AI: An Emerging Class of AI Workloads and their Characterization. *arXiv (Cornell University)*. 2109.06133

Symons, T., Straiton, N., Gagnon, R., Littleford, R., Campbell, A. J., Bowen, A. C., Stewart, A. G., Tong, S. Y. C., & Davis, J. S. (2022). Consumer perspectives on simplified, layered consent for a low risk, but complex pragmatic trial. *Trials*, *23*(1), 1055. Advance online publication. DOI: 10.1186/s13063-022-07023-z PMID: 36578070

Tabassi, E. (2023). *Artificial Intelligence Risk Management Framework (AI RMF 1.0)* (No. NIST AI 100-1; p. NIST AI 100-1). National Institute of Standards and Technology (U.S.). DOI: 10.6028/NIST.AI.100-1

Tartaro, A., Panai, E., & Cocchiaro, M. Z. (2024). AI risk assessment using ethical dimensions. *AI and Ethics*, *4*, 105–112. DOI: 10.1007/s43681-023-00368-6

Temel, D., Kwon, G., Prabhushankar, M., & AlRegib, G. (2017). *CURE-TSR: Challenging Unreal and Real Environments for Traffic Sign Recognition*. DOI: 10.48550/ARXIV.1712.02463

Thurzo, A. (2025). Provable AI ethics and explainability in medical and educational AI agents: Trustworthy ethical firewall. *Electronics (Basel)*, *14*(7), 1294. DOI: 10.3390/electronics14071294

Tramèr, F., Zhang, F., Juels, A., Reiter, M. K., & Ristenpart, T. (2016). Stealing machine learning models via prediction APIs. Proceedings of the USENIX Security Symposium, 601 to 618. https://www.usenix.org/conference/usenixsecurity16/technical-sessions/presentation/tramer

Tsipras, D., Santurkar, S., Engstrom, L., Turner, A., & Madry, A. (2018). *Robustness May Be at Odds with Accuracy* (Version 5). arXiv. DOI: 10.48550/ARXIV.1805.12152

Tsymbal, A. (2004). The problem of concept drift: Definitions and related work. Computer Science Department. *Trinity College Dublin*, *106*(2), 58.

U.S. White House. (2023). Executive order on the safe, secure, and trustworthy development and use of artificial intelligence. https://www.whitehouse.gov/briefing-room/presidential-actions/2023/10/30/executive-order-on-the-safe-secure-and-trustworthy-development-and-use-of-artificial-intelligence/

Ukai, Y., Hirakawa, T., Yamashita, T., & Fujiyoshi, H. (2023). Toward prototypical part interpretable similarity learning with ProtoMetric. *IEEE Access : Practical Innovations, Open Solutions*, *11*, 62986–62997. DOI: 10.1109/access.2023.3287638

UNESCO. (2021). Recommendation on the ethics of artificial intelligence. UNESCO. https://unesdoc.unesco.org/ark:/48223/pf0000373434

Valente, F., Paredes, S., Henriques, J., Rocha, T., De Carvalho, P., & Morais, J. (2022). Interpretability, personalization and reliability of a machine learning based clinical decision support system. *Data Mining and Knowledge Discovery*, *36*(3), 1140–1173. DOI: 10.1007/s10618-022-00821-8

Vancisin, T., Orr, M., Clarke, L., & Hinrichs, U. (2025). Provenance visualization as an entry point to the history and curation of information collections. *Journal of Visualization and Interaction*, *1*(1). Advance online publication. DOI: 10.54337/jovi.v1i1.8436

Vaswani, A., Shazeer, N., Parmar, N., Uszkoreit, J., Jones, L., Gomez, A. N., Kaiser, L., & Polosukhin, I. (2017). Attention is all you need. *arXiv (Cornell University)*. 1706.03762

Vayyala, R. (2025). Data lineage: Tracing data across systems. In *Data governance, DevSecOps, and advancements in modern software* (pp. 73–98). IGI Global. DOI: 10.4018/979-8-3373-0365-9.ch004

Veale, M., & Binns, R. (2017). Fairer machine learning in the real world: Mitigating discrimination without collecting sensitive data. *Big Data & Society*, *4*(2), 1–17. DOI: 10.1177/2053951717743530

Vinoth Kumar, C., Selvaprabhu, P., Baska, N., Vivek Menon, U., Babu Kumaravelu, V., Chinnadurai, S., & Ali, F. (2024). Ethereum Blockchain Framework Enabling Banks to Know Their Customers. *IEEE Access : Practical Innovations, Open Solutions, 12*, 101356–101365. DOI: 10.1109/ACCESS.2024.3427805

Vivek, M. U., & Poongundran Selvaprabhu. (2022). *Role of Telecommunication Technologies in Microgrids and Smart Grids*. 325–364. DOI: 10.1002/9781119760597.ch14

von Zahn, M., Liebich, L., Jussupow, E., Hinz, O., & Bauer, K. (2025). Knowing (not) to know: Explainable Artificial Intelligence and human metacognition. *Information Systems Research*, •••, 1–23. DOI: 10.1287/isre.2024.1431

Wachter, S., Mittelstadt, B., & Floridi, L. (2017). Counterfactual explanations without opening the black box: Automated decisions and the GDPR. *SSRN, 31*(2), 841–887. https://jolt.law.harvard.edu/assets/articlePDFs/v31/Counterfactual-Explanations-without-Opening-the-Black-Box-Sandra-Wachter-et-al.pdf. DOI: 10.2139/ssrn.3063289

Wang, Y., Zhang, T., Guo, X., & Shen, Z. (2024). Gradient based Feature Attribution in Explainable AI: A Technical Review. *arXiv (Cornell University)*. 2403.10415

Wang, A., Hertzmann, A., & Russakovsky, O. (2024). Benchmark suites instead of leaderboards for evaluating AI fairness. *Patterns (New York, N.Y.), 5*(11), 101080. DOI: 10.1016/j.patter.2024.101080 PMID: 39568473

Wen, J., Zhang, Z., Lan, Y., Cui, Z., Cai, J., & Zhang, W. (2022). A survey on federated learning: Challenges and applications. *International Journal of Machine Learning and Cybernetics, 14*(2), 513–535. DOI: 10.1007/s13042-022-01647-y PMID: 36407495

Widmer, G., & Kubat, M. (1996). Learning in the presence of concept drift and hidden contexts. *Machine Learning, 23*(1), 69–101. DOI: 10.1023/A:1018046501280

Winfield, A. F. T., & Jirotka, M. (2018). Ethical governance is essential to building trust in robotics and AI systems. *Philosophical Transactions of the Royal Society A, 376*(2133). Advance online publication. DOI: 10.1098/rsta.2018.0085 PMID: 30323000

Wu, X., Peng, S., & Li, J. (2024). Causal inference in the medical domain: A survey. *Applied Intelligence, 54*, 4911–4934. DOI: 10.1007/s10489-024-05338-9

Yan, R., Ma, T., Fokoue, A., Chang, M., & Julius, A. (2022). Neuro-symbolic Models for Interpretable Time Series Classification using Temporal Logic Description. *arXiv (Cornell University)*. 2209.09114

Yang, W., Wang, S., Cui, H., Tang, Z., & Li, Y. (2023). A Review of Homomorphic Encryption for Privacy-Preserving Biometrics. *Sensors (Basel), 23*(7), 3566. DOI: 10.3390/s23073566 PMID: 37050626

Yao, A., Pal, S., Li, G., Li, X., Zhang, Z., Jiang, F., Dong, C., Xu, J., & Liu, X. (2025). FedShufde: A privacy preserving framework of federated learning for edge-based smart UAV delivery system. *Future Generation Computer Systems, 107706*, 107706. Advance online publication. DOI: 10.1016/j.future.2025.107706

Yazdinejad, A., Dehghantanha, A., Karimipour, H., Srivastava, G., & Parizi, R. M. (2024). A robust privacy-preserving federated learning model against model poisoning attacks. *IEEE Transactions on Information Forensics and Security, 19*, 6693–6708. DOI: 10.1109/TIFS.2024.3420126

Yedavalli, V., Salim, H. A., Mei, J., Lakhani, D. A., Balar, A., Musmar, B., Adeeb, N., Hoseinyazdi, M., Luna, L., Deng, F., Hyson, N. Z., Dmytriw, A. A., Guenego, A., Faizy, T. D., Heit, J. J., Albers, G. W., Lu, H., Urrutia, V. C., Nael, K., & Llinas, R. (2024). Decreased quantitative cerebral blood volume is associated with poor outcomes in large core patients. *Stroke, 55*(10), 2409–2419. DOI: 10.1161/STROKEAHA.124.047483

Zaeem, R. N., & Barber, K. S. (2020). The Effect of the GDPR on Privacy Policies: Recent Progress and Future Promise. *ACM Transactions on Management Information Systems, 12*(1), 1–20. DOI: 10.1145/3389685

Zahid, I. A. (2025). Explainability, robustness, and fairness in user-centric intelligent systems: A systematic review. *IEEE Transactions on Emerging Topics in Computational Intelligence, 9*(6), 3728–3753. DOI: 10.1109/TETCI.2025.3567604

Zemel, R., Wu, Y., Swersky, K., Pitassi, T., & Dwork, C. (2013). Learning fair representations. In *Proceedings of the 30th International Conference on Machine Learning (ICML)* (pp. 325–333).

Zhang, B. H., Lemoine, B., & Mitchell, M. (2018). Mitigating unwanted biases with adversarial learning. In Proceedings of the 2018 AAAI/ACM Conference on AI, Ethics, and Society (pp. 335–340). DOI: 10.1145/3278721.3278779

Zhang, H., Torres, F., Sicre, R., Avrithis, Y., & Ayache, S. (2023). Opti-CAM: Optimizing saliency maps for interpretability. *arXiv (Cornell University)*. 2301.07002

Zhang, Y., Liao, Q. V., & Bellamy, R. K. E. (2020). Effect of confidence and explanation on accuracy and trust calibration in AI-assisted decision making. *Proceedings of the 2020 Conference on Fairness, Accountability, and Transparency*, 295–305. DOI: 10.1145/3351095.3372852

Zhou, J., Su, Z., Ni, J., Wang, Y., Pan, Y., & Xing, R. (2022). Personalized Privacy-Preserving Federated Learning: Optimized Trade-off Between Utility and Privacy. *GLOBECOM 2022 - 2022 IEEE Global Communications Conference*, 4872–4877. DOI: 10.1109/GLOBECOM48099.2022.10000793

Zuboff, S. (2019). *The age of surveillance capitalism: The fight for a human future at the new frontier of power*. PublicAffairs.

About the Contributors

Rahul K. Patel is a cybersecurity and information systems management expert with over 25 years of experience in high-tech, banking, and government sectors. An Adjunct Industry Associate Professor at the Illinois Institute of Technology, he is the author of AI Frameworks and Tools for Software Development and Essential Information Systems Service Management, and has published widely on AI applications, digital literacy, blockchain security, and privacy-preserving architectures. Dr. Patel holds a PhD in Management of Information Systems from Northcentral University and multiple professional cybersecurity certifications.

***

Shidiq Al Hakim received a Ph.D. degree in computer science from the University of Indonesia in 2021. He is currently a researcher at the Research Center for Artificial Intelligence and Cyber Security, National Research and Innovation Agency (BRIN) and a Lecturer at Bakrie University. His research interests include text mining, knowledge management, user experience, and recommender system. He is also a reviewer for the VINE Journal of Information and Knowledge Management Systems and some national journals

Rajesh Lingam is a software engineering leader with 22 years' experience across AI evaluation, test infrastructure, DevOps, and web platforms. He specialises in turning product goals into reliable delivery through baseline-gated CI/CD, quality gates, and developer-centric tooling. His work includes a source-to-test mapping approach that replaced brittle browser stacks ($\approx$1,600 engineer-hours saved per release and >75% effort reduction), local orchestration that reduced cloud usage by ~30%, and reusable, resolution-aware UI frameworks adopted across enterprise products. Rajesh mentors engineers via written growth plans, publishes practitioner articles, and contributes to civic-tech projects. He holds an MS in Computer Science

(Boston University) and a B.Tech in Electronics & Communication (JNTU). Certifications: PCAP (Python) and Prefect Associate. Research interests: trustworthy AI evaluation, MLOps, reliability engineering, and developer experience.

Cahyono Nugroho is a researcher at the National Research and Innovation Agency (BRIN), Indonesia, specializing in the Artificial Intelligence (AI) for Cybersecurity research group. As an expert in network security and information systems, he contributes to the development of cyber threat detection technologies, particularly in Internet of Things (IoT) networks and application security verification. He is affiliated with Budiluhur University and can be reached via his verified official email at the brin.go.id domain. His research encompasses the application of hybrid feature selection for botnet attack detection, the development of security assessment systems based on the Application Security Verification Standard (ASVS), and the design of mobile applications for business management

Shashank Parmar is a Machine Learning Engineer specializing in Generative AI at VISA Inc., where he spearheads the development of enterprise-scale AI solutions, including the "MyAssistant" agent and a corporate data classification platform. Shashank has authored numerous publications in high-impact, peer-reviewed journals and conferences, with work spanning interpretable AI, retrieval-augmented generation (RAG), computer vision, and novel algorithms for data similarity and plagiarism detection. His research contributions are complemented by several filed patents in AI-driven payment and verification systems.

P Geetha obtained her B. Sc degree from Nesamony Memorial Christian College, Marthandam, M S university. She received MCA degree from MK University. She obtained her ME degree in Computer ScieIndnd Engineering from RVS college of Engineering and Technology, Anna University. She obtained her PhD from Kalinga University. She is having more than Eleven years of teaching experience. She is now currently working as Assisant Professor (SG), in Department of Computer Science and Engineering, Saveetha School of Engineering, Saveetha Institute of Medical and Technical Sciences, Saveetha University, Saveetha Nagar, Thandalam, Kanchipuram - Chennai Rd, Chennai, Tamil Nadu 602105. Her research areas are Wireless Sensor Network, Image Processing and Cloud Computing.

Hemasri S is currently doing her B.Tech Artificial Intelligence and Data Science at V.S.B College of Engineering Technical Campus, Coimbatore. Her Research area includes Artificial Intelligence, Internet of Things and Cloud computing.

S.V. Divya M.E, Ph.D., is currently working as a Professor in the Department of Computer Science & Engineering in V.S.B College of Engineering Technical

Campus, Coimbatore, TamilNadu, India . She has the teaching experience of more than 16 years and had published more than 20 research papers in SCI/Scopus indexed journals, 2 Patents and 2 text books. She had published more than 15 papers in National/International Conferences.She received her B.Tech Degree in Information Technology from Jayamatha Engineering College, Aralvoimozhi and M.E Degree in Computer Science and Engineering from Mepco Schlenk Engineering College, Sivakasi in 2005 and 2007 respectively. She received her Ph.D in Computer Science and Engineering at Noorul Islam Centre for Higher Education in 2017 under the area of Cloud Computing and guiding four research scholars. Her research area includes Wireless Communications, Cloud Computing, Big Data and Cyber Security. Acted a s reviewer in many journals and IEEE conferences. She is a Life member of ISTE

T Saju Raj received the BE degree in Computer Science and Engineering from Dr. Babasaheb Ambedkar Marathwada University, India in 1995 and ME degree in Computer Science and Engineering, from Madurai Kamraj University, India in 2002. He has completed his PhD degree from Anna University, India. He has more than twenty five years of teaching experience. He is Currently working in the Department of Computer Science and Engineering, Vel Tech Rangarajan Dr. Sagunthala R&D Institute of Science and Technology, Avadi-Vel Tech Road Vel Nagar, Avadi, Chennai, Tamil Nadu 600062 His area of interests are reliability in grid computing, Cloud Computing, Automata theory, Machine Learning, Wireless Sensor Network, parallel and distributed computing.

Ajit Kumar Singh is a seasoned Technical Architect and Technical Delivery Manager with over 13 years of experience designing and delivering large-scale, mission-critical platforms across FinTech, Digital Payments, and Core Banking. His expertise spans Java full-stack engineering, cloud-native architectures, microservices, API-driven ecosystems, and high-availability payment systems. He holds a Bachelor of Technology in Information Technology from VITAM Berhampur, India, under the Biju Patnaik University of Technology. Ajit is also actively expanding his skills in Artificial Intelligence to build next-generation, intelligent enterprise solutions.

Parikshit Kumar Singh is a multifaceted Solution Architect, Product Owner, Scrum Master, RTE, and Enterprise Agile Coach, as well as an accomplished educator, author, and practitioner in Agile, DevOps, SRE, and AI. With over 17.5 years of industry experience, he has led large-scale digital transformation programs and architected high-performance, enterprise-grade solutions. He is the creator, innovator, and primary implementer of the GrowAAE (Grow Agile Architecture & Engineering) framework within Capgemini, driving organization-wide agility and engineering excellence. Parikshit holds a Bachelor of Technology in Computer

Science and Engineering from GIETU (formerly GIET), Gunupur, India, under the Biju Patnaik University of Technology. He also carries a strong portfolio of certifications, including CAL, CSP-SM, CSP-PO, CSP-D, TOGAF, Certified Architect, and Certified Engagement Manager. He is currently associated with Capgemini in Chicago, contributing to advanced enterprise transformation and next-generation AI-driven delivery practices.

Seema Parikshit Kumar Singh is a highly accomplished Solution Architect specializing in DevOps, with 17 years of experience leading end-to-end delivery, automation initiatives, and enterprise-scale digital transformation. She is actively expanding her expertise in Artificial Intelligence to align with emerging engineering and automation trends. Seema holds a Master of Computer Management (MCM) degree from Rashtrasant Tukadoji Maharaj Nagpur University and a strong portfolio of industry certifications, including SAFe RTE, CSM, TOGAF, and several advanced technical credentials.

Vivek Menon U received the master's degree in communication engineering and the Ph.D. degree in interference management strategies in 5G mobile communication systems from Vellore Institute of Technology, Vellore, Tamil Nadu, India, in 2019 and 2024, respectively. He is currently a Postdoctoral Fellow with the University of Modena and Reggio Emilia. His main research interests include interference alignment in wireless communication systems, interference management in massive MIMO communication systems, radar systems, reconfigurable intelligent surfaces, blockchain, and the Internet of Things.

P. Venkadesh M.E, Ph.D., is currently working as a Professor in the Department of Artificial Intelligence & Data Science in V.S.B College of Engineering Technical Campus, Coimbatore, TamilNadu, India . He received his M.E Degree in Computer Science & Engineering from Sathyabama University, Chennai, TamilNadu, India in 2007. He completed his Ph.D at Noorul Islam Centre for Higher Education in 2017 under the area of Network Security . He is guiding five research scholars and three scholars received their Ph.D degree under his guidance. His research area includes Network Security, Image Processing, Wireless Communications and Cloud Computing. He has a teaching experience of more than 22 years and had published more than 30 research papers in SCI/Scopus indexed journals . He has published more than 30 Patents and two patents were granted. He has published more than 5 text books, 5 SCOPUS indexed Book Chapters He is a life member of ISTE

Index

www.ingramcontent.com/pod-product-compliance
Lightning Source LLC
LaVergne TN
LVHW081522300926
849161LV00006B/1261
* 9 7 9 8 3 3 7 3 6 9 3 5 8 *